SECRET MUSEUMS

EL GRECO
&
FERNANDO ARRABAL

Translated from spanish
by Andrew Hurley

XVI
century

FLOHIC
– EDITIONS –

WARHOL

In 1881, the director of the Prado Museum called El Greco's paintings "absurd caricatures" and complained that he was "not allowed to throw them out of the Museum." Francisco Mateos Gago, a prestigious critic of the time, bemoaned the fact that the painter hadn't stayed in Greece, or in Crete where he came from: "We've no need of his sort of extravagances here." El Greco's paintings, "left to molder in the basement" of the Prado, were catalogued as "Venetian" until well into the twentieth centu-

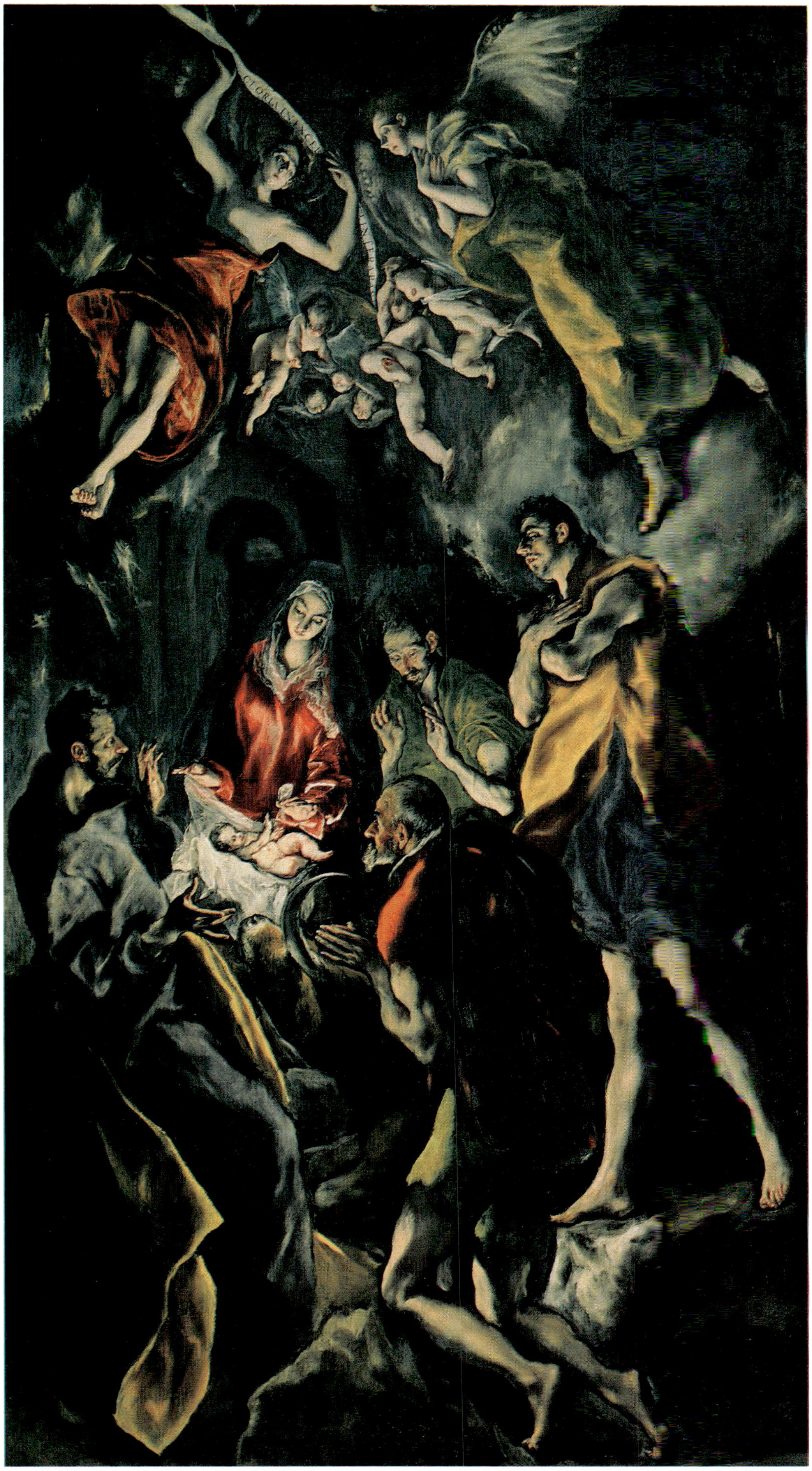

THE SHEPHERDS' ADORATION
1612-14. Madrid, Prado.
319 × 180 cm

ry. *The Annunciation* was not even left to molder in the Madrid museum — it was thrown out with great fanfare.

For three hundred years, silence or outright animosity greeted the work of this man who was, in my opinion, a painter apart, and who indeed is still one of the greatest painters the world has ever known.

In March, 1982, as Makos' book records, I had a conversation with Andy Warhol in Paris. "El Greco," he said to me, "is the God of Painting." I asked what led him to such high praise, and his answer was that "hundreds of years before me, El Greco did what I'm trying to do today — invert the relationship between man and art."

Recently, examining El Greco's work closely and recalling Warhol's words, I think I've been able to guess some of the reasons behind the fury and contempt the paintings inspired. El Greco changes the meaning of human relations, alters the rational order of the world, muddles roles, turns the universe upside-down, transforms Everything into Nothing and Nothing into Everything, and sets our ideas, beliefs, and certainties on their ear. He is the creator of inversion in art. Of the myriad possible, here are seven examples:

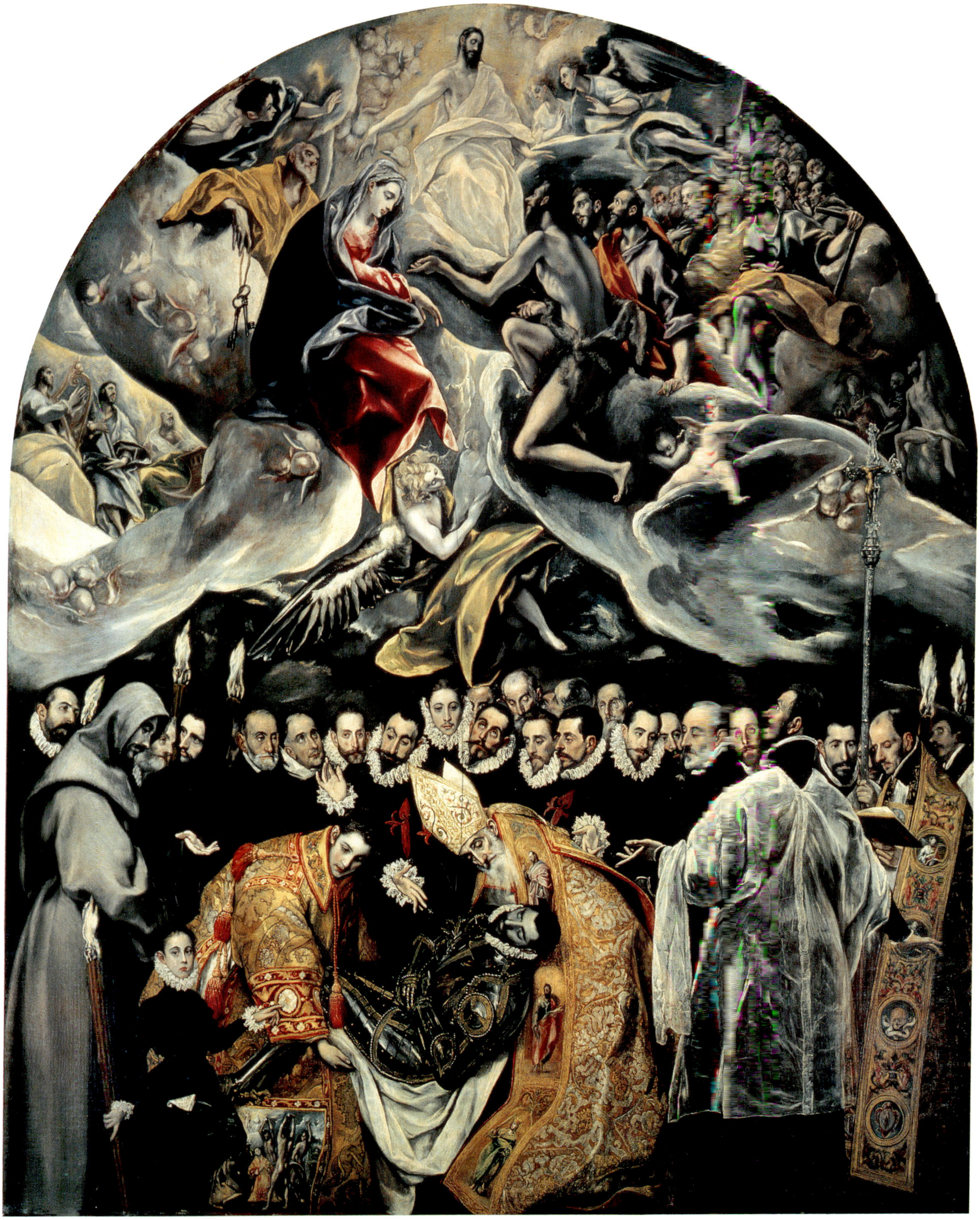

COUNT OF ORGAZ' BURIAL
1586-88. Toledo, Santo Tomé.
460 × 360 cm

• Beside a decapitated Theban warrior, the painter places a naked youth, who in order to offer himself more openly has his legs spread and his hands behind his back. A bearded warrior has laid his head in the youth's lap, and is kissing, or licking, his pubis. The immolation of the tortured man and the survivor's orgasm invert the meaning of the two figures. *(The Martyrdom of St Maurice and the Theban Legion,* El Escorial)

• In the landscape of Toledo, El Greco inverts the topography in order to mold it to his own ends. The painter has set the Cathedral between the Bridge of Alcántara and the Alcázar, while in reality the Cathedral lies to the right, the west, of the Alcázar. *(View of Toledo under Storm,* Metropolitan Museum, New York)

The right hand of the half-naked St Jerome grasps a thick sausage-like bulge of flesh, the tip of which emerges at the height of his breastbone. The hermit saint's ecstasy is inverted into onanism. *(St Jerome Penitent,* El Prado)

• In a dislocation of the object of their wor-

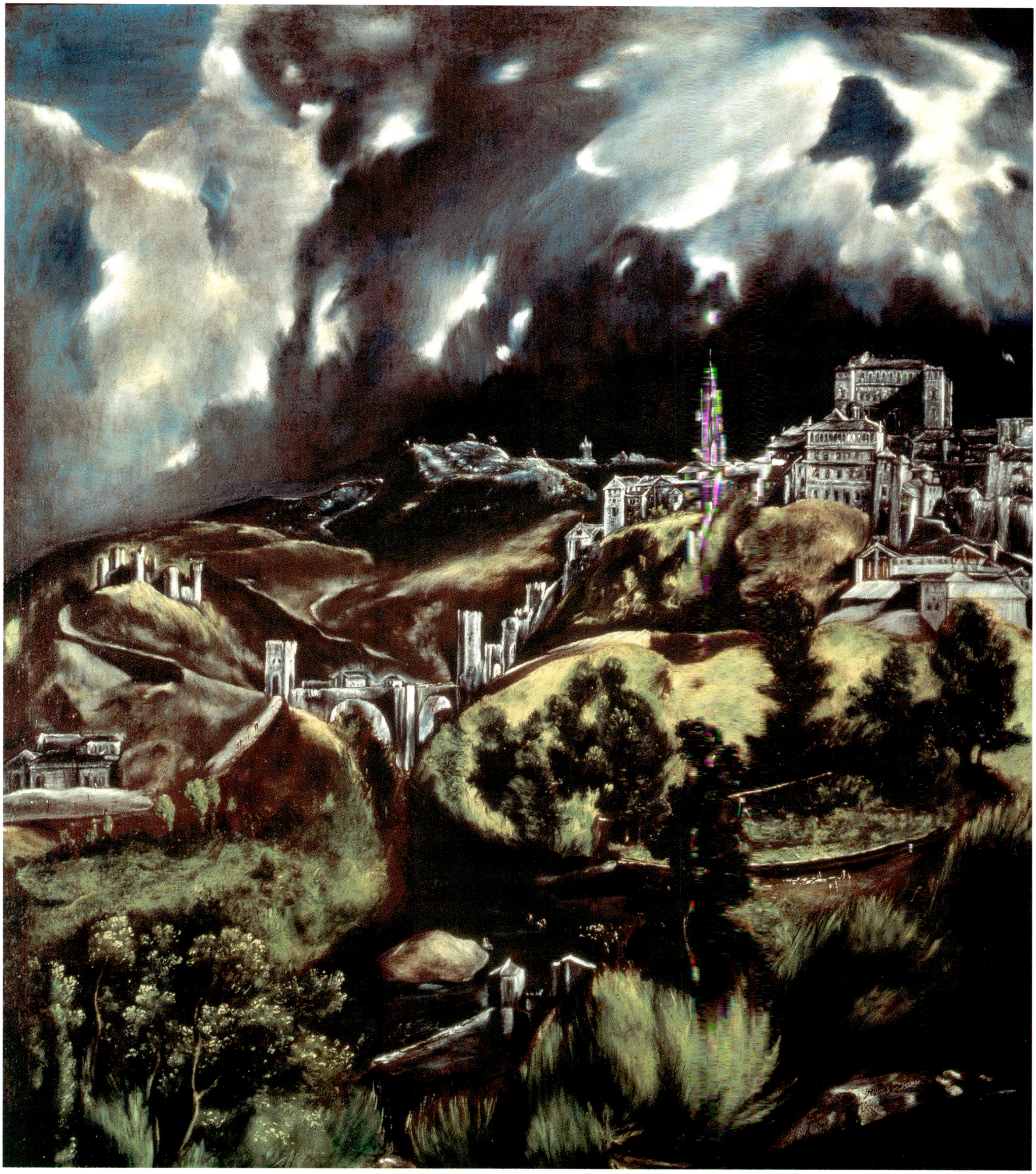

VIEW OF TOLEDO
1595-1610. New York, Metropolitan Museum.
121 × 190 cm

ship, the shepherds in the Adoration bow down before a gigantic phallus not at all well camouflaged as a cow's muzzle. *(The Adoration of the Shepherds,* El Prado)

• Above St Romuald and St Benedict in the *Allegory of the Camaldolite Order* there floats, like a cloud, the plan of the first community of the monastic order founded by the saints, with the individual monks' cells all in rows. El Greco inverts the meaning, and the image is transformed into a menorah, a Talmudic candelabra of seven branches. *(Allegory of the Camaldolite Order,* Valencia)

• St Stephen inverts the temporal order: on his robe is painted a scene depicting his own stoning. His martyrdom is transformed into a dramatic and sophisticated tableau: three beautifully naked athletes are holding stones aloft with studied affectation while another, also naked, is gazing upside-down at the backside of his neighbor. *(The Burial of the Conde de Orgaz,* Toledo)

• A naked Nazarene, upside-down, trades the

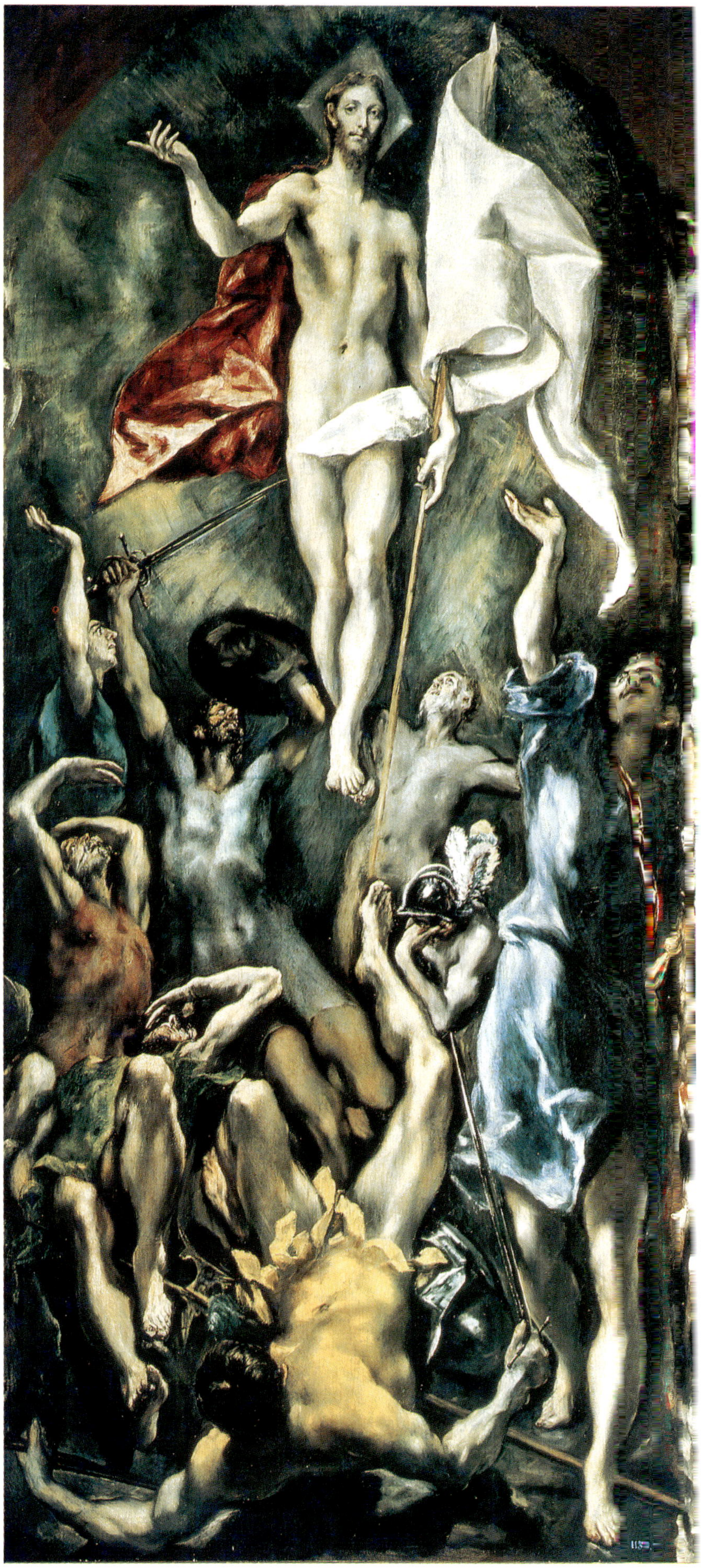

RESURRECTION
1605-1610. Madrid, Prado.
275 × 127 cm

mystical state of ecstasy for carnal pleasure: the foot of another Nazarene has slipped between his cheeks in the act of what is called in New York "foot-fucking." *(The Resurrection,* El Prado)

The "rehabilitation" of El Greco could only have been brought about by avant-garde movements seeking to regain the right to invert the values held by society. In 1840 the French *Romantics and Symbolists* —Delacroix, Baudelaire, and Gautier, among others — impassioned with the "madman-genius of Toledo," began to claim him as a precursor, and to use him to chip away at the foundations of the "vulgar" world that surrounded them.

In 1894, in a ritual of amends-making, the Catalonian *Modernistas,* with Rusiol at their head, triumphantly bore several El Grecos, mounted on poles and in the midst of flags and banners, to Rusiol's house-museum, Cau Ferrat, in Sitges. "El Greco was the *modernista* of his age!" they proclaimed. Zuloaga became the master's most impassioned panegyrist, and in Montparnasse he forwent food in order to continue his proselytizing. Rilke, Jorda, Uranga, and

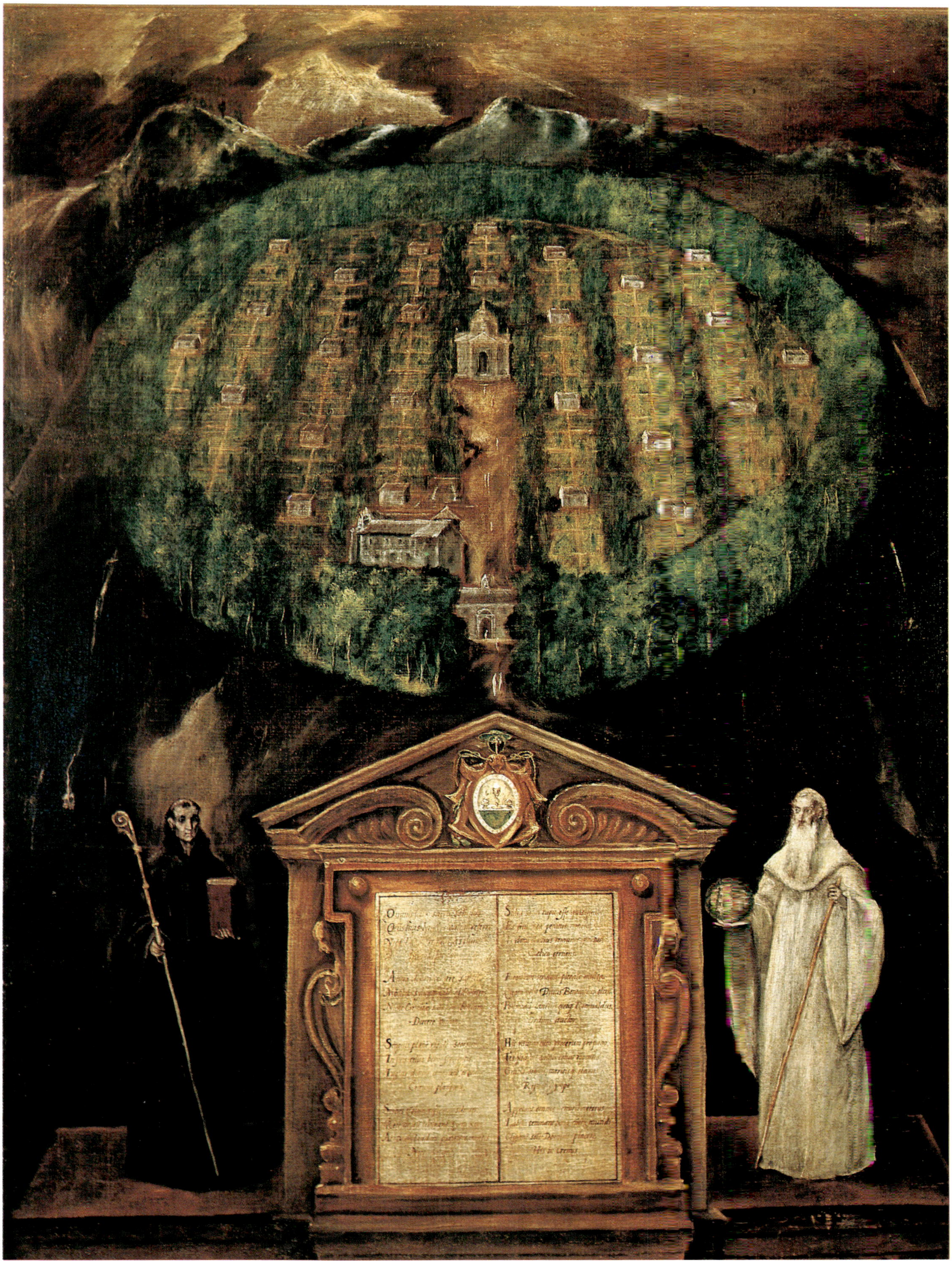

ALLEGORY OF THE CAMALDULES' ORDER
1597. Valencía, Colegio del Patriarca.
138 × 108 cm

even the Salon d'Automne in Paris were won over to the cause. For the Spanish "Generation of '98" admiration for El Greco was a religion... until 1903. A visit to Toledo would be "of foremost importance in the evolution of the school." Baroja, Galdós, and Unamuno waxed enthusiastic over him. He made Azorín "weep for admiration," and in 1902 Azorín begged that El Greco be given a gallery in the Prado. For these men El Greco represented "the epitome of essence." With El Greco they inverted the idealistic realism of Spain and turned it into spiritual naturalism.

With El Greco the "Instituto Libre de Enseñansa," that "Free School" created by Giner de los Ríos which was so important for the cultural life of Spain at the turn of the century, inverted the past — it raised that creator theretofore disdained higher than those theretofore consecrated, and at the same time proclaimed its faith in education. Giner often paid tribute to "the Toledan," and Cossío wrote a prophetic book on him, the first great study of the painter El Greco.

From that day on, controversy over El Greco has never abated. Maurice Barrès trembled in ec-

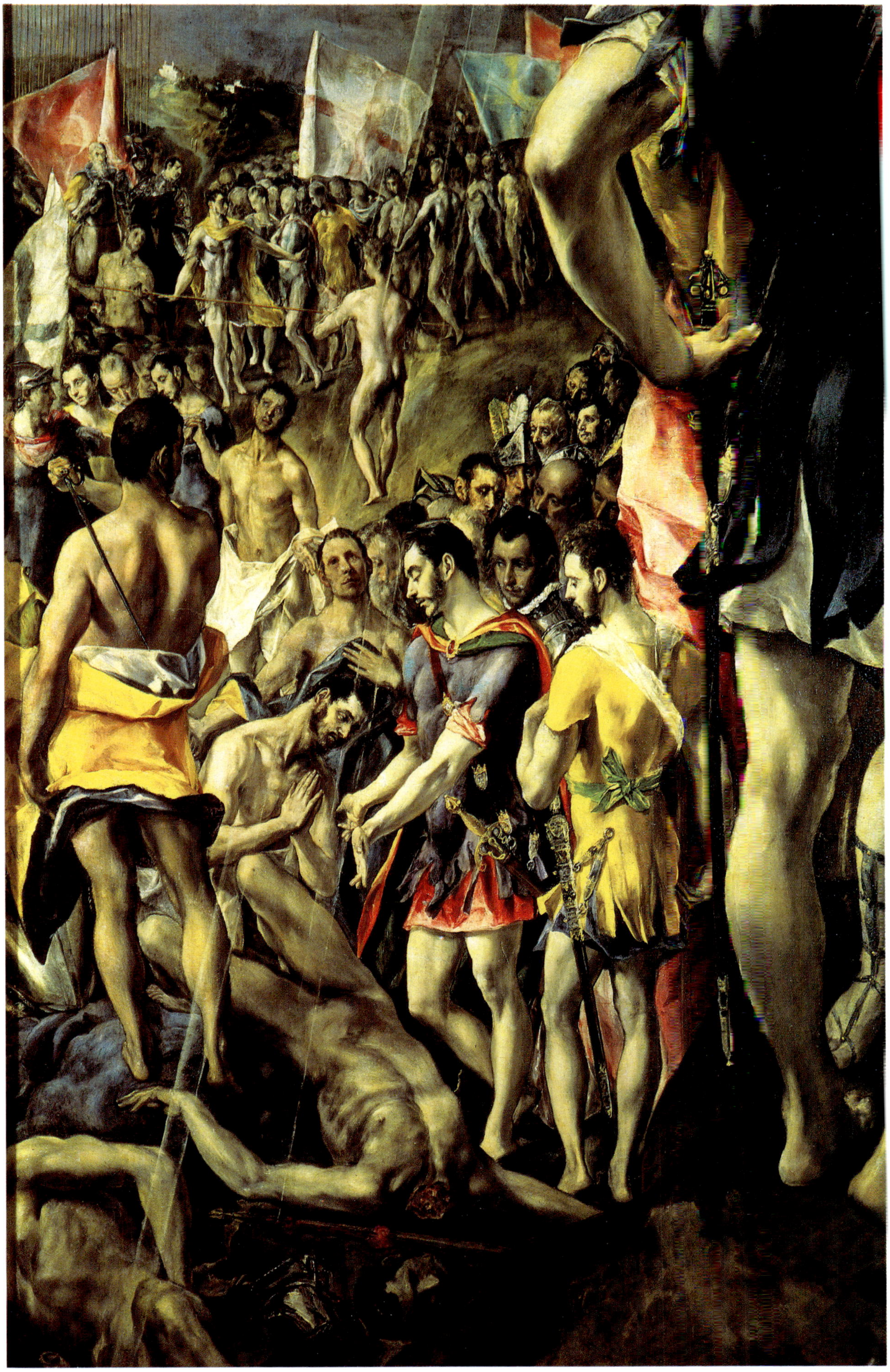

SAINT MAURICE'S MARTYRDOM
1580-82. Escurial Monastery.
detail

stasy before the sacred madness of his favorite painter, while Ortega y Gasset, more reticent, defined the *Pentecost* as an "attack of nerves" at the "frenzied height of a spasm." But it will be said that his detractors did after all define the reasons for their irritation; let us give ourselves the pleasure of reading these reflections on his work: Aldous Huxley wrote that "all has been transformed by El Greco into peritoneal mucosities,... like a resurrection of the digestive tract." Claudel was exasperated by "the unleashed purgatory." Woman, he said, "plays no role in these athletic exhibitions." Cocteau, in fury, lashed out against El Greco, snarling that "he is no painter,... he is an erotic geometer. The *Martyrdom of St Maurice* is a *massif* of members in erection. In its day, it was a scandalous canvas, and it still is today." In his diary for March, 1943, Cocteau wrote, "Without El Greco's name, and the respect paid snobbism today, his work would make us howl with laughter... It is an oddity one might pick up at a flea market, a canvas by the Independents, a monster from the madhouse or the reformatory, an advertising broadside for some fair."

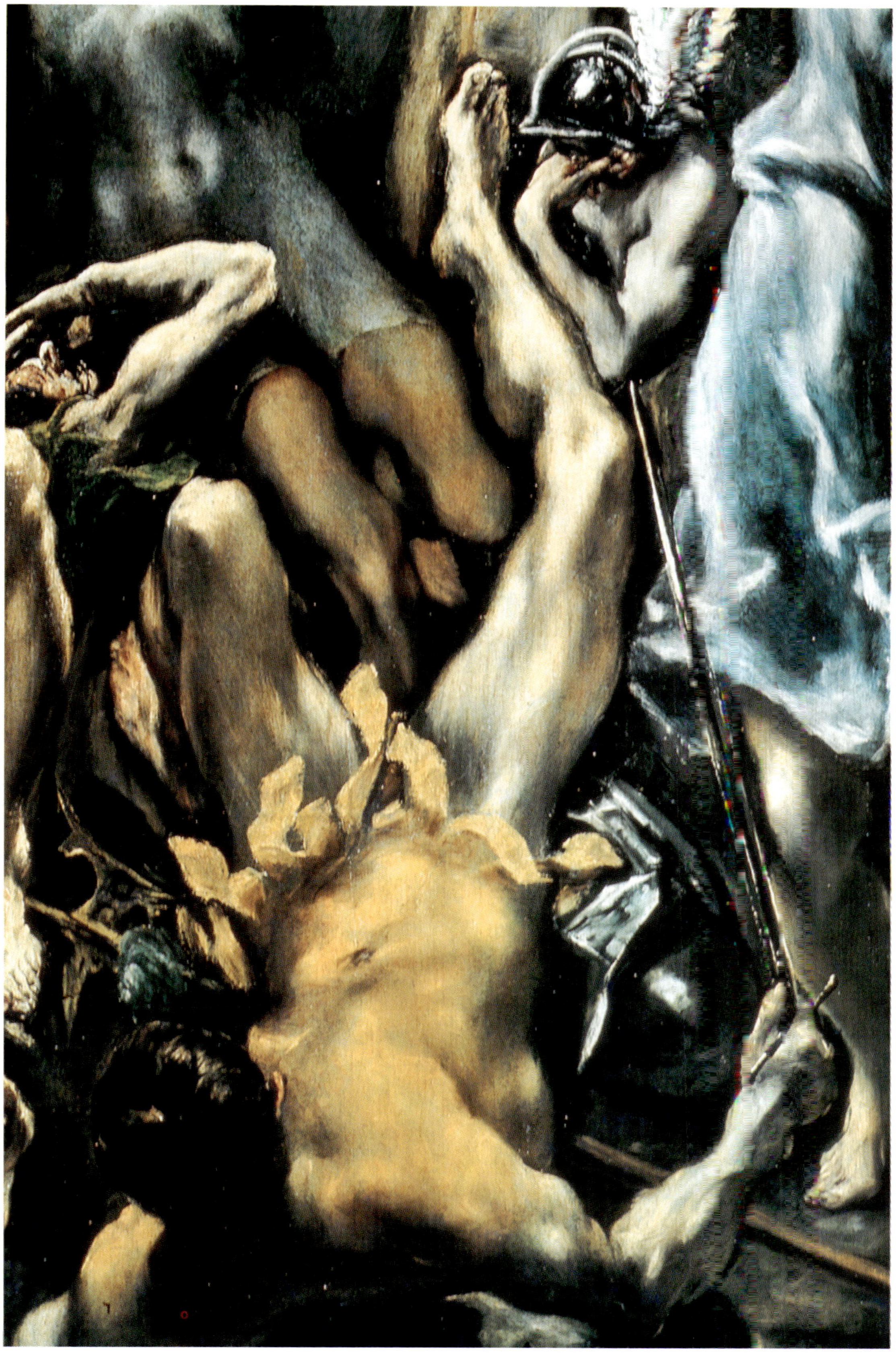

RESURRECTION
1605-10. Madrid, Prado.
detail

LIFE

No one could ever have banished El Greco, for he was born in exile, in stellar silence. Seven years after the death of his lover, the Italian Francisco Preboste (or even, as the memoirs and memoirists sometimes more elegantly denominate him, *de* Preboste), El Greco died in Toledo, on April 7, 1614. His entire fortune, Jusepe Martínez tells us, may be rendered as some two hundred canvases "begun by his hand." The two inventories taken after El Greco's death reduce the quantity but increase the quality, and most of his paintings appear not "begun" or "drafted" by his hand, but "finished." The painter was fated to die (and, alas, to live) in "a very old and ramshackle house" that he rented from the Marquise de Villena, ten steps from the synagogue in the Jewish section of Toledo. El Greco's home, fodder for entropy, oblivion's domain, has little by little been transformed into the setting for children's games by day and lovers' trysts by night, under a sign that reads Paseo de Tránsito. (Every inversion must have its transit). A few yards

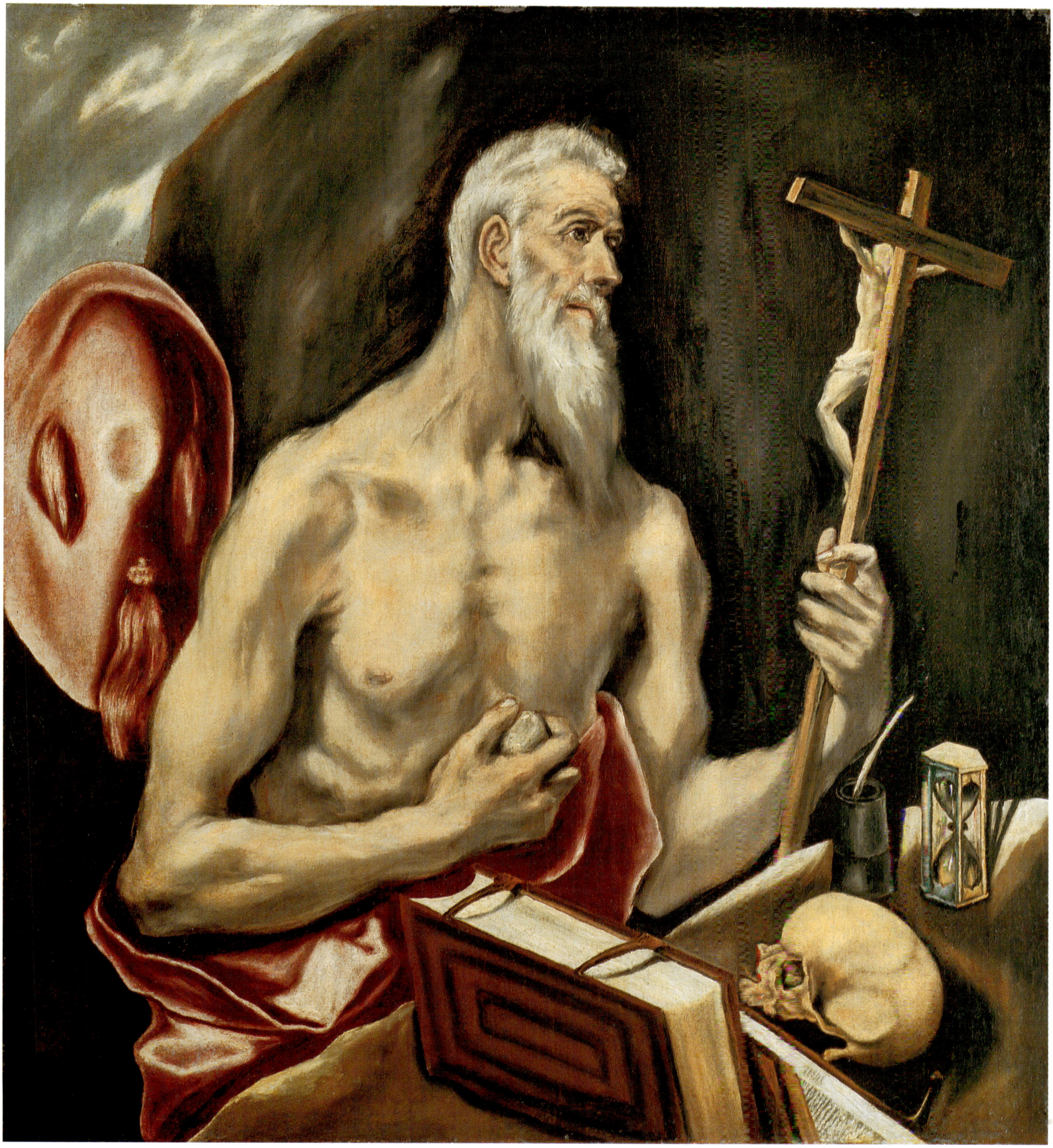

PENITENT SAINT JEROME
1595-1600. Edinburgh, National Gallery of Scotland.
104 × 97 cm

from the place where, at its own pace, yet inexorably, the mill of time was reducing the relics and ruins of the ramshackle old house to dust, there now rises a mansion-like establishment whose alias is *The House of El Greco.* Geography (and even reality) shifts, and shortcuts through reason appear, allowing the traveler to pick up trails that lead to the meaning of the works. The studio in which El Greco painted *The Burial of the Conde de Orgaz,* a place today exposed to the elements, is, then, nothing — or perhaps better, Nothingness: *le Néant, la Nada.*

At thirty-six, "Domenikos" was on the verge of triumph in Rome, or, what amounted to much the same thing, of failure. There were to be laurels from the Pope and swipes of the broomstick from his fellows — from Muse and from Jealousy, two faces of *la Nada* — when he abandoned it all, except his library and his true love. They went off together, the three of them, and for thirty-seven years they lived in exile, in Toledo, the ancient capital of the Kings of Castile. El Greco was a painter of some culture, though never affected, never one of the precious and euphuistic "culteranos," for though

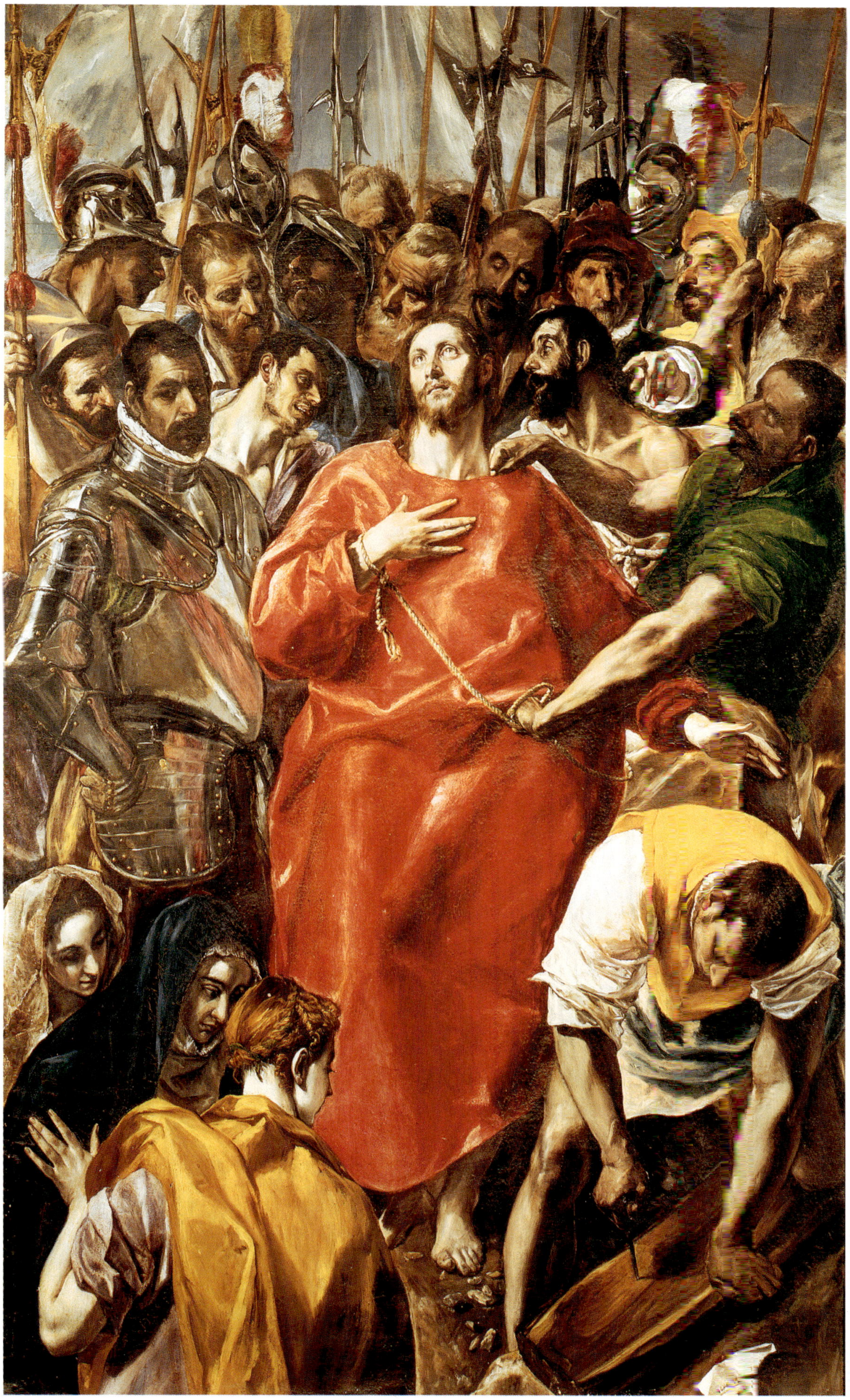

THE CUTTING OF CHRIST'S TUNIC (Espolio)
1577-79. Toledo, Cathedral.
285 × 173 cm

Góngora was to write a sonnet about him, the title of no Castilian book in his library has been recorded. Knowledge of the classics, and of his own time, permeates his work as it does his life. On the shelves one might find books read and re-read: nineteen volumes on architecture, Hippocrates, Botero's *La Relazione Universale,* treatises on painting and on military discipline, Plutarch's *Lives,* Homer, Euripides, Demosthenes, Isocrates, Æsop, Lucian, the Bible, Petrarch, Ariosto, Tasso, Aristotle's *Politics* and *Physics,* Plutarch's *Moralia,* a Greek lexicon, and so on. With these books, which must have cost him some effort to carry from Rome to Toledo, he lived the best moments of his life, until at the age of seventy-three he was to live, by the act of dying, even better ones. Without will, witness, or last words, freed from his own time and place, he might at last speak, in the silence of that last moment, the word "Nothing"... while in his paintings, Everything appears Little. The laconic death certificate reads: *"En siete del falesció dominico greco no hizo testam..."* [*"On the seventh,"* that is, *"died Dominico Greco made no wil..."*] We know the month and the year (April, 1614) because this

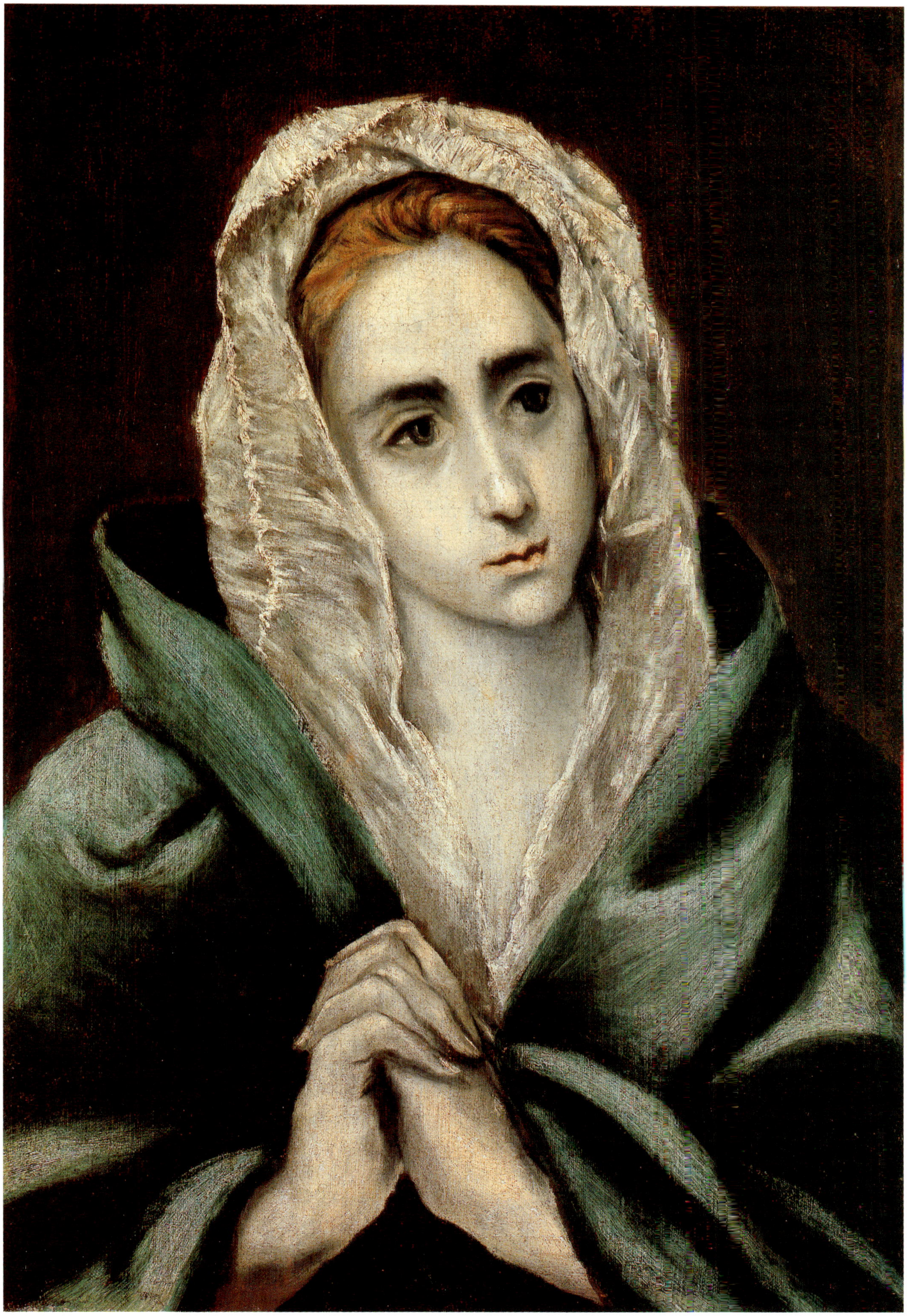

MATER DOLOROSA
1585-90. Berlin-Dahlem. Staatliche Museen.
62 × 42 cm

entry is preceded by one which says: *"En cuatro días del mes de abril de mil y seix cientos y catorce años felesció María hija de p° Ruiz de ocho meses."* [*"On the fourth day of April of one thousand and six hundred and fourteen years, died María the daughter of Ruiz at eight months."*]

Turning Beginning into End, passing through and pausing in a time turned inside-out, El Greco, the man who was to become the symbol of the Modern, was buried in the Church of Santo Domingo el Antiguo, St Dominic the Old. But at the same time, what better church to bury him in than that which, in Toledo, bears his (Spanish'd) name? It was in this church that Domenikos the Greek took brush in hand for the first time in Spain, and in it his body, rendered dust, was to disappear forever, as his works were to disappear from the History of Art for centuries. Our world brings forth such a delirium of strange and inexplicable events that it can come as no surprise that thirty-nine years after creating the paintings for the three great *retablos* of the Church's High Altar and two transept altars, he would be buried under those same scenes, in the same ritual (routine) used to bury

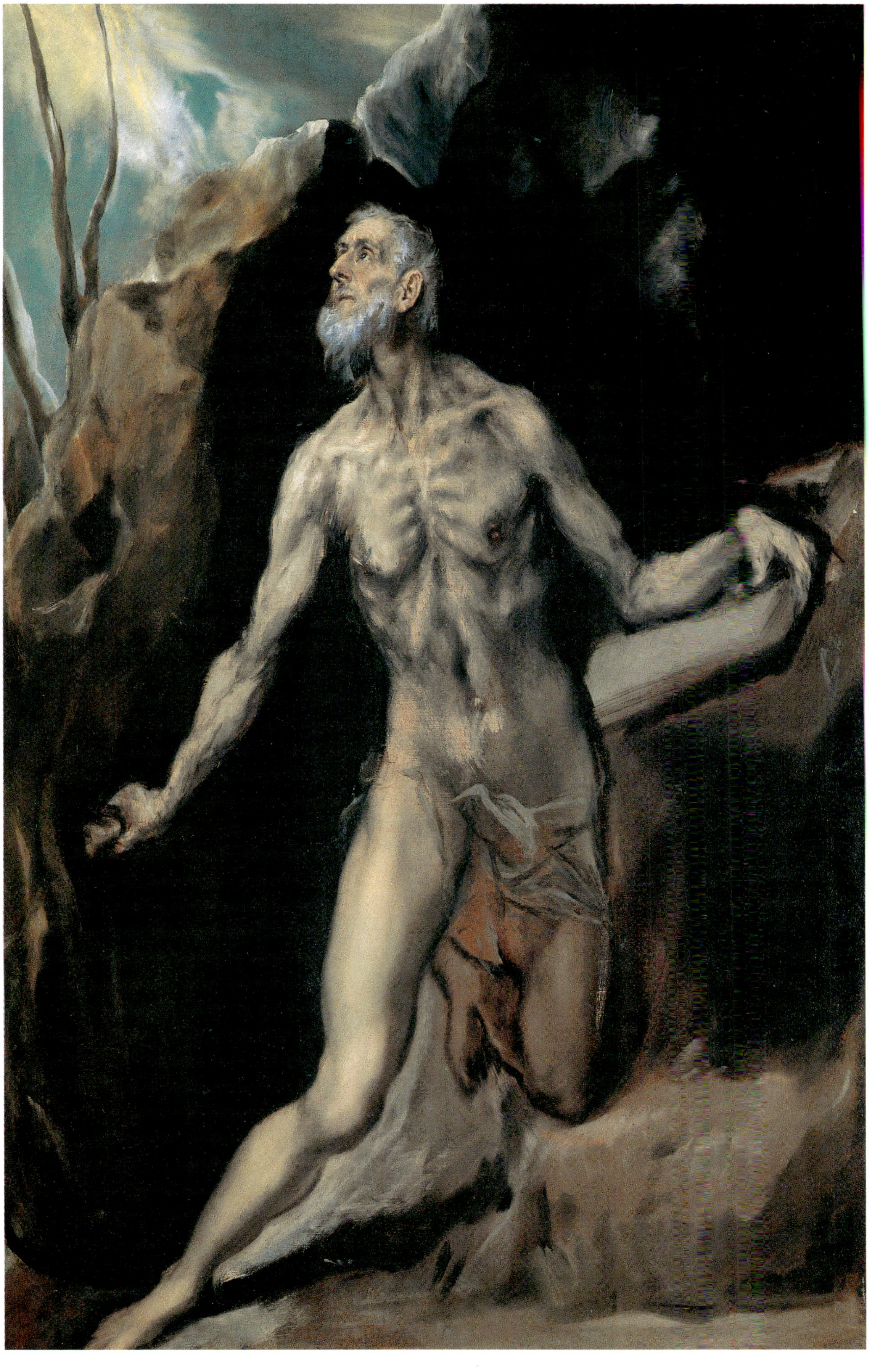

PENITENT SAINT JEROME
1612-14. Washington, National Gallery.
168 × 110,5 cm

an unknown eight-month-old baby girl.

The paintings are *The Assumption, The Trinity, St John the Evangelist, St John the Baptist, St Benedict* and *St Bernard, The Holy Face, The Adoration of the Shepherds, The Resurrection.* The *retablos* of gilded wood were also traced by El Greco; today, thanks to the nuns of the Church, they are adorned with criss-crosses of large-diameter electrical cords and have huge screws screwed into them, like so many comic mass-production examples of an unfairly unknown Art of the Nuns School. Of the nine paintings painted by El Greco, only three remain; into this long night of speculation in which we have the fortune to live, the others have disappeared.

The first contract given El Greco in Spain was signed with this church, and for the production of these very *retablos.* His lover could not help him, nor does he appear as a witness as he does so often elsewhere. And yet El Greco grants Francisco Preboste the power to bind him to "undertake to do any *retablos* or [other] works of painting and architecture." El Greco was to have the misfortune to commit himself to two contracts with this church, his first and his last

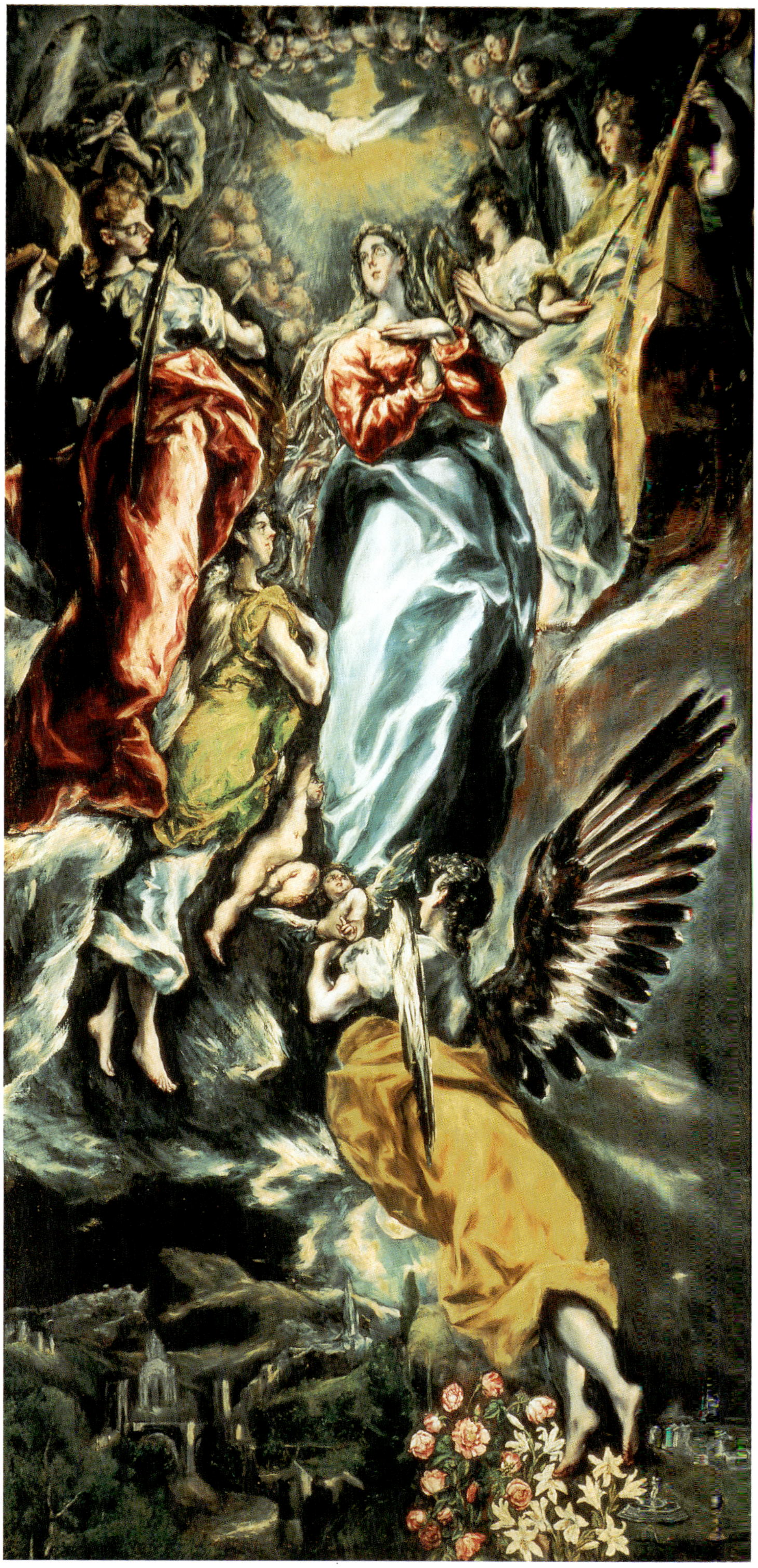

ASSUMPTION
1607-13. Toledo, Santa Cruz Museum.
347 × 174 cm

in Spain... and neither was ever to be fulfilled. Once the *retablos* had been painted, the law of "the strongest man wins" came into play: after a long tug of war, the Church at last dragged El Greco over the line. We know that when El Greco was finally paid his four pennies — borne to him by hands covered with excrement — he did not even reply "and my heart and my flesh embraced by your pullulating flesh your rotting kiss."

Thirty-nine years after that first suit, El Greco made the decision to trust the Church of Santo Domingo el Antiguo again. He purchased the rent "in perpetuity" of a sepulchre where his earthly remains would rest "for always and forever." One can easily believe that, depressed and resigned, El Greco imagined that he might in this way assure himself an end without the usual prolegomena to immortality. He was buried in an underground crypt, under the chapel of the Gómaras. No monument of any kind, no tombstone or marker or inscription, records this fact. In 1629 his place was taken by another occupant, no more dead than El Greco but from a well-to-do family — and a "Franciscan cleric" in the bargain. With this last legal act, the name

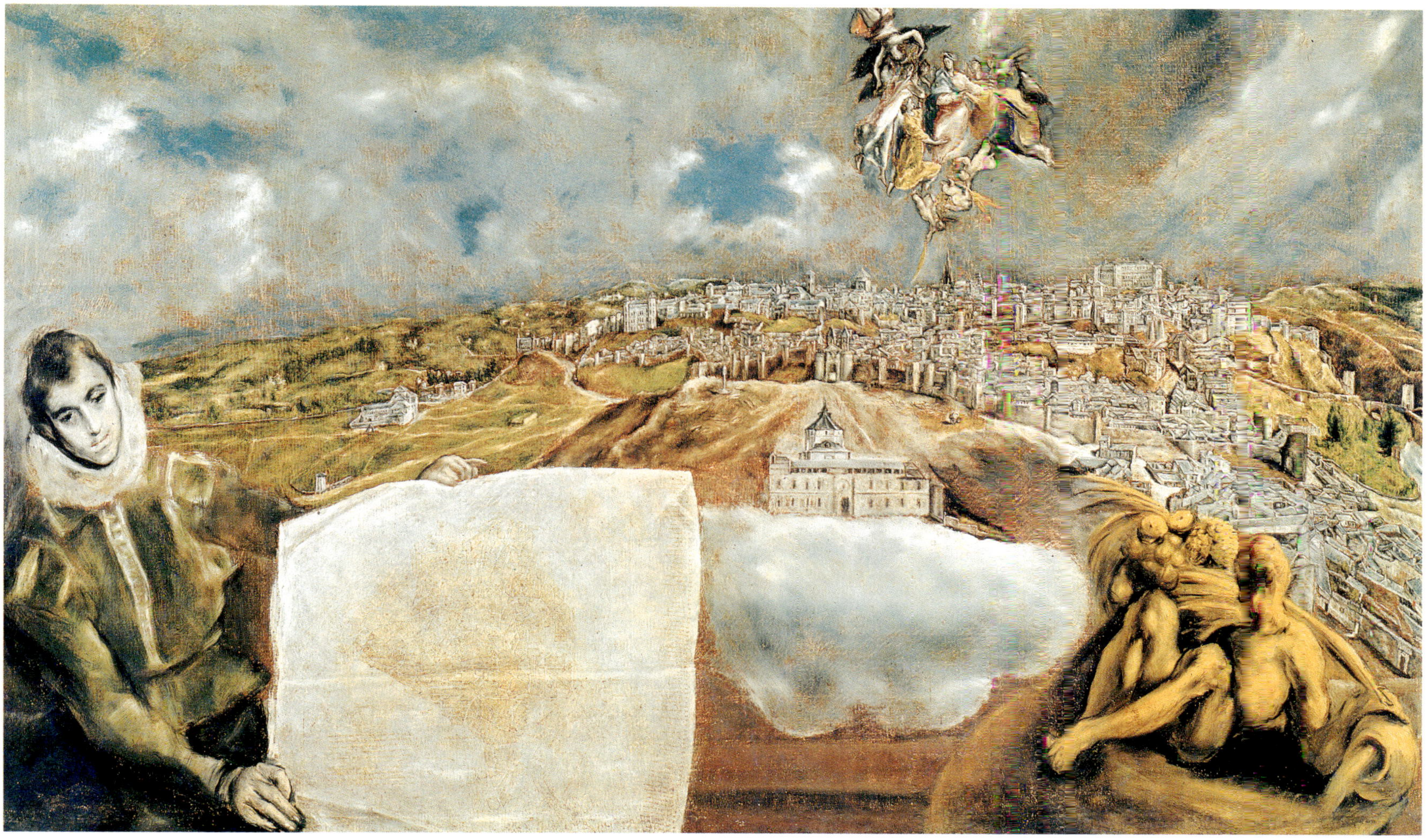

VIEW AND MAP OF TOLEDO
1608-14. Toledo Cathedral.
132 × 228 cm

of El Greco disappeared from the book of the dead as it had from the roll of painters, and his mortal remains vanished into the abyss of the Void. He had been transformed, without his (or even Orwell's) permission, into a bodiless non-person. Today when our admiration for El Greco moves us to make All out of the Nothingness, invert the rhythm of Time and turn on its head the verdict of the Past, what we find is a false "House of El Greco," a false sepulchre, a false country, and, if my information in the matter is correct, until just a while ago the false bones of El Greco, unveiled to the greater glory of Official Painting.

But why did he leave Italy at thirty-nine years of age and go to Spain? What was it that made him decide to go off into yet another exile, when he had already known two? In 1579, during the suit he was forced to undergo in order to recover his payment for the *Espolio,* or as it is also known, *The Disrobing of Christ,* we find this exchange:

DIEGO DE ORENSE (attorney): Is it true that you were brought to this city to make the retablo for Santo Domingo el Viejo, which is now

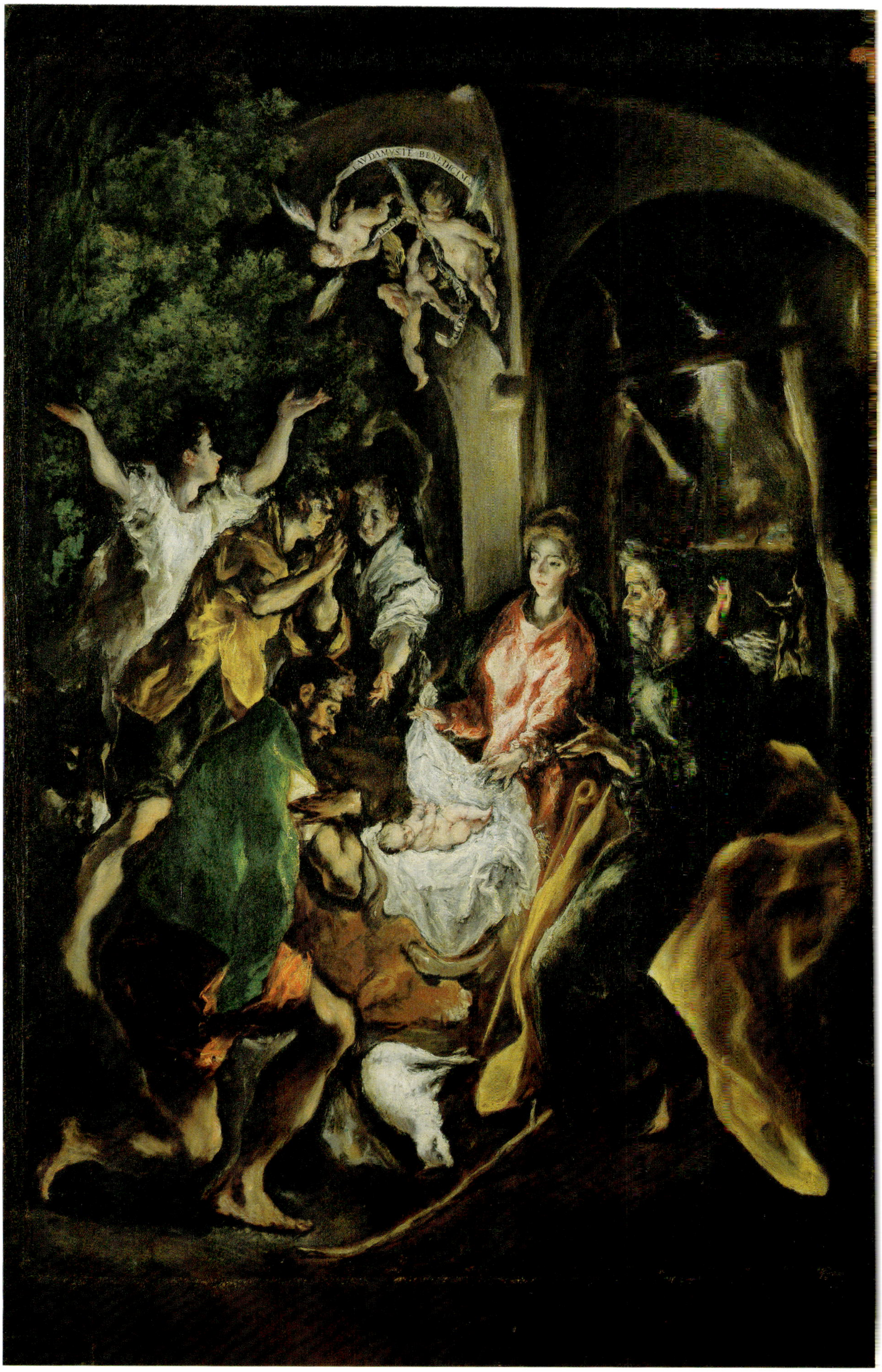

THE SHEPHERDS' ADORATION
1594-1604. New York, Metropolitan Museum.
111 × 65 cm

finished and hung in that church?

EL GRECO: I am not obliged to render account of my reason for coming to this city, and as for other questions that you may put me, I do not have to answer them either, for it is not required.

El Greco's quiet determination to invert values and meanings had provoked an incident in Rome, among the painters there, that concerned Michelangelo's *Last Judgment.* "If the entire work were demolished," he had declared, like Joseph before his brothers, "I would paint it again, and no worse for the painting, either." Others said that he had urged the Pope to have Michelangelo's frescos scraped off the walls so that he might paint over them. Mancini states that "all the painters and connoisseurs so resented him that he was forced to go to Spain." Fury seized them by the tail, they stood face to face with rage, and so they could not see, much less admire, El Greco.

In Rome, Mannerism, the Baroque, and Michelangelo were the fashion, but El Greco liked El Greco, and if he had had to choose a contemporary he would have chosen Tintorel-

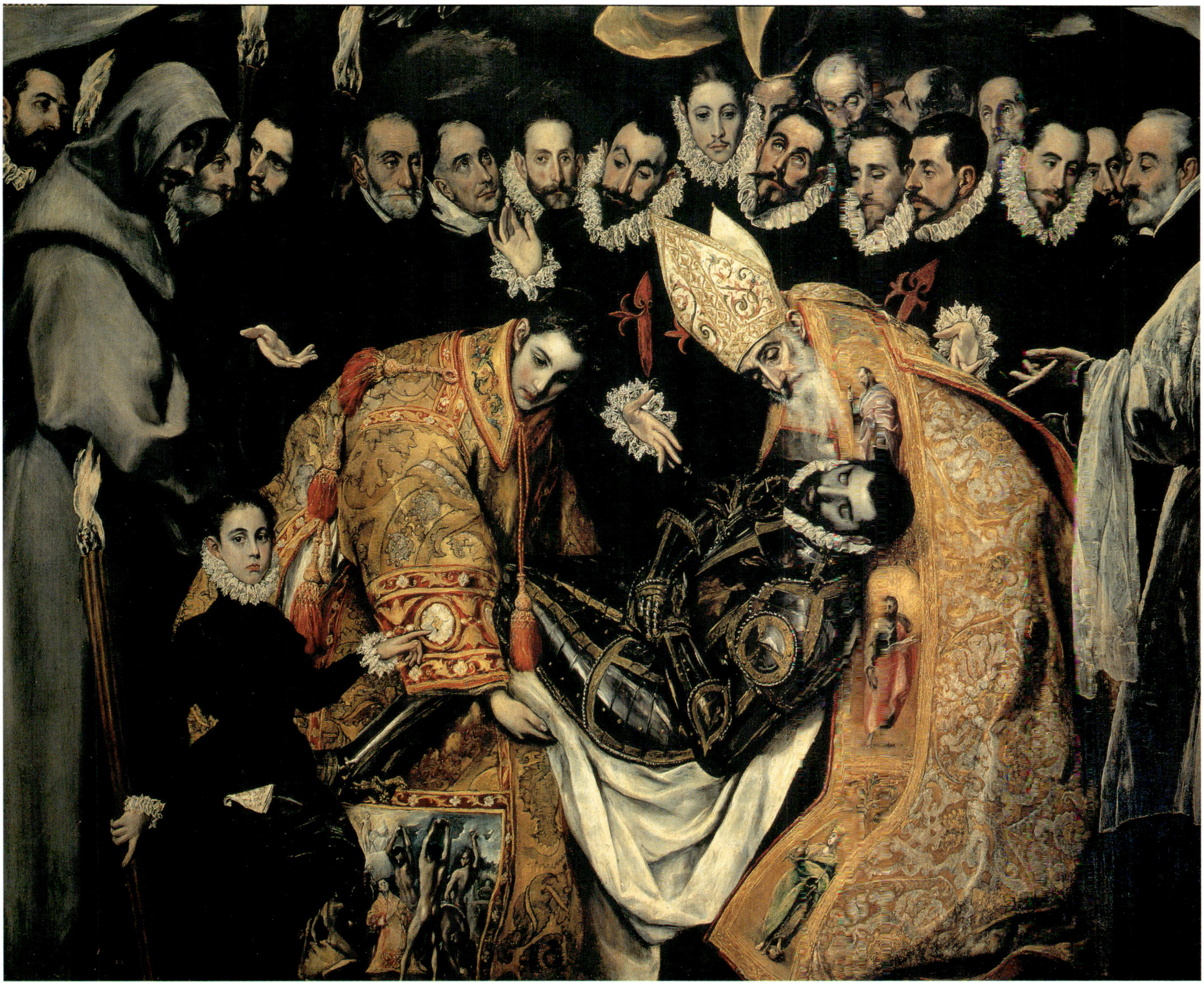

COUNT OF ORGAZ' BURIAL
1586-88. Toledo, Santo Tomé.
detail

lo. In order to secure his independence, he entered the Roman Academy of San Lucas as a "*pittore a carta,*" which is to say miniaturist; he had trained his hand in Crete as a youth painting wooden icons. But in Rome, thanks to the Pope and the painters mired in conformism, El Greco found the only person who might have been able to teach him something, if he'd only known how to paint. Benito Arias, "El Montano," knew how to live, how to think, how to reason, how to seduce. He frightened some people and intimidated many with his title, and for good reason: he was psychiatrist to the President of the Empire, or, translated four hundred years, the confessor to Philip II, King of Spain. This "compleat man," El Greco's elder by fourteen years, so watchfully cultivated the cult of discretion that he has been virtually swallowed up by History. He was Extremaduran, though born in Andalusia, not far from the square on which, in the chessboard of the Universe, the World Champion Ruy López was set. Thanks to his talent and his arts, after a long trial which he underwent to determine whether there were Jewish ancestors in the closet, "El Montano" at last managed to have himself made a priest.

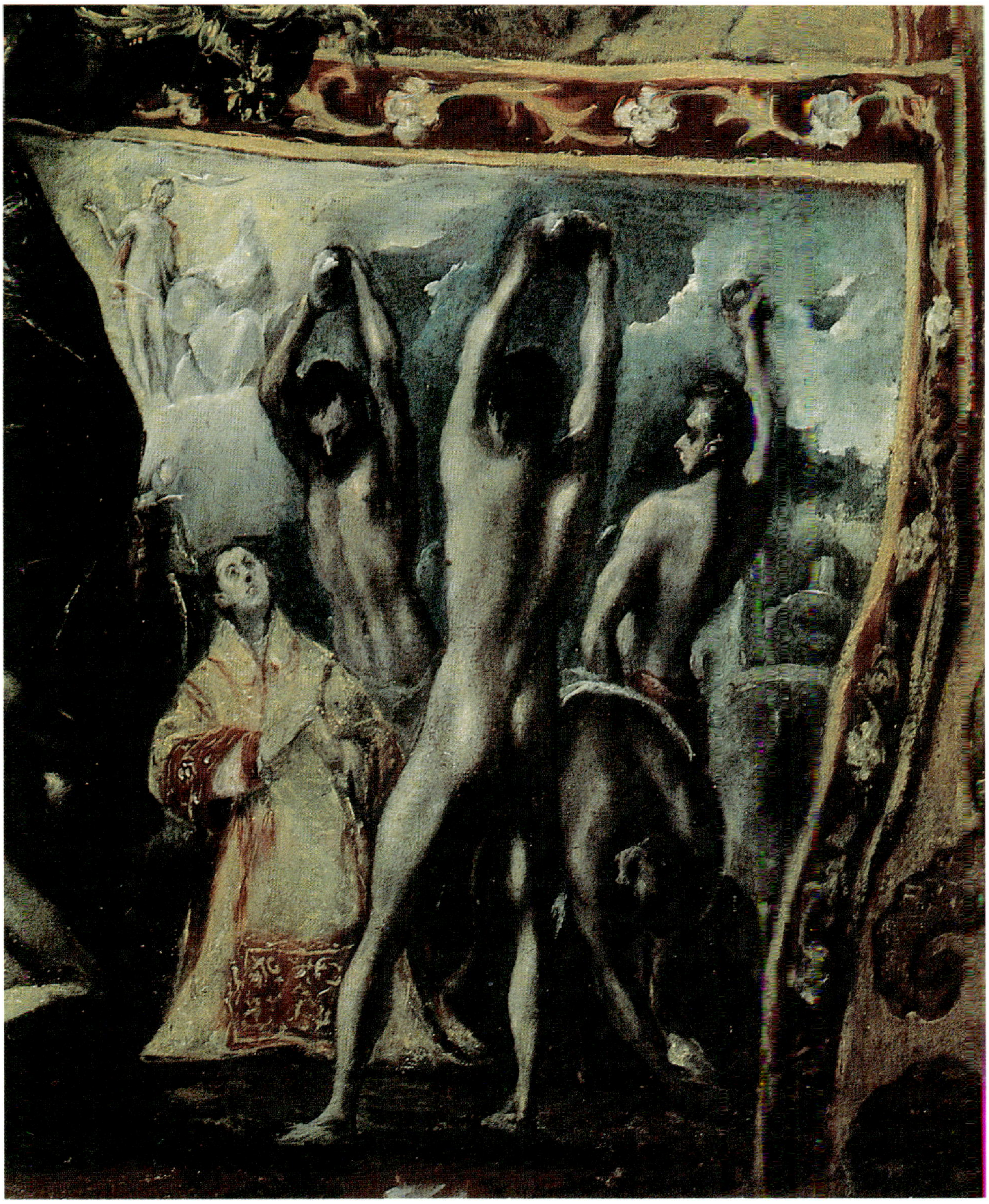

COUNT OF ORGAZ' BURIAL
1586-88. Toledo, Santo Tomé.
detail

There where his blood might have betrayed him, his money and his powers of seduction managed to camouflage and even to ennoble him. Under the very nose of the Inquisition he created a secret sect called the Family of Love: "He that walks among men must have the cunning of the serpent," the circle of its initiates intoned. They were but a small group, which inverted the relationship of religion and society; listening to the Voice of God, which was its guide and its treasure, the Family of Love considered itself above churches (whether Tridentine or Protestant) and the usual creeds, and even showed contempt for them. This club, its members gathered together in the name of Love, suited El Greco: it subverted the relationship between the spiritual and the temporal. His understanding stood in admiration and his will was inflamed.

This unusual painter and the seditious confessor had met in the Vatican; both believed that behind the walls of Reality there were locked chimeras, illusions, errors, and ravings. On this trip to Rome, El Montano intended to carry out the mission his master the King of Spain had charged him with: he was to secure the Pope's approval for a polyglot Bible in five languages,

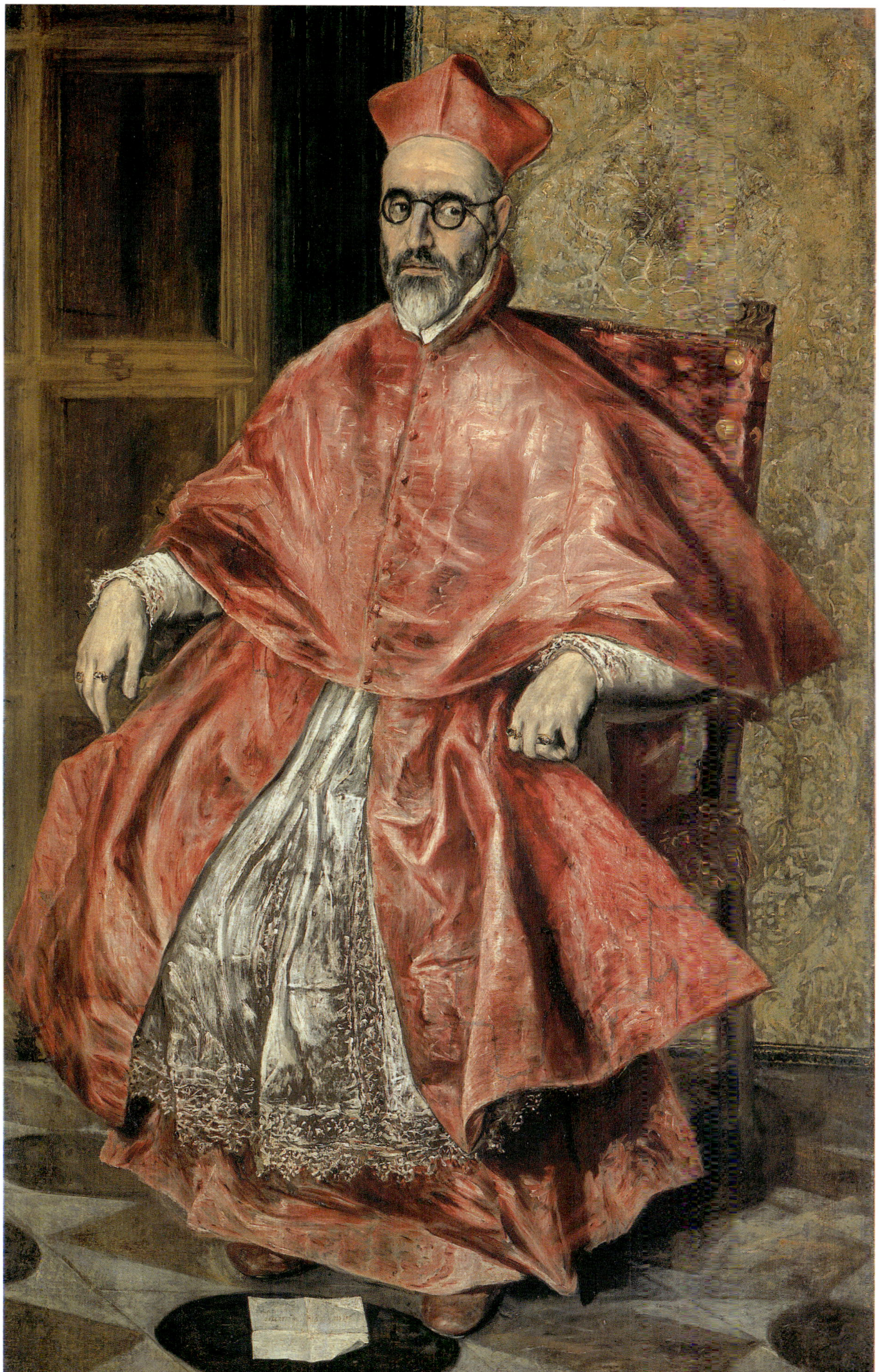

PORTRAIT OF CARDINAL NINO DE GUEVARA
1596-1600. New York, Metropolitan Museum.
171 × 108 cm

the Bible to be produced by the Flemish printer Plantino with scrupulous faithfulness to the Hebrew original. The Hebraicists of the University at Salamanca, captained by León de Castro, and exchanging their professorial gowns for constable's warrants, denounced this deicidal book to the Inquisition. Fray Luis de León opposed his colleagues, and was imprisoned in a Salamancan dungeon for his pains. Benito Arias, with the cunning of a serpent, managed to thwart the plans of these enemies of tolerance — who, as is often the case, were those men in all of Rome most mistrustful of intelligence. El Greco, in silence, admired his maneuvers. In his attempt to convince his friend to cross the sea and journey to Spain, El Montano spoke an intriguing prophecy: "Great is the adornment of thy caparison, greater still that of thy destiny."

After his first exile in Venice and his second in Rome, this third and definitive remove to Toledo was to change his life and his work forever, though not so his identity or his signature. "El Greco" never took to that name, which was a nickname about as justified as "The Gypsy" is to its Belgian owner centuries later. In the language of his forebears, in the hand of his

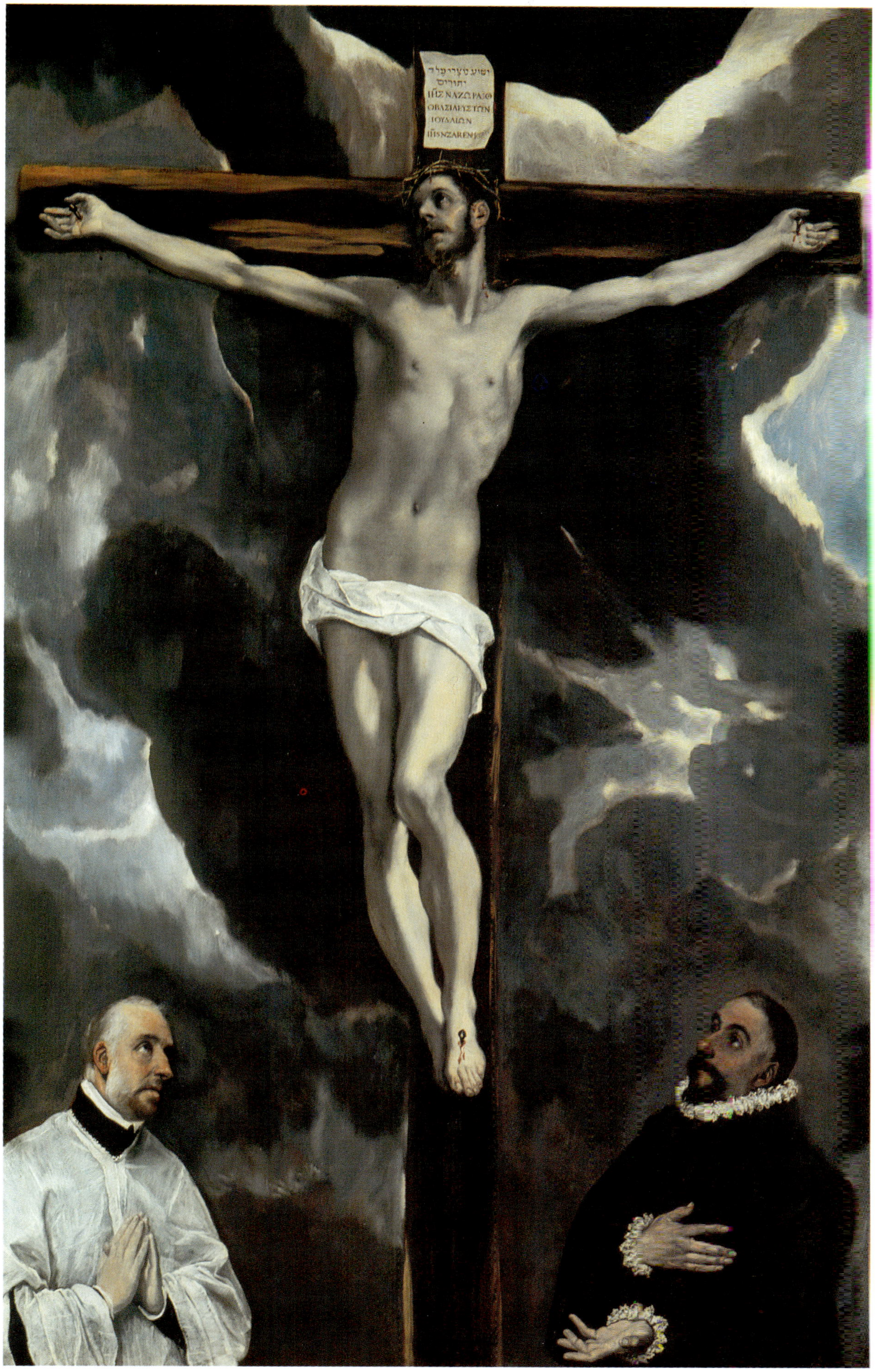

CHRIST ON THE CROSS
1585-90. Paris, Louvre.
250 × 180 cm

grandparents, and in the Greek alphabet, he always set his name on his paintings, or had it put down as it sounded on legal documents. Sometimes the scrivener of the moment would Latinize or Spanish-ize his name, turn the *K* of his surname into a more domesticated *C,* and call him *Domenico* or *Dominico,* but "El Greco" always signed his paintings:

DOMENIKOS THEOTOKOPOULOS

Sometimes he would add expressions such as EPOIEI (*"made it"*), or KRES (*"the Cretan"*), or KRES EPOIEI (*"the Cretan made it"*). Apparently, he didn't want to be classified as Castilian. But if he had ever gone back to Crete, he would have done everything in his power not to be written off as a Cretan, either. El Greco inverted his relationship with the place in which he lived. He lived in a place without being of that place, inside a space recreated by him, the theater of his own extraordinary abilities, in which he would weave his immortality out of the secretions of his own genius.

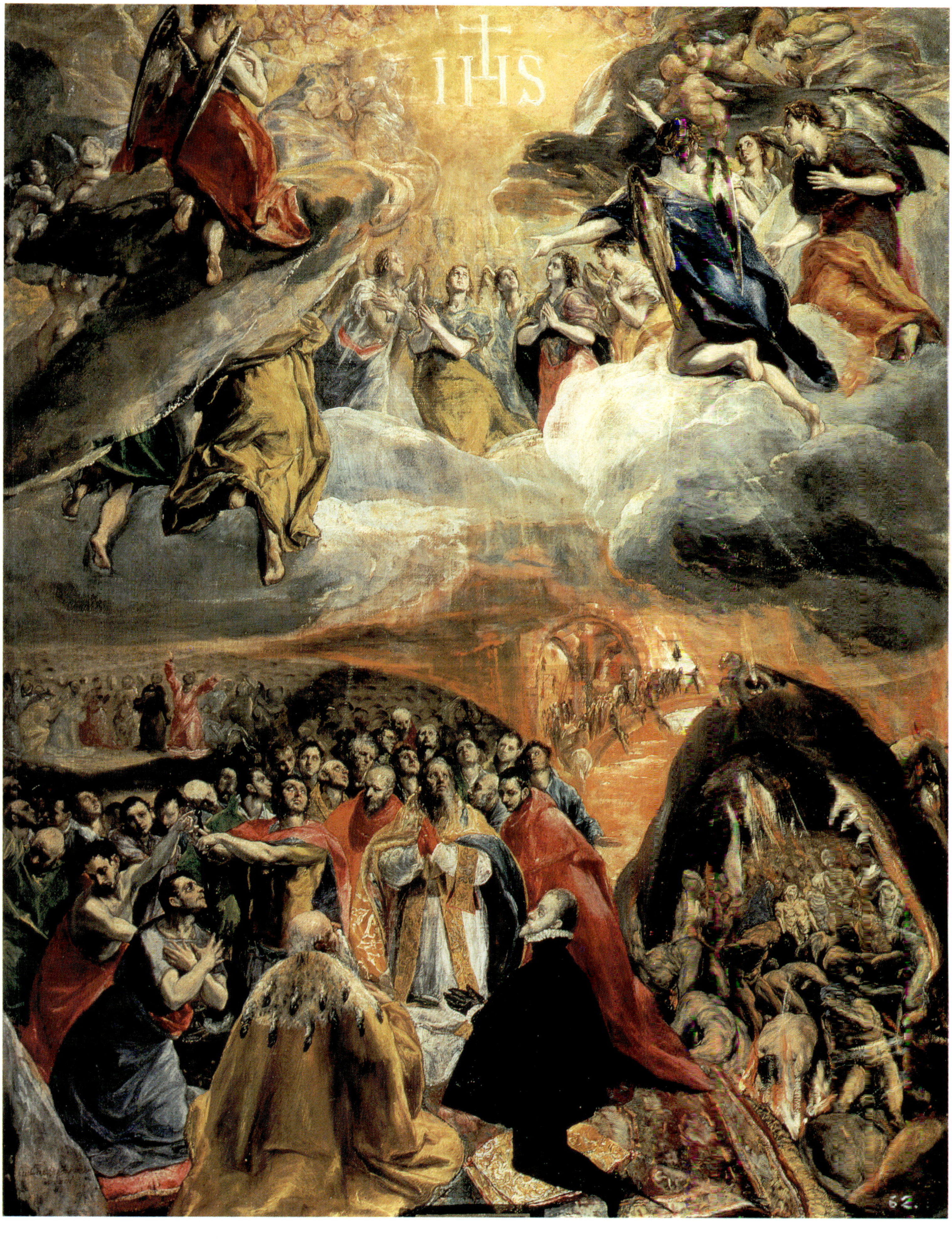

FELIPPE II'S DREAM (Allegory of the Holy Alliance)
1579. Escurial, Monastery.
140 × 110 cm

His nickname was to be "El Greco," the words in Italian, and not, as one would think more reasonable, *"El Griego,"* in Spanish. Thanks to this shift in his pseudonym, Domenikos achieved one last exile — into Italian. For the Spaniards, he was not an emigrant Greek (*"El Griego"*), but a Greek exile from Rome, to be known by his Italian denomination "El Greco", as though three hundred years before Mateos Gago, Spain were to make the painter a foreigner squared: "We've no need of his sort of extravagances here." The only name that this Son of the Mother of God (THEOTOKOPOULOS) could have deservedly carried would have been "El Cretense" — "The Cretan." *KRES,* El Greco signed his work, thereby declaring to posterity "I am Cretan, not Venetian, as the Prado will announce one day." Venice was the duchy that had turned the island of his birth into a province. El Greco's own history leads to hesitancy. He was a mass of so many contradictions when he was born... and there were many more to come. Years after his death, we find historians of art who in order to add yet another paragraph to the chapter of confusions, call him *Domenico della greche,* and still

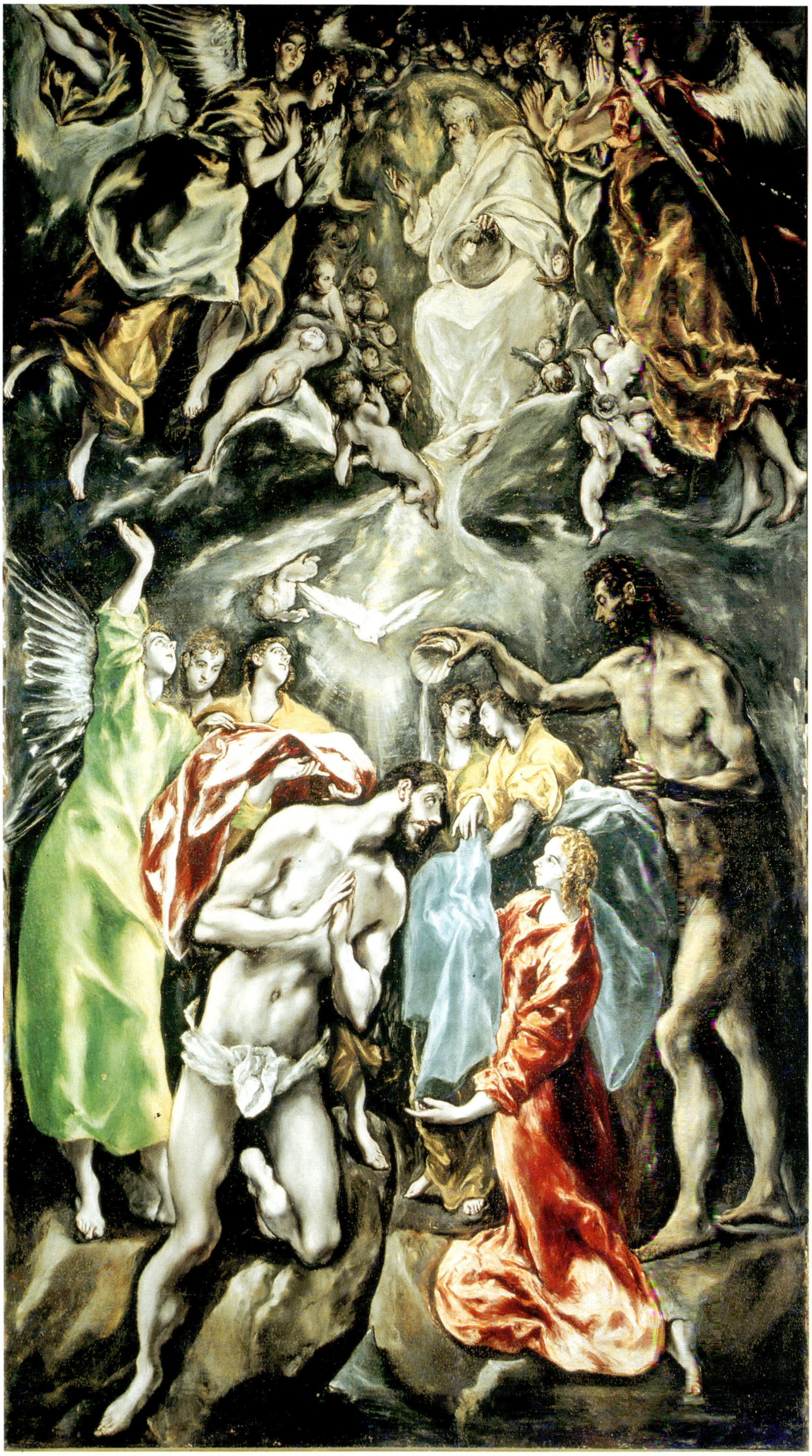

CHRIST'S BAPTISM
1608-14. Toledo, Tavera Hospital.
330 × 211 cm

others *El Grechi.*

If we continue to follow the itinerary which has been leading us step by step from the painter's death in Toledo to Rome, and thence to Venice, in an upside-down chronology (as El Greco might have liked, in fact), we come at last to the day of shivering solitude, the day of his birth.

El Greco was born in Candia (now Iráklion or Heraclion), the capital of the island of Crete. Crete itself is called Candia in Italy, and so it is with good reason that he is sometimes recorded as "a Candiot." In the year in which that dark hopper of Fortune, after so many near-misses, at last spat out our number and bestowed upon us mortals the Grand Prize in Painting — that is, in 1541 — Domenikos came into the world, opening his eyes to the Aegean Ocean and the banners of ducal Venice. "And to great honor!" most Cretans would have cried. Venice was at the time the least bad of Crete's invaders. It "protected" the island in much the same way the colonial powers at the turn of this century "protected" their subject "protectorates." Yet many Cretans liked the idea of being the sentinels of Venice — and better still, of the entire

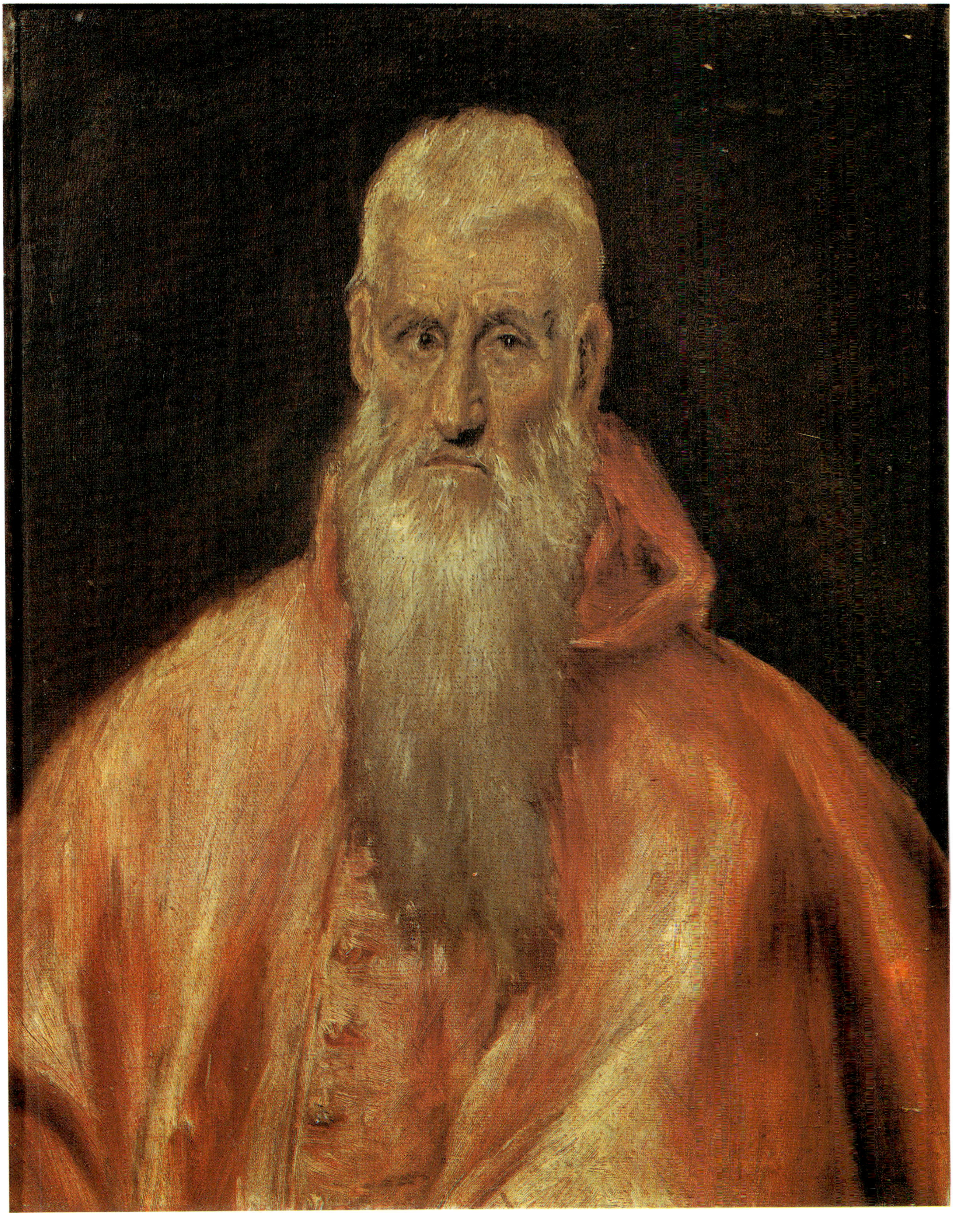

SAINT JEROME
1600-10. Bayonne, Bonnat Museum.
30 × 24 cm

"civilized" Western world — against the Turkish Empire, which had already, and without the Ottomans' even knowing it, created the dreaded figure of the *bogeyman.* "The Turks'll get you," Western mothers cautioned their children, as the mothers of Constantinople warned their children to "watch out the Christians don't get you."

Crete, planted there absurdly on the front lines of this drawing-room battle, knew a great deal about relativity, and even about metamorphosis. Crete was a stopover and refueling station for messengers sent secretly by the Spanish Christian emperor to the Sultan of the Ottoman Turks, and vice-versa, while for the consumption of the masses the monarchs could find no words in the dictionary vile enough to insult their enemies, nor weapons in their arsenals sufficiently terrible to destroy them "for always and forever." In this climate of neither-yes-nor-no, of winners losing, of a game of lies whose sequel was to be blood, sweat, and tears (or what amounted to the same in those days — torture and enslavement), young Domenikos opened his eyes, and gave a shrug of absolute recognition. From the cradle his mind was formed to the measure of that *mare magnum*

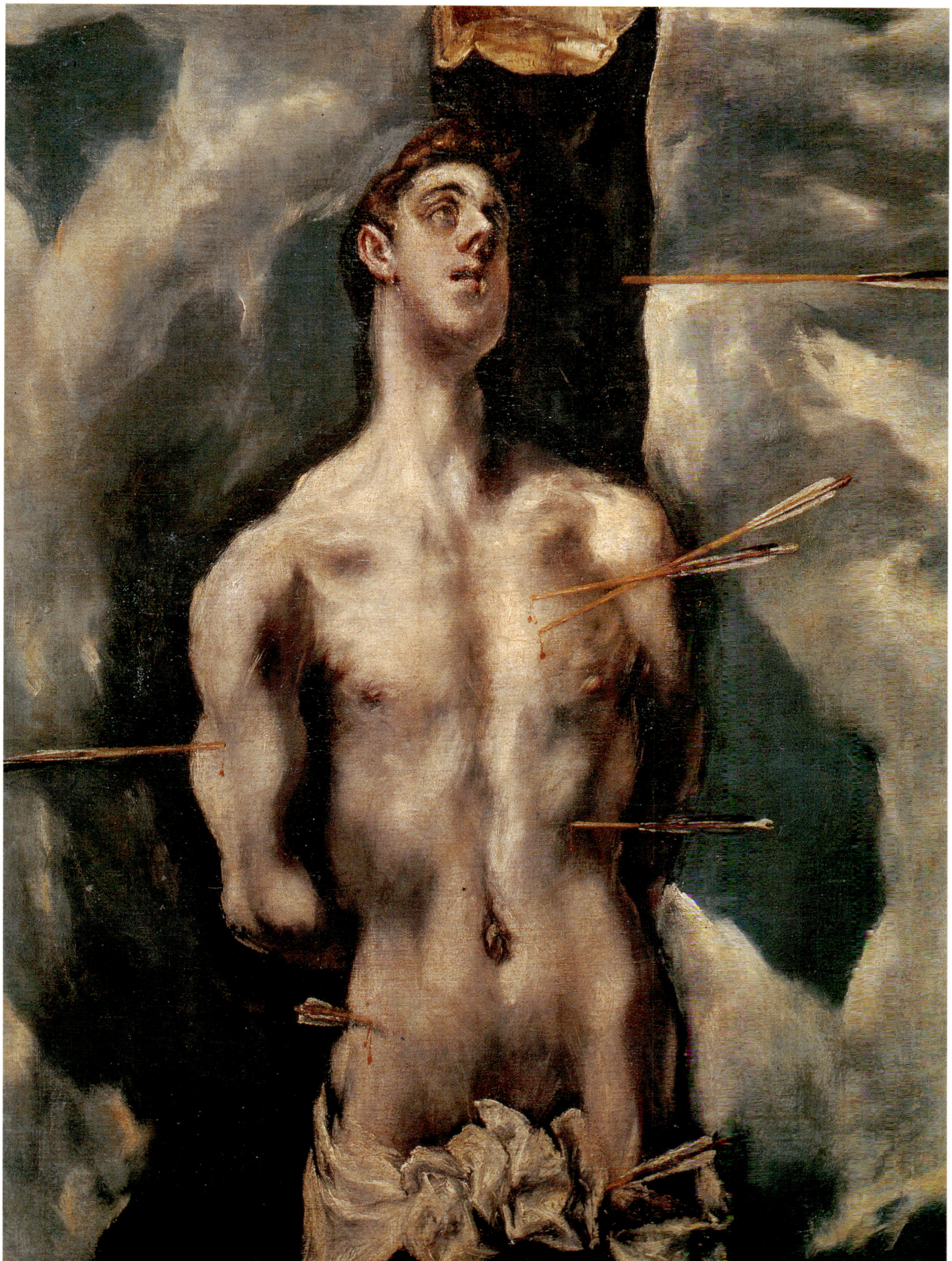

SAINT SEBASTIAN
1610-14. Madrid, Prado.
115 × 85 cm

which was the world that lay around him, and where, to the sound of the trumpets of the armies, the lines that connected reality to thought could be scrambled in the wink of an eye. Warriors sketched the topography of the hand of chaos, in a barren plain of raw eternity.

About El Greco's mother, nothing has ever been known, not even her name. About his father we know two bald facts: one, that he was named Jorghi, and two that he "must have" died in 1566. St George, who as we know stood docile before the marvel, was able to bring the dragon to its knees — a deed which, recently, dullards have doubted and dyed-in-the-wool agnostics, who don't know enough to take refuge in dreams, have laughed at. Surely St George's duel, so often talked about *en famille,* made El Greco not laugh, but think, for the stars are a landscape, too. If I have learned from Luce Moreau's doctorate (or her dissertation, anyway) that the wisest and most intelligent man of his time, Isaac Newton, once organized an expedition to the Alps to look for dragons, I can hardly be surprised that the young Greco, shifting the grounds of the relation between "sacred" history and reason, should go out hunting dragons

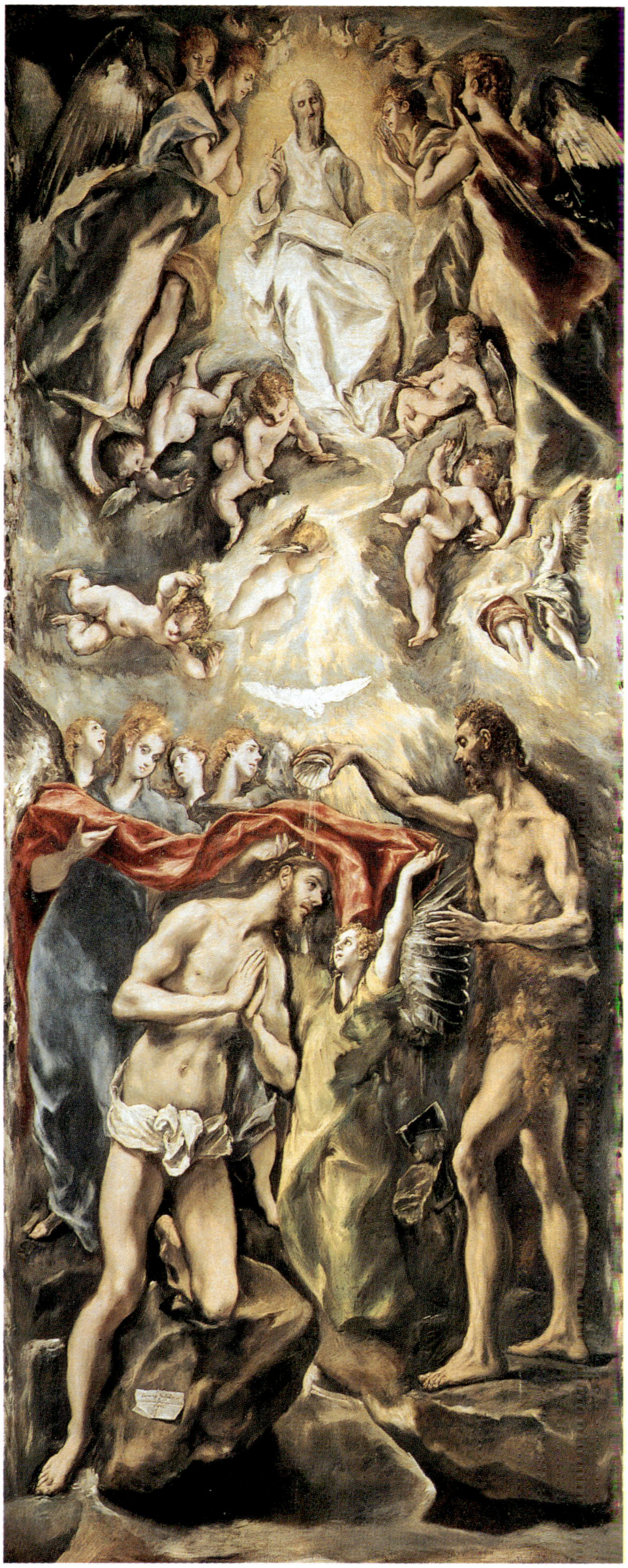

CHRIST'S BAPTISM
1897-1600. Madrid, Prado.
350 × 144 cm

on the top of Mount Athos, rising mythically before his house — the ultimate example of positivistic investigation with a touch of madness. El Greco was never to be consoled by what was reasonable, but rather by the silent grace of things.

El Greco's brother was named Manoussos. He was a tax collector... for Venice; it was a position sufficiently equivocal for a citizen of the colony of Crete that it made a mark on the younger brother's education in the field of ambiguity. Sixty years later, when it looked as though he were destined to be just one shadow more in the life of Domenikos, Manoussos appeared in Toledo, like a warm whisper. It was now the seventeenth century (if only just), and El Greco had figured out that beauty demands patience. Manoussos was shepherding a group of Greeks who had come to Castile as beggars, but beggars *de luxe.* In his charge there were princes, archbishops, captains, bishops, and governors, come to plead for alms. In all the History of Mendicancy, no pack of panhandlers has ever received such welcome, or enjoyed such success, not even those international organizations of charlatans and swindlers who, mount-

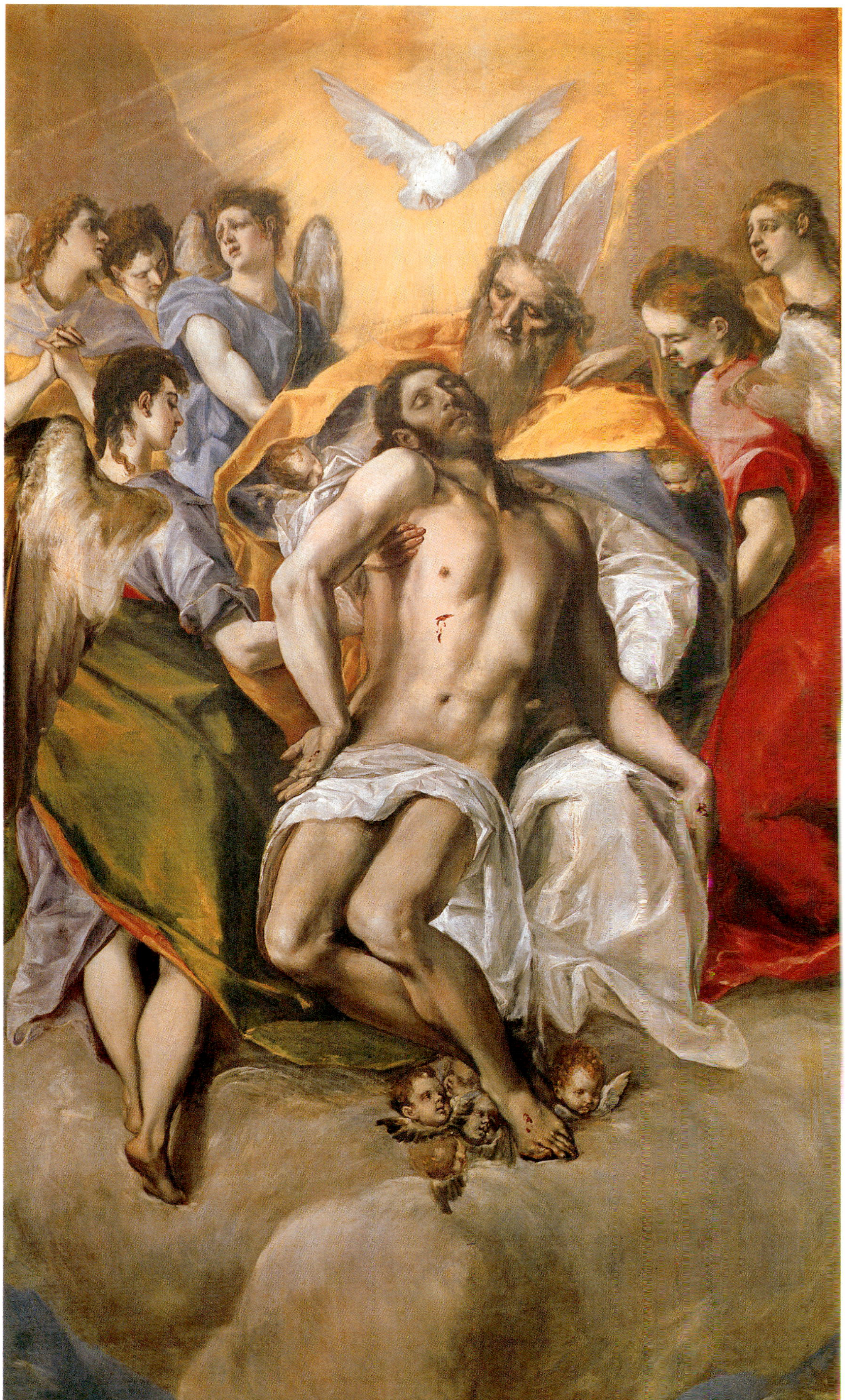

SORROWFUL TRINITY
1577-79. Madrid, Prado.
300 × 179 cm

ed on the ass of charity, live like nabobs at the expense of yet other asses. There had occurred to these grand and stately moochers an infallible ruse: the money collected was to be used to pay for the destruction wrought by the Turks. They were thus giving the pagan Castilians the chance to prepare for their swift ascent into Heaven astride the mule of charity, and at the same time to shore up their triumphant racism. Manoussos would remain in Toledo, to the great satisfaction of his brother, and together (as El Greco's lover was now dead) they would go down into the plain of the Tagus in search of a Paradise Lost.

It was at the Greek School in Crete that El Greco took his first steps, like a sturdy oak among poplars. Instead of specializing, as his brushmates did, in the very small or the very grand, he swung between the two poles as though they were two postulates of one theorem. Thus he practiced the technique of *fresco* on the exterior walls of monasteries and churches while simultaneously mastering the miniature form in the studios of icon-copiers. The tiny gave him a vision of the entire spectrum of the universe, and vice-versa. If he had

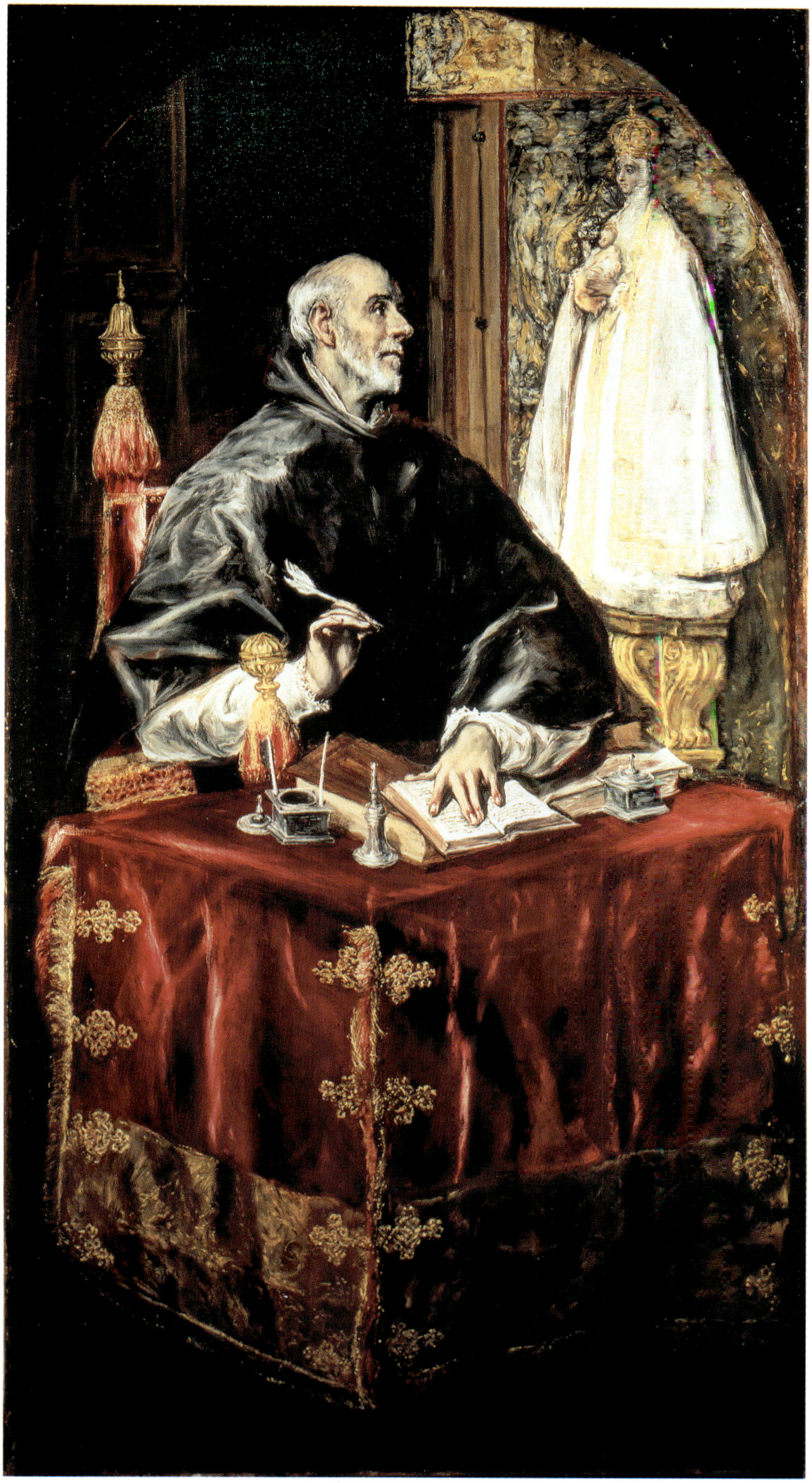

SAINT ILDEFONSE
1603-05. Illescas, Charity Hospital.
187 × 102 cm

devoted himself to the Exact Sciences, he would have invented Fractals, without waiting for Newton or Leibnitz to invent the Calculus.

It was precisely one day of the Feast of the Holy Innocents, December 28, in 1566, when the least naive painter on the face of the earth sold his first work. Eyes closed, he was awaiting his fate, when one of his icons was bought; it was to be the grand prize in the Island lottery. Thus he was to learn at first hand that art is a lottery, a crap-shoot as the vulgar say, in which the best or the worst can win the pot and gain immortality, or shoot the snake-eyes of indifference and oblivion, as the rules of confusion dictate. The name of El Greco suddenly burst upon the pages of the History of Art; it boarded the alchemical Shooting Star of Vicissitude during the ritual of the Lottery of Babylon.

While thanks to the various exiles in his life El Greco was to come to know several cultures — their greatnesses, their meannesses, their heroisms, and their fanaticisms — even in Crete he had the fortune to live among Jews, orthodox Christians, and Muslims, in the snowy, radiant desert of time. The Noise and Passion of histo-

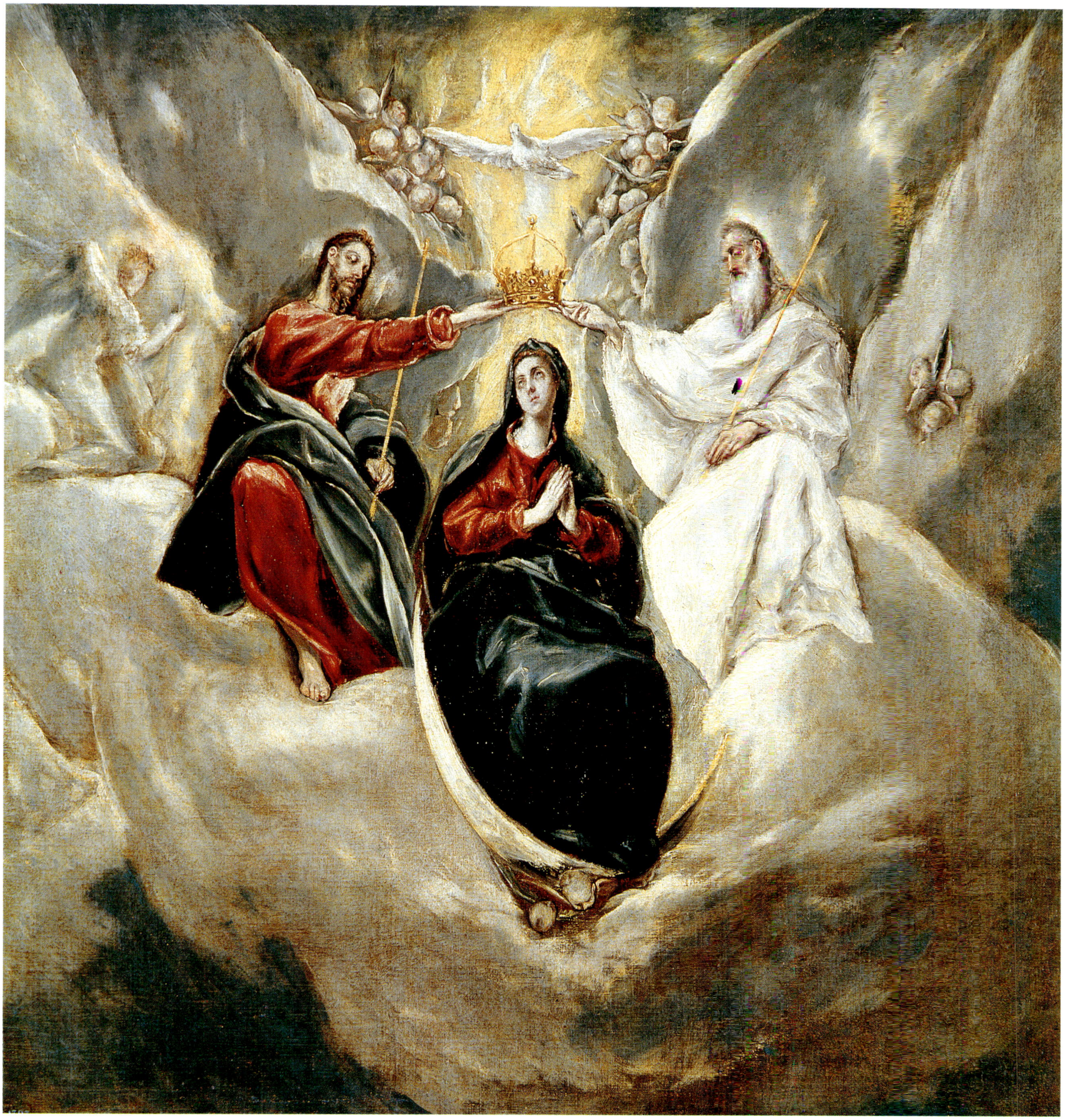

THE CORONATION OF THE HOLY VIRGIN
1590. Madrid, Prado.
90 × 100 cm

ry had set the island just at the faultline where the empire of the Christian King Philip II and that of the Muslim King Suleyman met. In 1565 Crete received news, decked out in a wealth of bloody exaggerations, from her sister island Malta. To our Candiot's ears came rumors of sacking and pillaging, defenders put to the invaders' swords, and other fell deeds of Christian conquerors. He knew that in Constantinople the conquered had told stories of torture and cruelty which sounded strangely the same. Hand in hand, marching right in step, each side cried down the other's carnage, while neither spoke of its own crimes. Domenikos fled Crete. He refused to become a spectator at the ruin of a country, an onlooker at one of those shivarees of war which might pave the island with corpses, and flood the Aegean with blood.

Five years afterward another great island in the area, Cyprus, a Venetian protectorate occupied by the Ottomans, was to serve as pretext for another mobilization of armies. The fleet of the Holy Roman Empire would proclaim victory in the Turkish-Christian War after winning the Battle of Lepanto, yet the Turks, every bit as enthusiastically, would claim victory as well — for

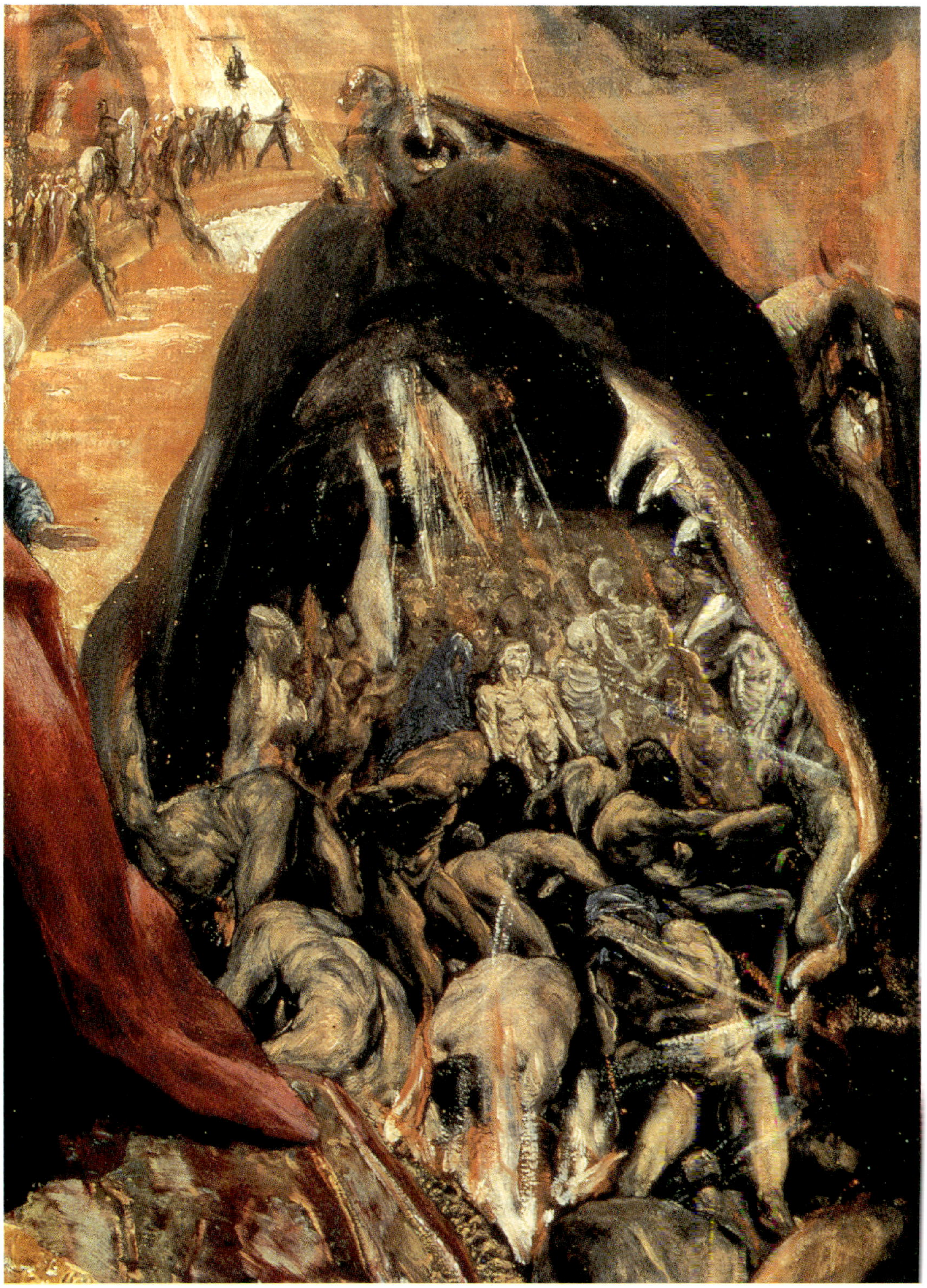

FELIPPE II'S DREAM (Allegory of the Holy Alliance)
1579. Escurial, Monastery.
detail

they had not only not yielded one foot of Cyprus, they had actually pinched off a few inches of Christian territory in North Africa. All around El Greco, inspiration, wreathed in the haze of war, was dying.

The Battle of Lepanto took place on October 7, 1571; five years earlier, El Greco had begun his life as an emigrant. His journey was to have three stages. For each remove, El Greco, much like an exile today, chose a bright shining city, a magical city where (so go the legends that candidates for exile feverishly whisper to each other) Gold, Immortality, Love, and Evil beckon. El Greco did not believe in these fairy tales, these stories for the children of the poor, and yet, adrift in the limbo of hope, he acted, and traveled, as though he believed in them.

His first remove carried him to Venice, the capital of the duchy, the great city which in his beloved, provincial Candia had shone brighter than the sun. His second took him to Rome, the center of Christianity, the navel of the Renaissance, a dazzling city in the eyes of every Venetian. His third and last remove was to transport him to the heart of the empire, to the side of

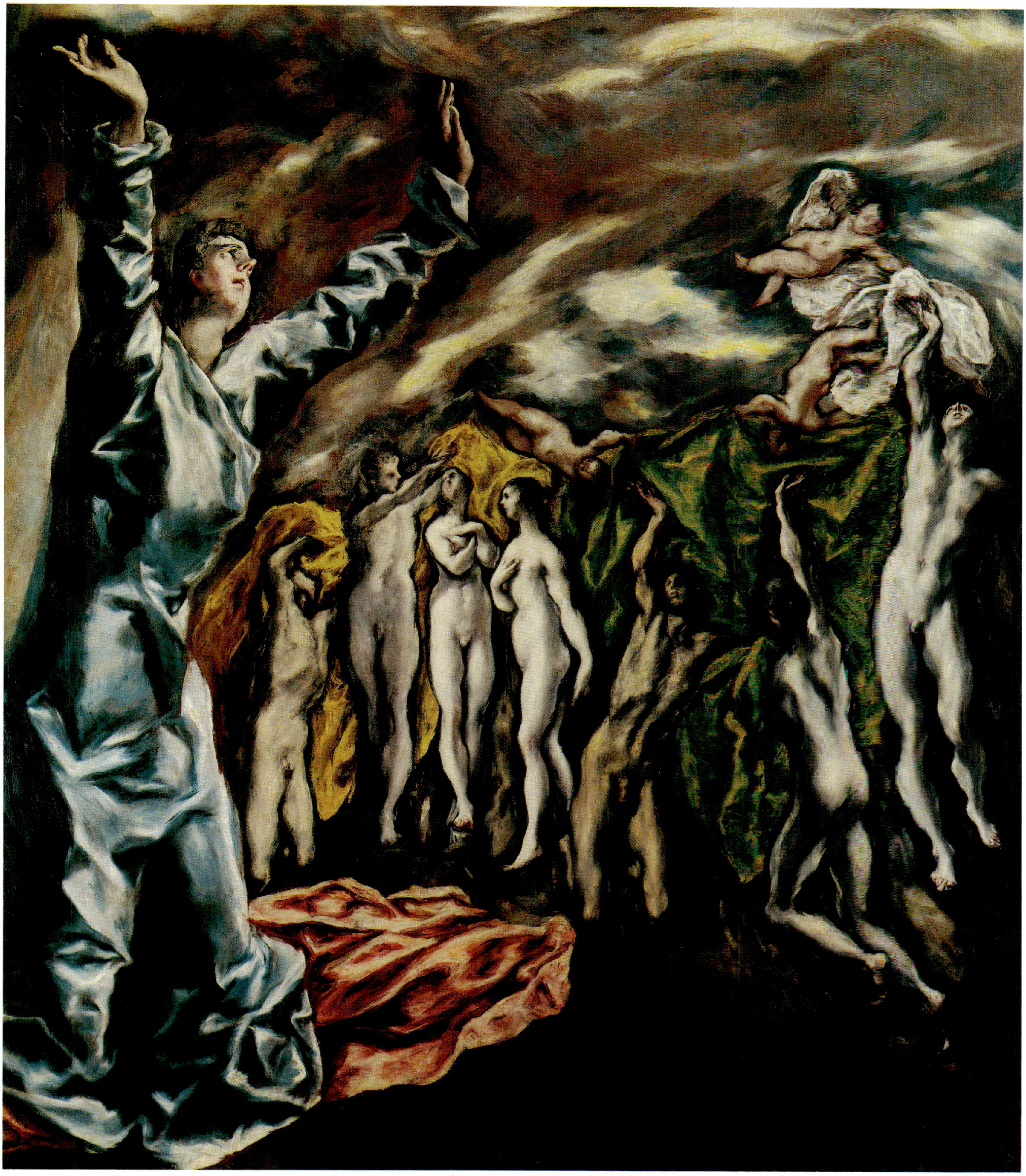

THE FIFTH SEAL OF THE APOCALYPSE
1608-14. New York, Metropolitan Museum.
225 × 193 cm

Philip II and the "eighth wonder of the world," the Escorial. What did it matter if in order to penetrate to the axis of the world one had to pass through the antechamber of Toledo! But the antechamber became the lodging, Toledo became his panacea, outside space and time.

There at the border of the Void, the palaces, cathedrals, and bridges of Toledo inverted, to El Greco's eyes, the order of geography. In several of his paintings, and in all of those in which the city figures, he moved the landmarks about. He was as much in Candia as in his great ramshackle rented house in Toledo, and the past was as present as the future.

In Venice, people always say, El Greco's teacher was Titian, and in Rome, Tintoretto; in Toledo, his teacher was to be Toledo. But the Talmud tells us that "one learns more from the students than from the teachers."

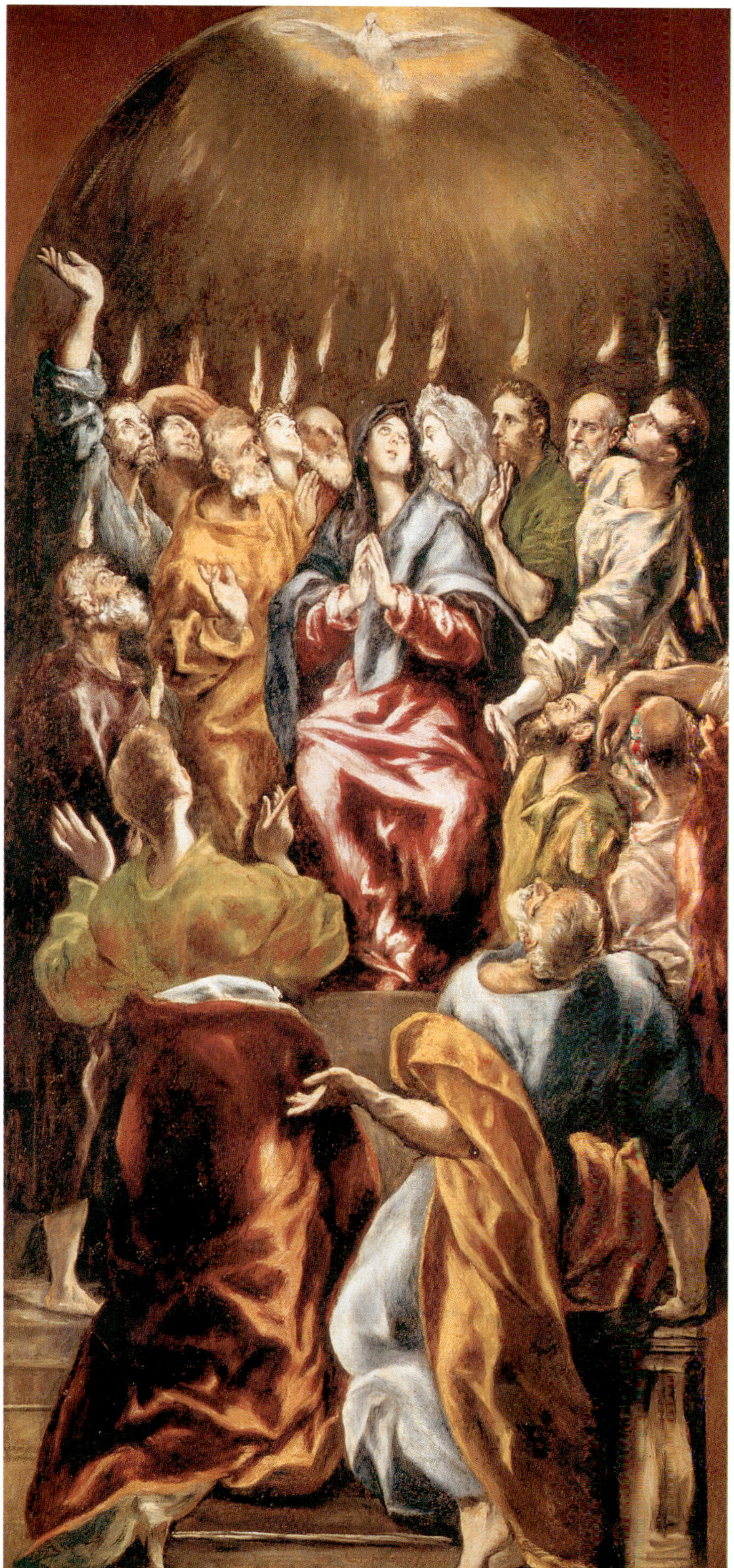

PENTECOST
1605-10. Madrid, Prado.
275 × 127 cm

TOLEDO

For El Greco, Toledo was a city of unreal bodies, equivocal pleasures, a confused presentness, a raw eternity.

When he arrived in Toledo, the city seemed chimerical yet autonomous, it seemed a region ruled by Natural Law. Of course Castile and Spain took for granted that it was a part of their lands, their sovereign realm.

The city sat atop a peak of ambiguity in the center of a region as violent as its precipices, its roads, its *cigarrales* (those eminently "Spanish" orchards and gardens), its abysses and its mountain summits. Predators and raptors, in choosing this region for their home, became impatient, empirical, and hungry for tangible fruits. Like El Greco, they adored the lightning which reduced the world to ashes... yet whose flashes illuminated it as well.

Everything he saw there was worthy of veneration, and became a model for his work, like the clouds at evening. And yet when El Greco arrived in Toledo a crushing fatalism possessed him, like that which had invaded the city. Dis-

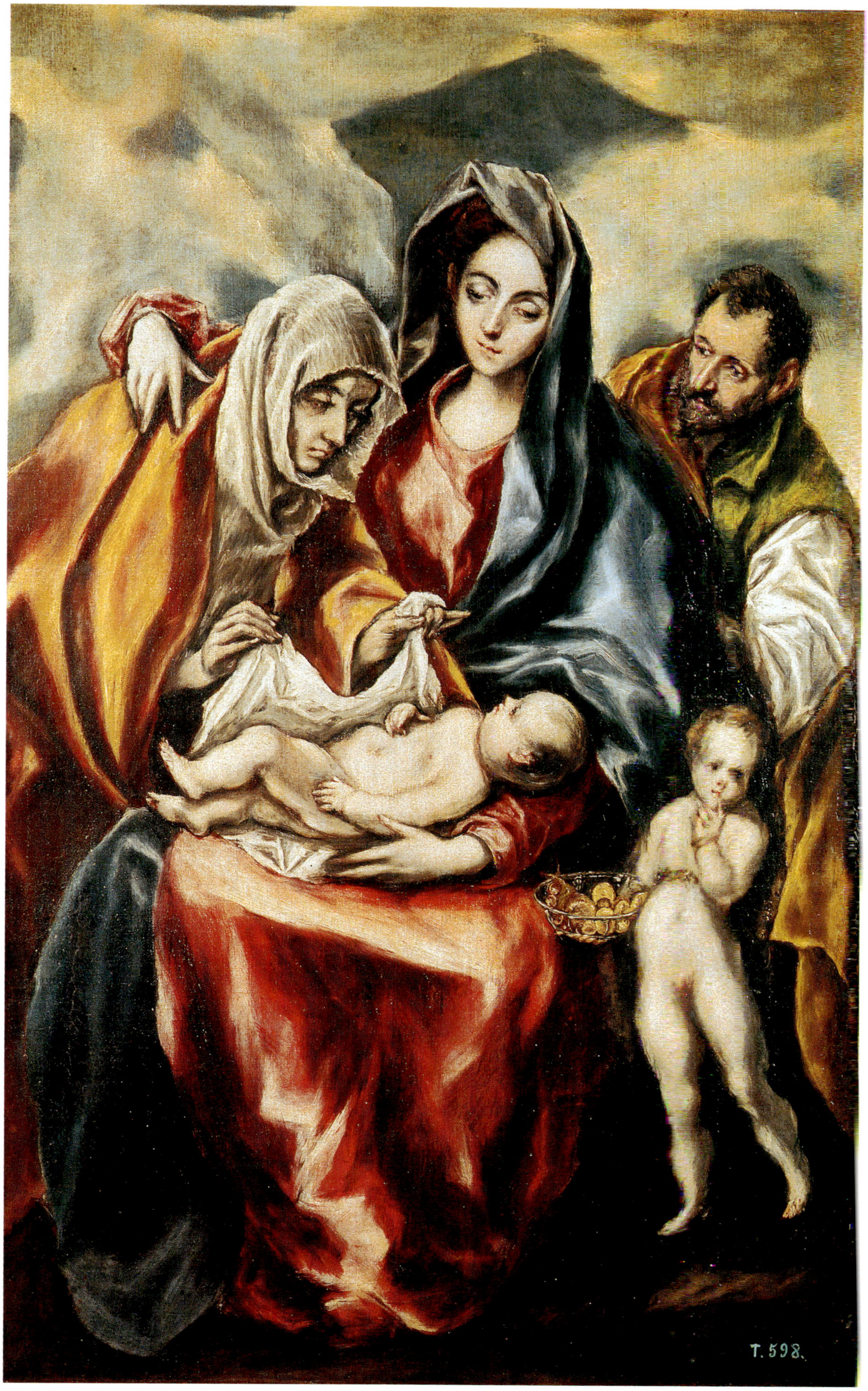

HOLY FAMILLY WITH SAINT ANNE AND SAINT JEAN BAPTISTE
1597. Valencia, Colegio del Patriarca.
107 × 69 cm

illusionment had wiped out the triumphant spirit of the former "capital of the Empire."

There wafted into this foreigner's studio certain alchemists' tales which circulated among a small group of "adepts." Toledo had only been built, they said, after a founding act of sacrifice. No one ever learned why History hid this legend among the white sheets of amnesia. Looking out upon the city, El Greco dreamed of that marvelous age of "long ago." The people that he lived among, so uncommunicative when he had first come, accepted the illusory, relative reality that surrounded them. But no one recognized it as a portent of essence. El Greco, in that wayside inn forgotten by the firmament, curled up to meditate, and he prepared to take wing.

The city had once enjoyed great prestige, but when that faded what was revealed, as though the prestige had worn transparent, was the full decadence of it, the organic and intemporal unity of The City. Synagogues, mosques, and churches cast their silhouettes against the sky, but when the trinitarian truce between the three religions ended under the hammer-blows of the Inquisition, that firmament became a labyrinth calcined and parched by intolerance. Locked

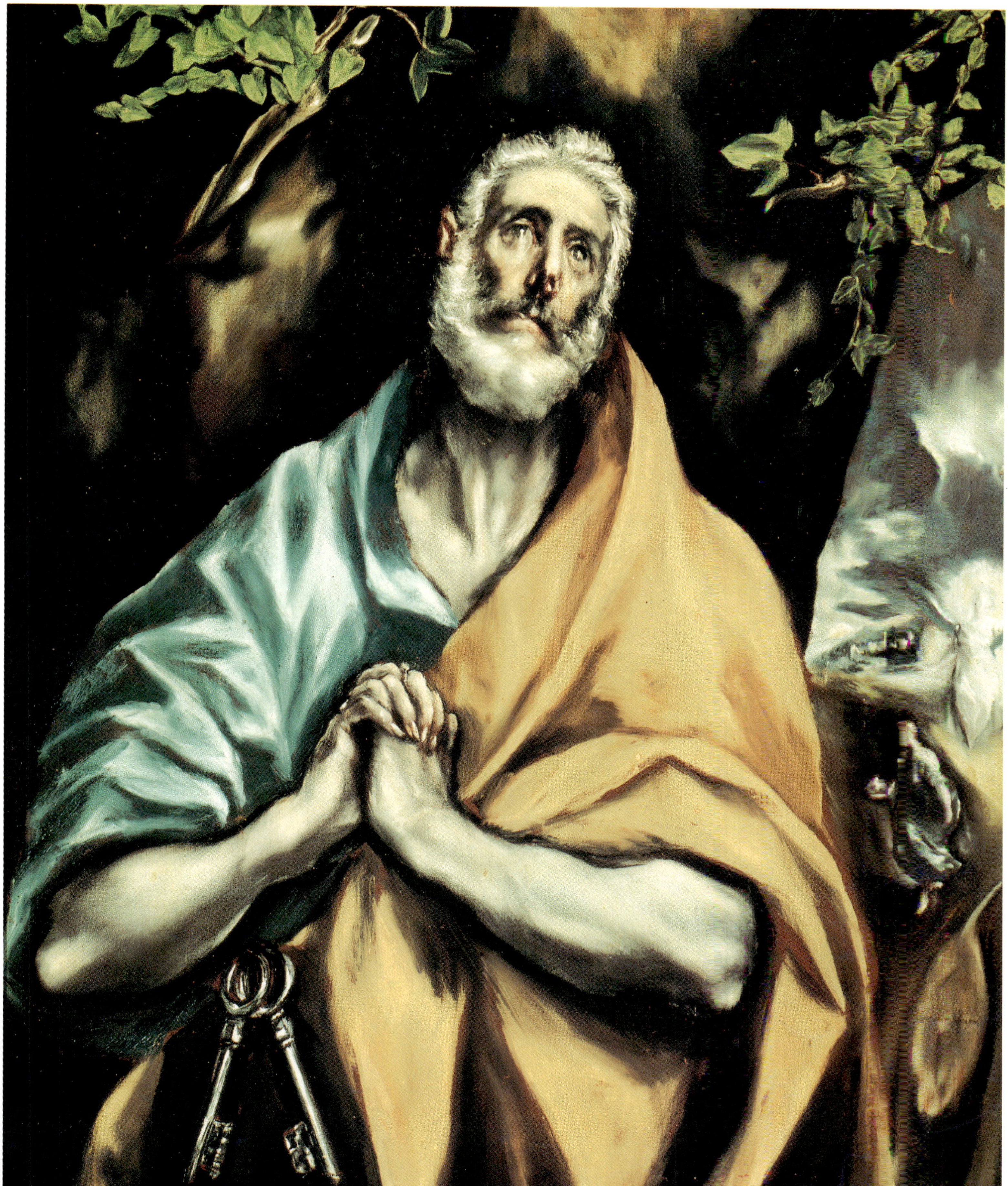

SAINT PETER'S TEARS
1605. Toledo, Tavera Hospital.
102 × 84 cm

within the walls of the morally ruined city, El Greco's creative fire would not be quenched by the fatality of its innocence.

Streets, houses, walls, paving-stones were the elements of a time lost within the labyrinth of memories. For the painter, things occupied not their geographical places, but their spiritual *loci.*

The city hovered between reality and fable. In altering the topography of his surroundings, El Greco transformed himself. But looking at the indestructible rock that circled the city, and which neither nicks nor disillusions had marked, El Greco asked himself: After what stretch of eternity will the last vestiges of the Alcázar or the Bridge of Alcántara mingle with the dust of a butterfly?

As he painted, high above the Tagus, he became fluid, light, as impalpable as the breeze, in love with his lover and above all with love. Holding tight to his imagination, and protected by his hunger for exactitude, he expected to ascend into the heavens of Toledo and float among the clouds. In the instant of creation, a snowflake could have changed his weight. Painting created him, and he was froth.

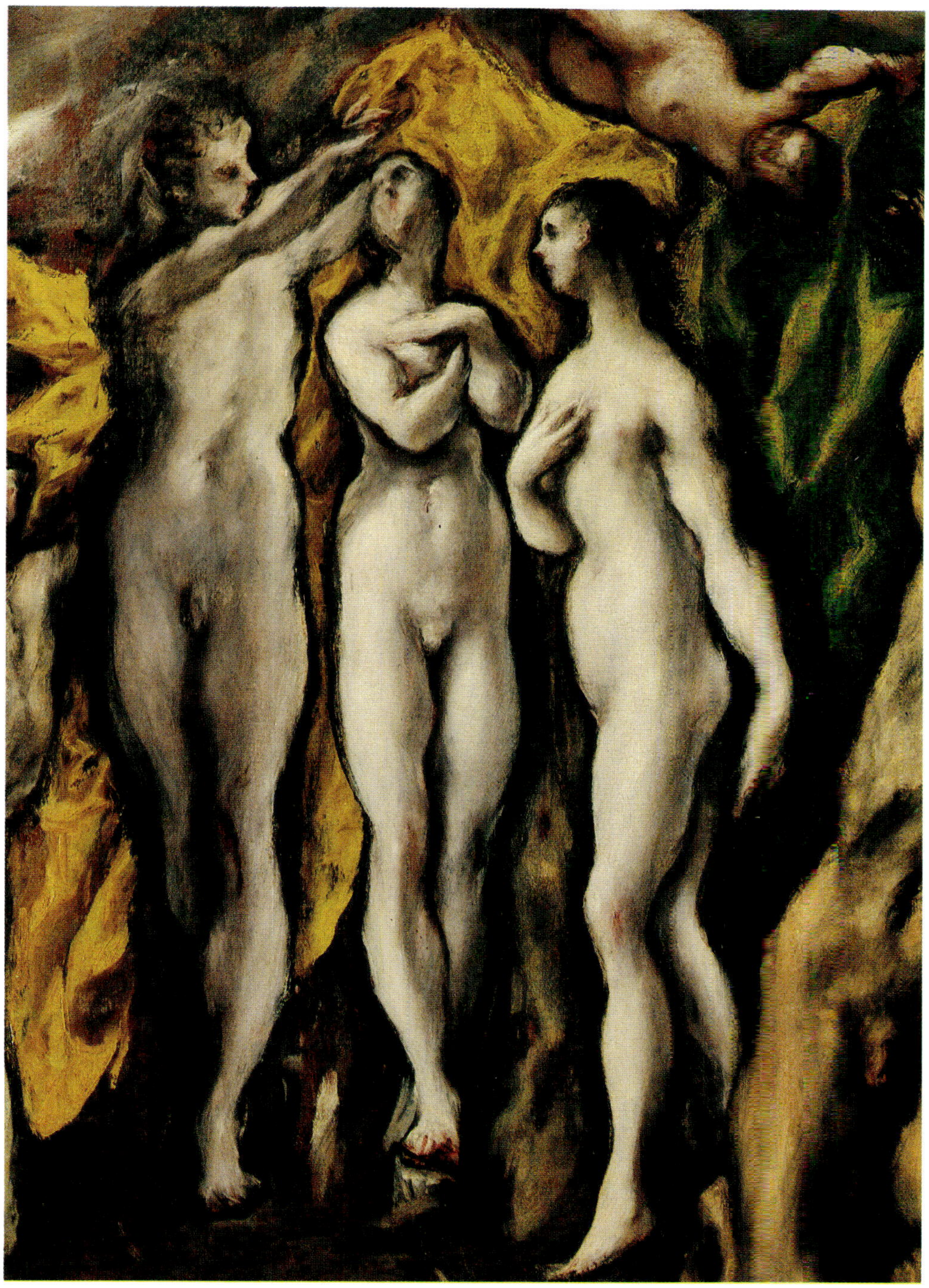

THE FIFTH SEAL OF THE APOCALYPSE
1608-14. New York, Metropolitan Museum.
detail

WORK

El Greco painted the way he was: a foreigner cubed, an exile among exiles, a countryless wanderer who had forded worldly fame on the ferry of ambiguity. Everything shimmered and wavered under the feet of this Cretan... even his own identity. "Candiot" by birth, he became, thanks to the Castilians, not a Spaniard's but an Italian's Greek. Everything and everyone slips away from reality.

The windows of his studio had looked out upon so many, and such different, cultures — Greek, Venetian, Turkish, Roman, Spanish! He had contemplated them, and he had wavered, though never dangerously, never at risk of foundering in perplexity or astonishment. He linked each one to the next, though he never lumped them, for he was convinced that each was unsurpassable. Sheltered within his intelligence, and his intelligence tempered with humor, he watched them face each other across the desert of jingoism.

Priests and bishops approached his workshop

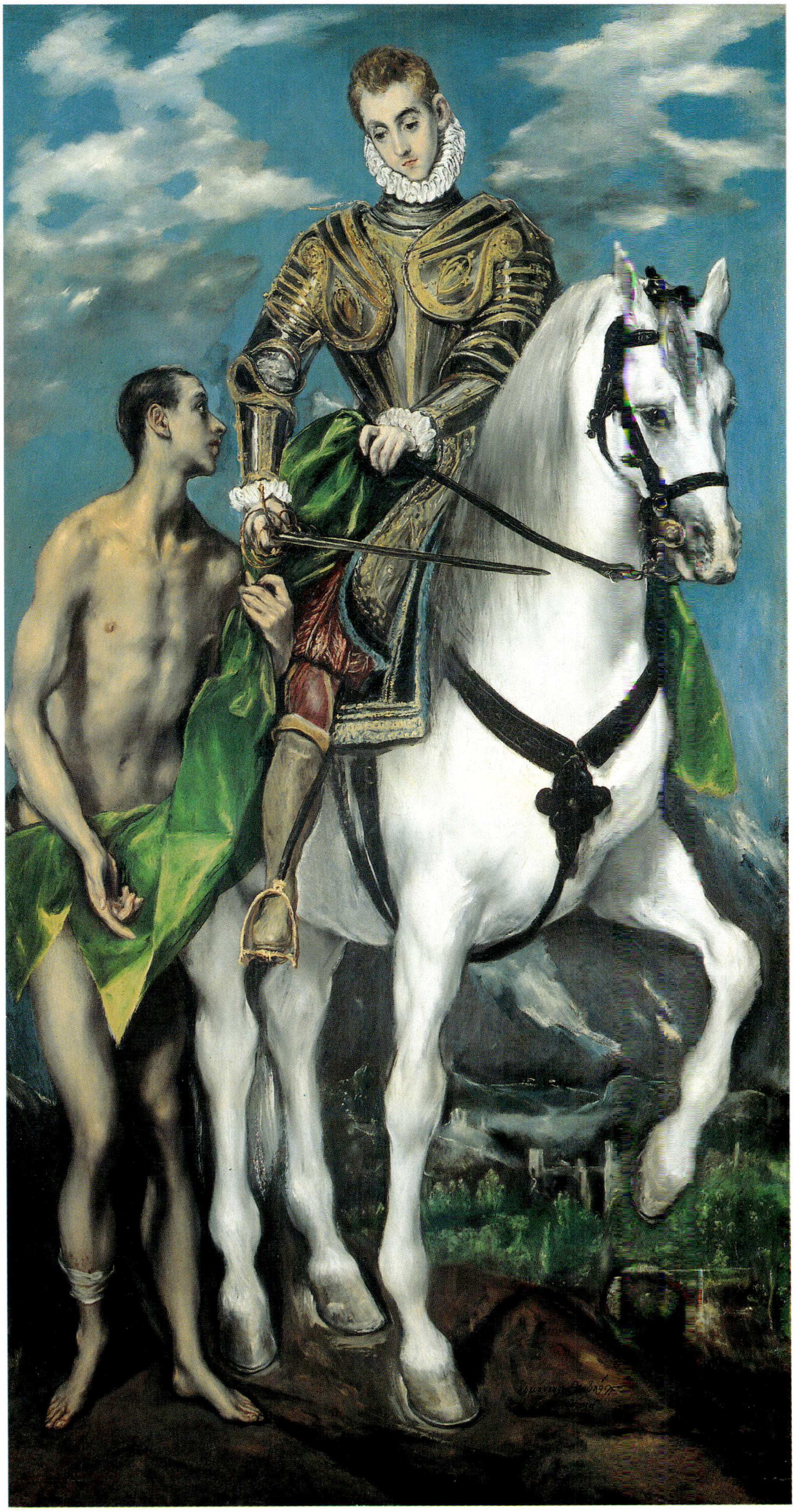

SAINT MARTIN SHARING HIS MANTLE WITH A POOR MAN
1597-99. Washington, National Gallery.
193,5 × 103 cm

in the hope of converting him to the one true doctrine. They managed only to inspire in him anger, disagreement, metamorphoses, inversions in his song of blasphemy. He had seen two separate sides, with this same faith, though with different images, commit murder, rape, and torture, all in the name of God. He had proved with his own flesh, his own spirit, that "unnatural" love could be as natural as that imposed by the dogmas that walled him about.

And when ambiguity had penetrated to the very marrow of his spirit, "El Montano" appeared in his life, bestowing letters of nobility and the secret kiss of the initiate upon the pariah of every creed, empire, capital, and culture of his age.

El Greco was to be a painter unique in all the world, and his fate has been equally without parallel. From prudence, good judgment, patriotism, and conformity he received the only rewards that one can receive without sullying oneself: contempt, indifference, and reprobation. He inverted the relationship between art and life just as his life was a constant shifting of the

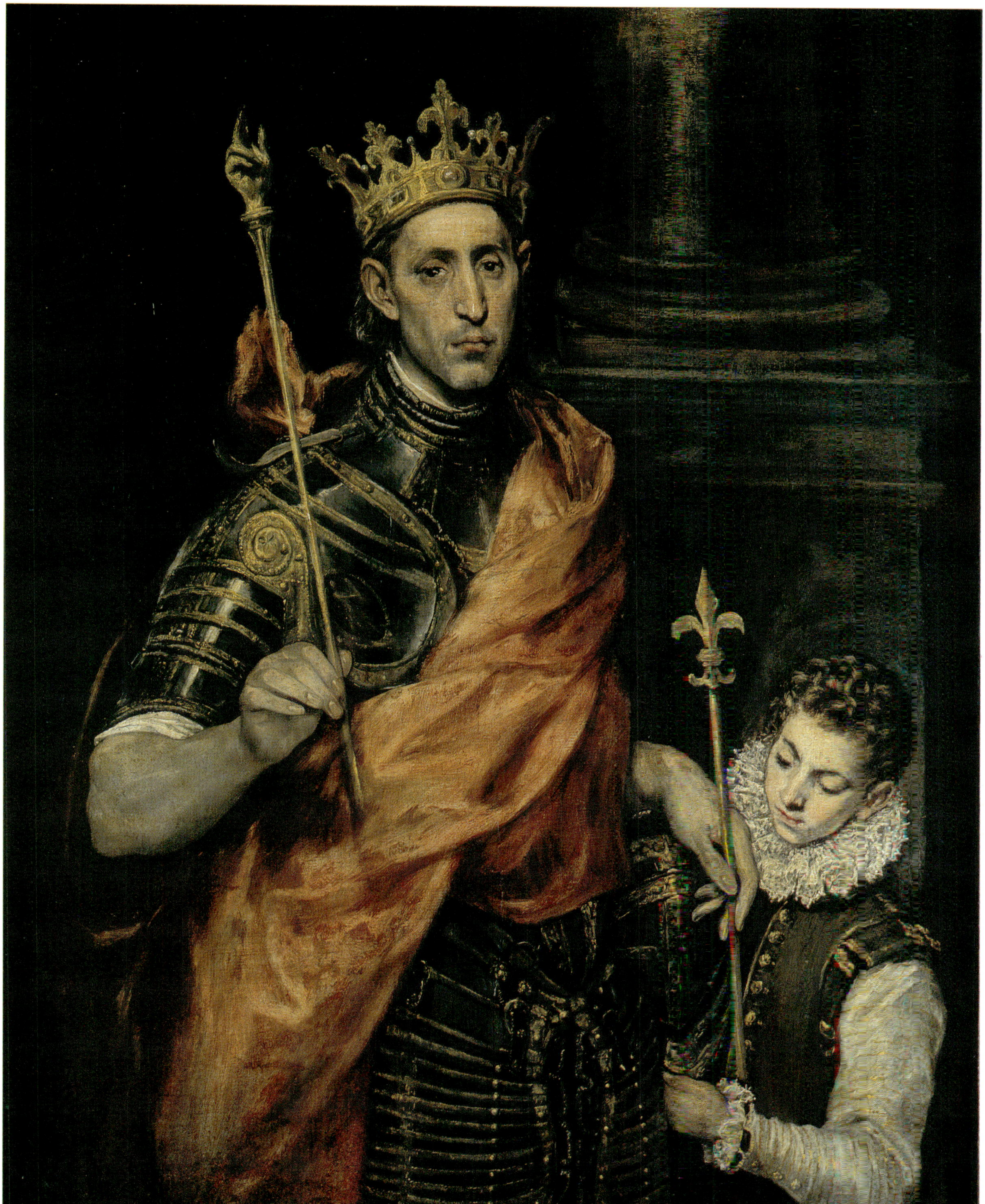

SAINT LOUIS KING OF FRANCE
1585-90. Paris, Louvre.
117×95 cm

reference-points between man and the world about him.

Within the rectangle of each of his paintings the essence of his work is concentrated, and eternity is suspended. The structure of every painting is the same, and its germ may be found on the other side of reason — in Genesis. El Greco painted in order to meditate, and he meditated in order to nourish himself on science, chimeras, and truth — and with what an appetite!

The form or composition of his canvases varies, and is modified *ad infinitum,* as in some Platonic harmony. El Greco offers up his brushstrokes, the colors, to the inspiration of the moment. This inspiration, like fantasy, plays the role of a disturbing, perturbing element in the creation of every painting. With it, Domenikos achieves perfection through sublimation in disorder. Any burning, glowing, whimsical, irrational, blasphemous, extravagant idea at all may enter his work, so long as that invariable structure remains.

Peripeteia, complicating the plot of the work, may seem to compete against its majesty, when

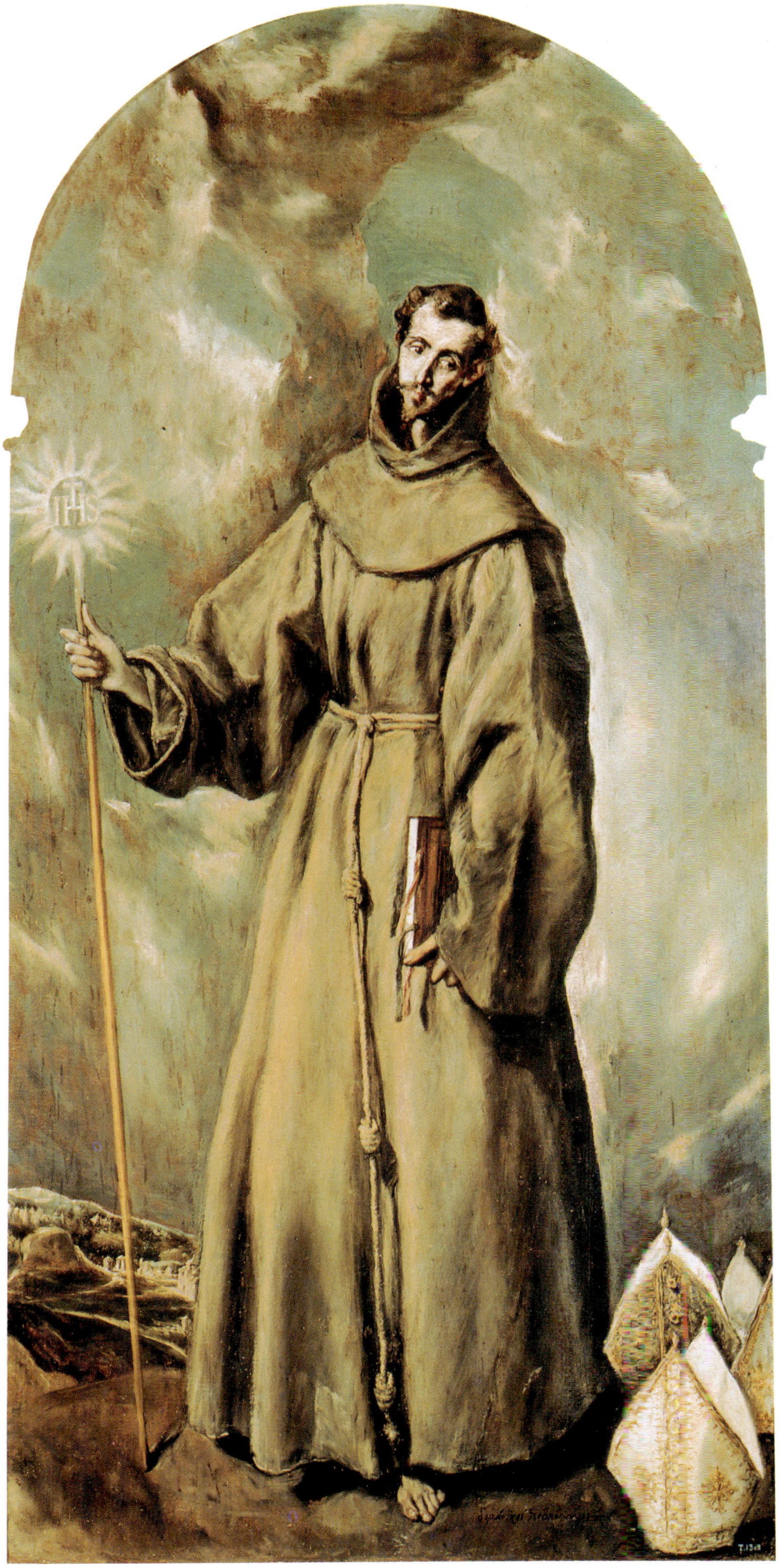

SAINT BERNARDIN
1603. Toledo, Museo del Greco.
269 × 144 cm

in fact it brings that majesty further to the fore. Balance was a dragon that lived off the fire of El Greco's zeal and excitation, the flames of his genius, but that nourished itself upon his everyday afflictions.

The order of his paintings and of the world cross and intertwine with total interdependence, outside time. Thus, to meditate over his work is to attempt to discover the fluctuation between the real and the imaginary. Proof against all delirium, El Greco inverted this oscillation. Through it, he could look into the heart of matter, as love contemplates the most secret and hidden places of the spirit.

Unlike the scientist, who through probing, trials, and doubt arrives at the concept, El Greco employed concepts from the first day he looked out upon the world around him in Candia. That is why, rather than concerning himself with things that happen and are gone, things that pass away, he preferred to capture the eternal and immutable law of things. Over and above events, things, properties, or symbols, El Greco's work personifies substance, the *stuff* it all is made from.

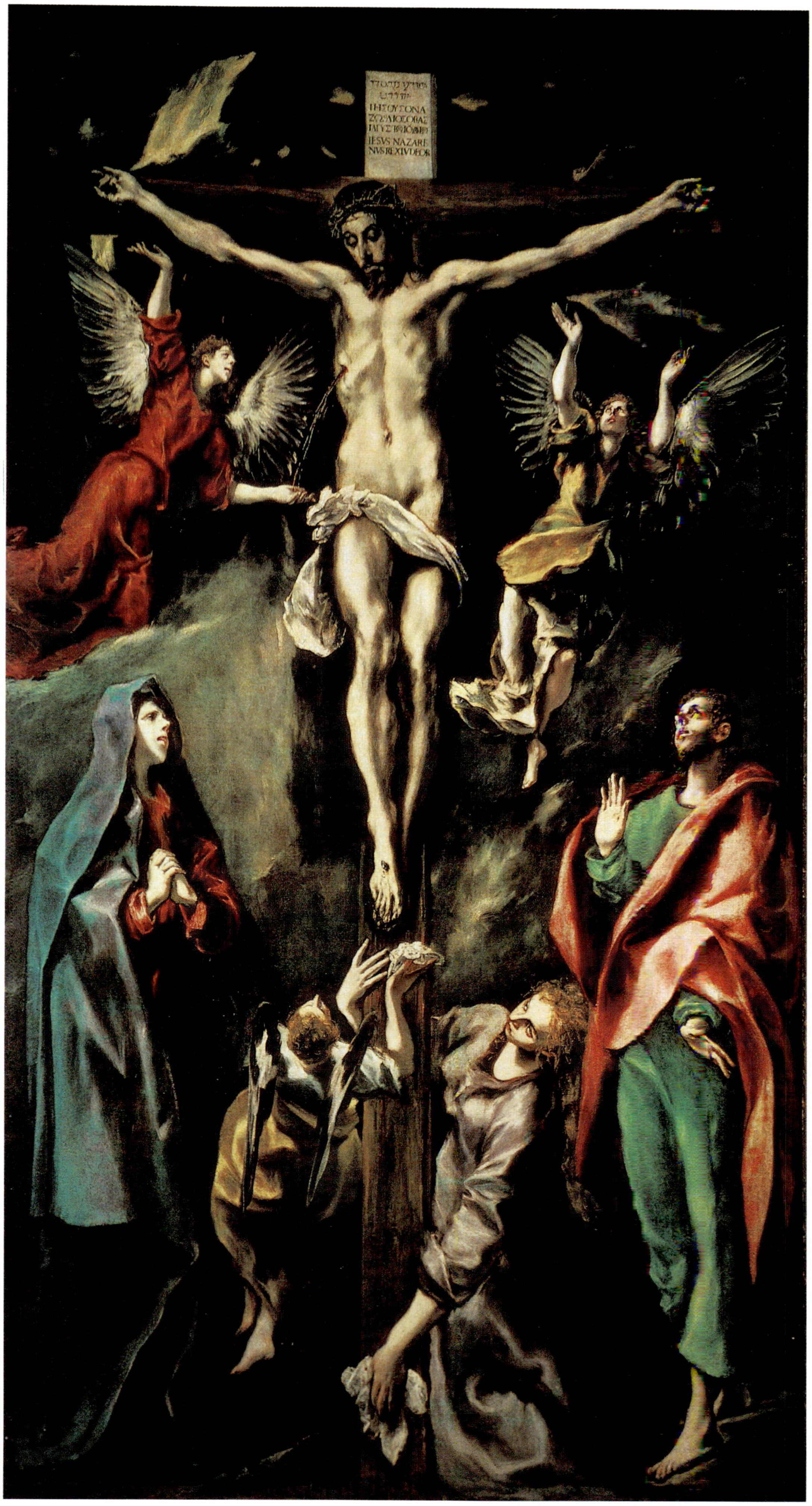

CHRIST ON THE CROSS
1590-1600. Madrid, Prado.
312 × 169 cm

If the word was made flesh so that it might live among us, El Greco's inspiration was made counterpoint so that it might define harmony. He was given the gift of painting as no one else ever was. Neither time nor entropy can corrode El Greco's work or wear it away; it can only be magnified, for it elevates the incombustible, incorruptible principles of art to the apex of ultimate purification.

El Greco is the active subject of his work confronting the passivity of the world around him. The uncertainties and doubts that assailed him were met, and bravely, the moment he picked up his brushes. At that instant, he suspended the values of society and internalized his global vision of the Universe.

El Greco was a cultured, invulnerable painter. His independence and his personality have often been misunderstood: "In an El Greco," says one of his detractors, "what we mainly see is El Greco. Velázquez, on the contrary, disappears after he gives the last brushstroke. That is the elegance of Velázquez: to be absent in the painting." It is true that each and every brushstroke, each and every intention, is signed "El Greco."

All that is manifested as love, all that is dis-

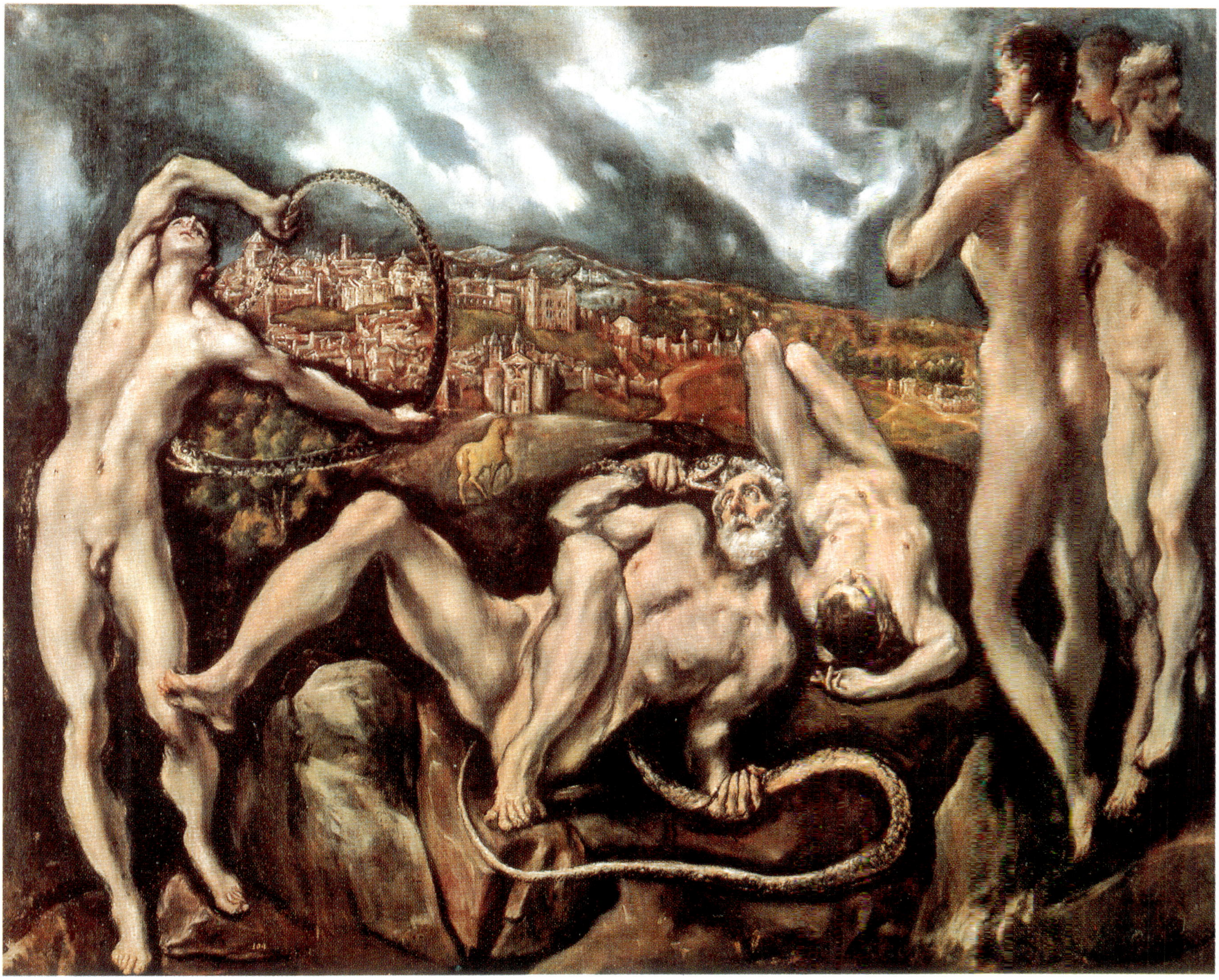

LAOCOON
1610-14. Washington, National Gallery.
137,5 × 172,5 cm

covered as memory, all that shines through as art, all that is meditated upon as science is enclosed within his work, and the work is so filled with genius that it appears filled with grace.

If God on the seventh day of creation had painted instead of rested, He would have painted with the grace of that rejected "Son of the Mother of God":

Theotokopoulos

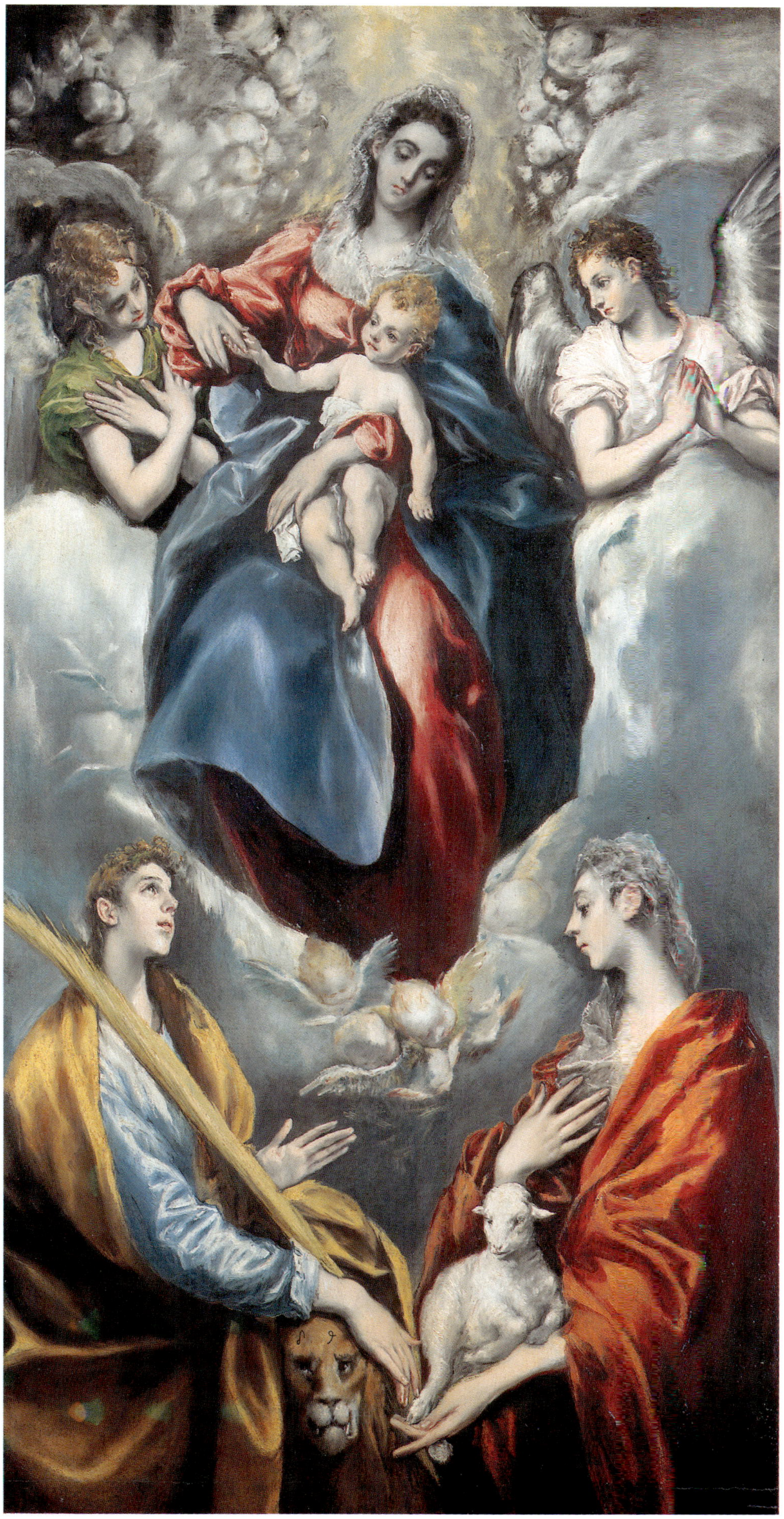

HOLY VIRGIN AND CHILD WITH SAINT MARTINE AND SAINT AGNES
1597-99. Washington, National Gallery.
193,5 × 103 cm

EL GRECO

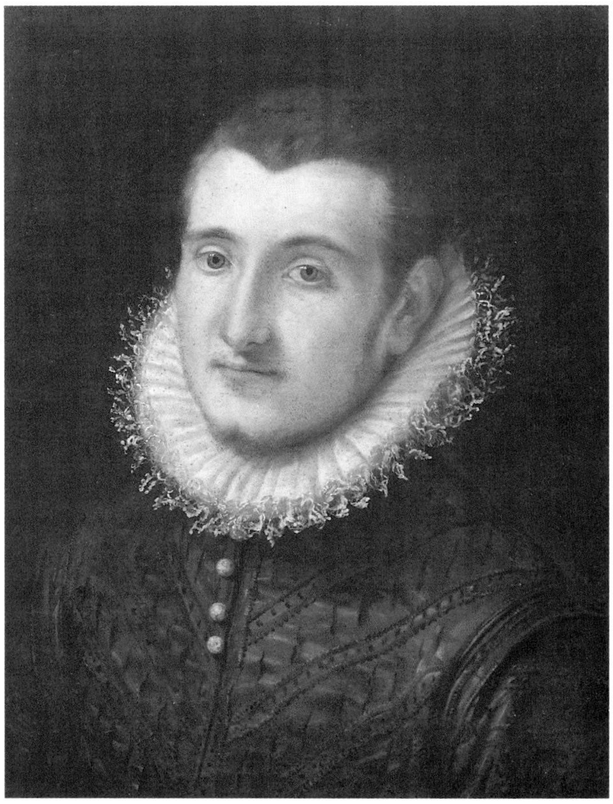

Self portrait. Oil on canvas,
private collection, Paris.

1541. All historians seem to agree that El Greco was born in 1541 at Candia in Crete, which was under Venitian rule at the time. The son of Jorghi Theotokopulos, he was christened Domenikos, El Greco was the family's second child. His brother Manussos was ten years his senior.

1566. A notarized document attests to the presence of El Greco at Candia, in which he was referred to as "master". On 26th December of the same year, the painter took one of his works to be valued for auction at the *Lottery*. The painting was valued at 80 ducats by the painter Giogio Klotza and 70 ducats by the priest Janni de Frossego.

1568. El Greco's name was first mentioned in Venice. A number of documents point to the possibility of his being a pupil of Titian.

1572. El Greco registered at the Accademia di San Luco, which was a focal point for Roman artists.

1573-75. It is thought that El Greco spent time in Venice.

1575-76. El Greco settled in Spain.

1577. El Greco went to Madrid. He painted *The Assumption* for the Santo Domingo el Antiguo at Toledo and was commissioned to paint the *Espolio (The Disrobing of Christ)* for the Cathedral at Toledo.

1578. Birth of Jorge Manuel, the son of El Greco and Doña Jerómina de las Cuevas, a young woman of noble birth. It is unlikely that the artist ever married her.

1579. El Greco completed the *Espolio,* Much controversy surrounded payment for the work.

1582. El Greco acted as interpreter at the trial of an Athenian tailor accused of being a muslim. On this occasion, the painter stated that he was a native of Candia.

1584. The priest of Santo Tomé in Toledo commissioned El Greco to paint *The Burial of the Conde de Orgaz.*

1585. The painter rented accommodation in Toledo from the Marquis de Villena.

1586. A contract dated 18th March drawn up between the priest of Santo Tomé and El Greco, under which the painter undertook to execute the work himself and complete it by Christmas was discovered.

1587. El Greco left his modest rooms for more spacious apartments in one of the Marquis de Villena's main residences.

1591. Arrival in Toledo of the painter's brother, Manussos, a former tax collector for the Venitian Republic in Crete. He would remain close by his brother's side until his death in 1604.

1592. El Greco completed the works for the church of Talavera la Viega.

1595. The painter received his first commission for the Tavera hospital in Toledo to produce a tabernacle for the high altar.

1596. El Greco hired his lover, Francisco Preboste, who had returned with him from Italy, to execute the high altar for the church of the Augustinian College of Doña Maria de Aragon in Madrid.

1597. Documentary evidence exists of the painter's links with Seville merchants to sale his works.

1598. El Greco finished the tabernacle for the Tavera hospital.

1600. Possible stay in Madrid.

1603. The Hospital de la Caridad at Illescas commissioned El Greco to decorate the high altar. The painter charged his son, Jorge Manuel, with the project for the altar at the Ermitage de Nuestra Señora del Prado at Talavera la Reina.

1604. Christening of Gabriel, son of Jorge and Alphonsa de los Morales, the painter's grandson. Death of Manussos Theotokopulos on 13th December.

1603-07. Luis Tristan studied under El Greco.

1605. El Greco assigned Francisco Preboste and Francisco Ximénez Montero, a public servant at the royal chancellery of Valladolid, to represent him in litigation which he had initiated concerning payment for commissioned works.

1608. El Greco signed a contract for the high altar and the lateral altars of the Tavera Hospital.

1611 : A royal edict was published describing the tomb executed by El Greco for Queen Margaret of Austria.

1612. Jorge Manuel arranged to lease a crypt in the church of Santo Domingo el Antiguo as the family burial place.

1613. El Greco finished the *Assumption of the Virgin* for the Chapel of Oballe. His work rate showed signs of decline and he appeared to be ill, although there is no documentary evidence of this.

1614. On 31st March, El Greco designated his son Jorge Manuel as sole heir, and entrusted him with making arrangements for his funeral and settling his debts.
He died on 7th April.

El Greco's work are exhibited in the following museums:

ARGENTINA

BUENOS AIRES, Museo Nacional de Arte Decorativo
Museo Nacional de Bellas Artes
ROSARIO, Museo Municipal de Bellas Artes

AUSTRALIA

MELBOURNE, National Gallery of Victoria

BRAZIL

SAO PAULO, Museu de Arte

CANADA

MONTREAL, Museum of Fine Arts
OTTAWA, National Gallery of Canada

CZECHOSLOVAKIA

PRAGUE, Narodni Galerie

DENMARK

COPENHAGEN, State Art Museum

FRANCE

AMIENS, Musée de Picardie
BAYONNE, Bonnat Museum
LILLE, Beaux Arts Palace
LYON, Beaux Arts Museum
PARIS, Louvre
STRASBOUEG, Beaux Arts Museum

GERMANY

BERLIN, Dahlem Staatliche Museen
DRESDE, Gemaldgalerie
MUNICH, Alte Pinakothek

GREECE

ATHENS, Benaki Museum
National Pinakothek

HUNGARY

BUDAPEST, Szepmüvészeti Muzeum

IRELAND

DUBLIN, National Gallery of Ireland

ITALY

BERGAMO, Galleria dell accademia Carrara
BOLOGNA, Pinacoteca Nazionale
FLORENCE, Galleria degli Uffizi
GENOA, Palazzo Reale
MILAN, Pinacoteca di Brera
MODENE, Galleria Estense
NAPLES, Gallerie Nazionali di Capodimonte
PARMA, Galleria Nazionale
REGGIO EMILIA, Civica Galleria d'Arte Parmeggiani
ROME, Galleria Nazionale di Palazzo Barberini

NETHERLANDS

AMSTERDAM, Rijksmuseum
OTTERLO, Rijksmuseum Kröller-Müller
ROTTERDAM, Museum Boymans van Beuningen

NORWAY

OSLO, Nasjonalgalleriet

POLAND

SIEDICE, Bishop's Palace

RUMANIA

BUCHAREST, Muzeul de Artà al Republicii Socialiste Romania

SPAIN

ANDUJAR (Jaen), Santa Maria
AVILA, Museo de la Cathedral
BARCELONA, Museo de Arte de Cataluna
BILBAO, Museo de Bellas Artes y de Arte Moderno
CADIZ, Hospital Nuestra Senora del Carmen
CUENCA, Cathedral Treasury
EL BONILLO (Albacete), Santa Catalina
MADRID ESCURIAL, Monastery
ILLESCAS, Charity Hospital
LOGRONO, Museo de Arte
MADRID, Academia de San Fernando
Biblioteca Nacional
Instituto de Valencia de Don Juan
Museo Cerralbo
Museo Lazaro Galdanio
Museo Nacional del Prado
San Gines
San Hermenegildo
MARTIN MUNOZ DE LAS POSADAS (Segovid) Parish Church
MONTFORTE DE LENIOS (Lugo), Colegio de la Compania
OLOT (Gerond), San Esteban
ORGAZ (Toledo), Parish Church
PALENCIA, Cathedral
PARADAS (Seville), Parish Church
PASTRANA, Cathedral
PONTEVEDRA, Museo Provincial
SAN SEBASTIAN, Museo Municipal de San Telmo
SEVILLA, Museo Provincial de Bellas Artes
SIGUENZA, Cathedral Chapter
SITGES (Barcelona), Museo del Cau Ferrat
TOLEDO, Casa Museo del Greco
Cathédrale
San José Chapel
Colegio de Doncellas Nobles
Tavera Hospital
Museo de Santa Cruz
San Ildefonso
Santo Domingo el Antiguo
Santo Tomé
VALENCIA, Colegio del Patriarca
Museo Provincial de Bellas Artes
VILLANUEVA Y GELTRU, Museo Balaguer

SWEDEN

STOCKHOLM, Nationalmuseum

SWITZERLAND

ZURICH, Koller Gallery

UNITED KINGDOM

BARNARD CASTLE (Durham), Bowes Museum
CARDIFF, National Museum of Wales
EDINBURGH, National Gallery of Scotland
GLASGOW, Pollok House, Stirling Maxwell's Collection
LONDON, National Gallery
Warwick House
UPTON HOUSE (Warwickshire), National Trust

UNITED STATES

BALTIMORE, Walters Art Gallery
BOSTON, Museum of Fine Arts
CAMBRIDGE, Fogg Art Museum
CHICAGO, Art Institute
CINCINNATI, Art Museum
CLAREMONT, Scripps College Art Galleries
CLEVELAND, Museum of Art
DES MOINES, Art Center
DETROIT, Institute of Arts
FORT WORTH, Kimbell Art Foundation
GRAND RAPIDS, Art Gallery
HARTFORD, Wadsworth Atheneum
INDIANAPOLIS, Clowes Foundation
KANSAS CITY, William Rockhill Nelson Galleries of Art and Mary Atkins, Museum of Fine Arts
LOS ANGELES, County Museum of Art
Art Galleries of university of California
MERION, Barnes Foundation
MINNEAPOLIS, Institute of Arts
NEW YORK, Brooklyn Museum
Hispanic Society of America
Metropolitan Museum of Art
OMAHA, Jocelyn Art Museum
PHILADELPHIA, Museum of Art
PRINCETOWN, Art Museum of University
PROVIDENCE, Museum of Art
Rhode Island School of Design
ROCHESTER, Memorial Art Gallery of the University
SAINT-LOUIS, City Art Museum
SAN ANTONIO, Marion Koogler Mc Nay Art Institute Museum
SAN DIEGO, Fine Arts Gallery
SAN FRANCISCO, De Young Memorial Museum
Palace of the Legion of Honor
SARASOTA, John and Mable Ringling Museum
TOLEDO, Museum of Art
WASHINGTON, Corcoran Gallery of Art
National Gallery of Art
Phillips Memorial Gallery
WEST PALM BEACH, Norton Gallery and School of Art
WORCESTER, Art Museum

U.S.S.R.

LENINGRAD, Ermitage
MOSCOU, Pouchkine Museum

SOUTH AFRICA

JOHANNESBURG, Art Gallery

By the same author

IN FRANCE

Théâtre
(Christian Bourgois et 10/18)

Oraison :
Les Deux Bourreaux
Fando et Lis
Le Cimetière des voitures
Guernica
Le Labyrinthe
Le Tricycle
Pique-nique en campagne
La Bicyclette du condamné
Le Grand Cérémonial
Cérémonie pour un Noir assassiné
Le Couronnement
Concert dans un œuf
L'Architecte et l'Empereur d'Assyrie
Le Jardin des Délices
Bestialité érotique
Une tortue nommée Dostoïevski
...Et ils passèrent des menottes aux fleurs
L'Aurore rouge et noire
Ars Amandi
Dieu tenté par les mathématiques
Le Ciel et la Merde
La Grande Revue du XXe siècle
Bella Ciao
La Guerre de mille ans
Sur le fil ou Ballade du train fantôme
La Tour de Babel
La Marche royale
Une orange sur le Mont de Vénus
La Gloire en images
Vole-moi un petit milliard
Ouverture orang-outan
Punk et Punk et Colegram
Mon doux royaume saccagé
Le Roi de Sodome
Le Ciel et la Merde II
L'Extravagante Réussite de Jésus-Christ
Karl Marx et William Shakespeare
Lève-toi et rêve
Les Délices de la chair
La ville dont le prince était une princesse
Bréviaire d'amour d'un baltérophile
Apokalyptica
La Charge des centaures
Les « Cucarachas » de Yale
Une pucelle pour un gorille
The Red Madonna
La Traversée de l'Empire

Poésie
(Christian Bourgois et 10/18)

La Pierre de la Folie, 1962
Cent Sonnets, 1965
Humbles Paradis, 1983

Romans
(Christian Bourgois, Grasset, Ramsay, Acropole et 10/18)

Baal Babylone, 1959
L'Enterrement de la sardine, 1963
Fête et rites de la confusion, 1965
La Tour prends garde, 1983
La Reverdie, 1984
La Vierge rouge, 1986
La Fille de King Kong, 1988
L'Extravagante Croisade d'un castrat amoureux, 1990

Documents
(Christian Bourgois, éd. du Rocher et 10/18)

La Panique, 1963
Le New York d'Arrabal, 1971
Lettre au général Franco, 1972
Sur Fisher : Initiation aux échecs, 1974
Les Echecs féeriques et libertaires :
Chroniques de l'Express, 1979
Echecs et mythe, 1983
Lettre à Fidel Castro, 1984

Is published in the United Kindom by *Calder and Boyars* in the United States by *Grove Press, Viking* and *River Run*

Photo credit: Lauros-Giraudon: cover, p. 63, 11, 19, 27, 43, 71 - Giraudon: p. 3, 5, 9, 13, 15, 25, 31, 33, 39, 45, 47, 49, 51, 53, 55, 59, 61, 73 - New York, Metropolitan Museum: p. 7, 29, 35, 57, 65 - Edimbourg, National Gallery of Scotland: p. 17 - Berlin-Dahlem, Staatliche Museen: p. 21 - Washington, National Gallery: p. 23, 67, 77 - Jean Bazière: p. 37, 69 - Fr Grandi Opere Srl: p. 75

 - Dépôt légal Avril 1991 - Imprimeur Campin, Tournai Belgique - Photocomposition ETNA Productions - I.S.B.N. 2-908958-03-1.

Rec'd August 1995, K. R. Dorn, Johnstown, NY

CLASSIC NATURAL HISTORY PRINTS

MAMMALS

ACKNOWLEDGMENTS

The author and publishers would like to thank the following for their help in the compilation of this book:
The National Museums of Scotland: Andrew Kitchener and David Heppell of the Department of Natural History; the Head of Library, Manjil V. Mathew and his staff. The Natural History Museum, London: the Head of Library Services, Rex Banks and his staff. The Linnean Society of London: the Council and Librarian, Gina Douglas. Ken Smith Photography (Edinburgh). Cavendish House, Carlisle: Una Dance, Robert Dance.

They would also like to thank the following for their kind permission to photograph the original prints in their possession:
The National Museums of Scotland, Edinburgh, for the plates appearing on pages 13, 27, 29, 31, 35, 37, 39, 41, 79, 93, 95, 97, 99, 101, 103, 105, 107, 109, 111, 113, 115, 117, 119, 121, 123, 125, 127. The Natural History Museum, London, for the plates appearing on pages 9, 11, 23, 33, 43, 45, 47, 49, 51, 53, 55, 57, 59, 61, 63, 65, 67, 69, 71, 89 and 91. The Linnean Society of London, for the plates appearing on pages 15, 17, 19, 21, 25, 73, 75, 77, 81 and 83. Una Dance, for the plates appearing on pages 85 and 87.

Classic Natural History Prints, *Mammals*
first published in 1990 by Studio Editions Ltd.
Princess House, 50 Eastcastle Street,
London W1N 7AP, England.

Printed and bound in Italy

ISBN 1 85170 389 6

CLASSIC NATURAL HISTORY PRINTS

MAMMALS

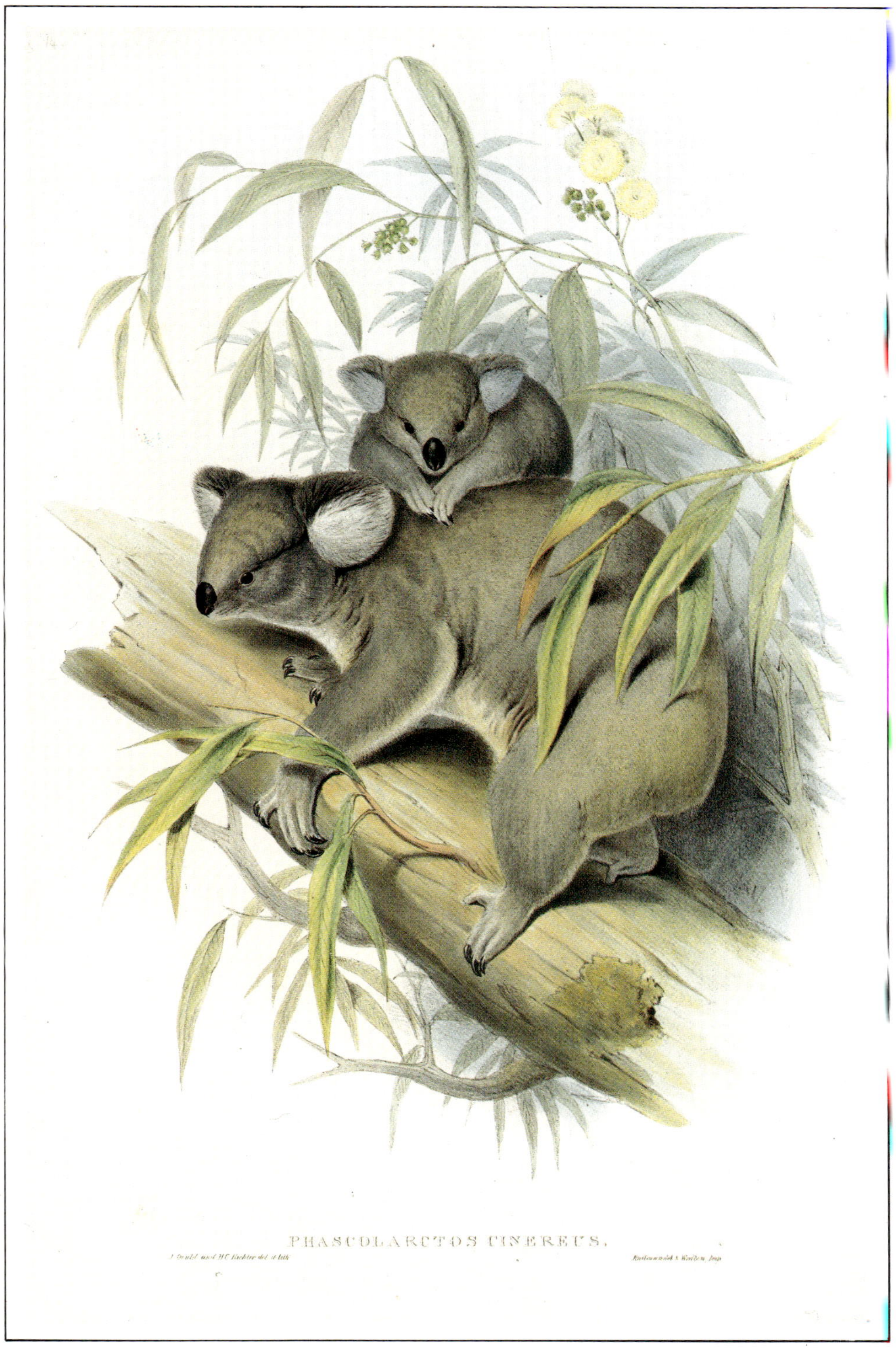

S. PETER DANCE

STUDIO EDITIONS
LONDON

LIST OF PLATES

INTRODUCTION

One day in September 1940 four lads from the little town of Montignac in south-western France scrambled through a small hole in a wooded plateau and found themselves in an underground cave. Returning the next day with a makeshift light they re-entered the cave and boggled at figures of strange animals, outlined in black and coloured with vivid reds and earthy browns, sprawling across the walls and ceilings. They had stumbled upon the Lascaux cave system and its wonderful series of palaeolithic paintings.

The discovery of this subterranean art gallery showed that, about 25,000 years before the Christian era, some of our ancestors had learnt to make bold, identifiable and life-like portraits of the larger animals sharing their environment. But were they drawn from life? One or two zoologists have argued that most must have been portraits of dead animals; and the way some are shown as though on tip-toe, an attitude they would never have adopted in life, supports that argument. But this does not diminish the stupendous artistic achievement of the troglodytes. The beasts portrayed so unforgettably in their gloomy cave must have meant a great deal to the ancient image makers of Lascaux.

Early civilisations in both East and West have left evidence of a widespread enthusiasm for animal art in one form or another. From Mesopotamia we have cylinder seals carved with lions and other animals dating from about 2000 BC. From China we have representations of a variety of animals carved into objects made from jade, marble, pottery and bronze dating from the same period. About 1500 BC paintings of domestic animals became a common feature of the civilisation of the New Kingdom in Egypt; and colossal stone lions and human-headed bulls characterised the might of the Assyrian empire. By then dolphins and other marine creatures were familiar motifs on pottery and on palace walls at Knossos in Crete when the Minoan culture was at its zenith. Austere but well-proportioned horses from the Parthenon typify Greek art of the millenium before the birth of Christ; and the sprightly animal portraits seen on wall paintings and mosaics unearthed from the ashes which buried Pompeii epitomise the very different, life-enhancing attitude to animals adopted later by the Romans.

So, thousands of years before the prints reproduced in this book appeared, the urge to make images of horses, lions, dolphins, bulls and other large mammals had been expressed in various and often wonderful ways. Further expressions of that urge may be seen in sculptures, carvings, hanging scrolls and illuminated manuscripts fashioned by artists of various cultures up to the time of the Renaissance. In Europe the first prints to portray animals were products of that time.

Some of the finest of the earliest prints of mammals produced in Europe were the work of the outstanding Renaissance artist Albrecht Dürer. His scientific approach to graphic art ensured that a drawing of a hare or a horse was minutely correct – although he was guilty of superimposing a tiny unicorn's horn on the back of a now famous study of an Indian rhinoceros. The woodcuts in Conrad Gessner's mid-sixteenth-century publication *Historia Animalium* were less scrupulously exact (many of them represented exotic creatures known only from their dead remains, from inadequate sketches or from hearsay) but became very popular and were still being reproduced in books two centuries later. During the seventeenth century many more woodcuts of animals appeared in books devoted to aspects of natural history but, with few exceptions, they were no more accurate and often aesthetically less pleasing than Gessner's. Unless specially commissioned, none of these publications was issued with the woodcuts coloured by hand: that was an eighteenth-century development.

Dürer had shown that the most accurate and most satisfying pictures of animals were those based on a close scrutiny of the animals themselves: so for a long time the best animal pictures were those of domestic subjects. Pictures of exotic animals were likely to be unsatisfactory by comparison because the subjects were scarce or in poor condition, and sometimes the artist had only inferior sketches, inadequate notes or oral descriptions to work from. In a European context, therefore, an artist could not produce a satisfactory portrait of, say, a lion, an elephant or a monkey unless he had access to a menagerie. Alternatively it was sometimes possible to gain access to preserved skins or mounted specimens in private collections of natural curiosities (there were no public ones before the middle of the eighteenth century), such as those amassed by the Englishman Hans Sloane and the Dutchman Albert Seba.

Sloane's collection eventually formed the nucleus of that in the British Museum; Seba sold his first collection to Peter the Great of Russia and his second was dispersed, but not before it had been described and illustrated in a massive four-volume book, now known as Seba's *Thesaurus*. The first plate in our own book comes from the copy of the *Thesaurus* owned formerly by Sloane, a copy specially hand coloured for him, and shows various hedgehogs from Seba's extensive collection. While artists worked from this kind of material their portraits of mammals and other animals were certain to be lifeless; and for most of the eighteenth century lifeless they were.

The *Histoire Naturelle des Mammifères* by E. Geoffroy Saint-Hilaire and G. F. Cuvier, published early in the nineteenth century, was the first large-scale illustrated treatise on mammals. Its hand coloured engravings were reproductions of drawings by highly accomplished artists employed to help professional naturalists working at the Jardin des Plantes in Paris. The engravings, three of which are reproduced here, were sensitively drawn and well coloured, but they showed mammals as though they were precious works of art displayed in an art gallery rather than animals made of flesh and blood shown against natural backgrounds. C. G. Ehrenberg's sensitive illustration of several Nubian ibex in their rocky stronghold, published in 1828, contrasts strikingly with the polished but static French illustrations of mammals published at about the same time. The engravings in James Wilson's *Illustrations of Zoology*, most of them by William Home Lizars (who engraved the first few plates of John James Audubon's *The Birds of America*), were also more lively, if occasionally less original than their French counterparts.

The invention of lithography, a process allowing prints to be taken from a design drawn directly onto a smooth stone surface and inked, came into commercial use in the 1820s. Our picture of the Bactrian camel, from the *Histoire Naturelle des Mammifères*, is an early example of its application to natural history illustration. By the late 1830s lithography had become the principal method used to illustrate the larger animals, the soft lines and subtle shadings of the process helping the artist to capture the essence of fur and feathers. The resulting prints had to be coloured by hand, in the same way as steel engravings, and even when colouring by the automatic process known as chromolithography came into general use in the second half of the century, hand coloured lithographs still illustrated the more expensive natural history books.

Lithography was not only speedier than other processes such as engraving on steel or wood, it was cheaper and easier to master. Soon it became the preferred method of illustrating the larger animals (it was less suitable when applied to smaller creatures such as insects, the lines being too coarse to define their more delicate structures). Here was a graphic reproduction process which could be used to illustrate some of the new and unusual creatures which travellers and explorers were bringing to Europe in large numbers from Africa, South America, India, Indonesia and other places rich in wildlife. As well as institutions such as the Jardin des Plantes in Paris and the Gardens of the Zoological Society in London, the private residences of wealthy men, such as the Earl of Derby's seat at Knowsley Hall near Liverpool, now often included menageries and aviaries crowded with exotic creatures. Animal artists could visit these establishments and make sketches of their living inhabitants and, soon afterwards perhaps, lithographs of their finished pictures could be in the hands of the colourists. It was not usually as simple as this, of course; to turn out a series of hand coloured lithographs of high quality required great skill and patience.

Lithography caught on quickly in the United States and, in Europe, only the French seemed slow to adopt it. While steel engravings illustrated the scientific reports of the French research vessels *Venus* and *Bonite* in the 1840s, the British in particular were busy publishing natural history works, some of them substantial, illustrated by lithography. David Low used the process with telling effect to illustrate his folio book *The Breeds of the Domestic Animals of the British Islands*. John Gould, well known for his series of magnificently illustrated bird books, all illustrated with lithographs, found time to bring out an equally impressive work, *The Mammals of Australia*. In the United States John James Audubon and the Revd John Bachman emulated Gould by describing and illustrating the entire mammal fauna of North America in their monumental publication *The Viviparous Quadrupeds of North America*. (Curiously, the scientific reports of the United States Exploring Expedition, including the *Mammalogy and Ornithology* report published in 1858, were illustrated with steel engravings, but these had probably been prepared long before publication.)

A series of folio-sized lithographs, from original drawings by Benjamin Waterhouse Hawkins, illustrating mammals then on display in the Earl of Derby's menagerie, were published in 1850. The three lithographs from the series reproduced here show that Hawkins had an excellent understanding of mammalian anatomy and pictorial composition. Other lithographs from the series, however, portray mammals with large, liquid eyes reminiscent of those we associate with heroines of Victorian melodramas. No one could say this about the mammal portraits executed by Joseph Wolf, one of the most outstanding of all wildlife artists, whose original drawings were ideal for reproduction by lithography.

Wolf produced the original watercolour drawings for many lithographs of mammals, perhaps the finest of them being those reproduced in Daniel Giraud Elliot's book, *A Monograph of the Felidae, or Family of the Cats*, published in 1883. Wolf's career as a wildlife artist, however, had begun many years before in his native Germany and he had been commissioned to produce illustrations for books, especially bird books, as early as 1830.

His subjects, whatever their place of origin, are always well observed and usually shown in naturalistic settings. It is difficult to believe that Wolf had never seen most of the exotic creatures he drew so skilfully in their native haunts: but the London Zoo provided him with endless opportunities to examine and sketch creatures from parts of the world inaccessible to him; and he used his fertile but disciplined imagination to place them in their own wild environment. Often he had only a single beast as his model but he could multiply it wonderfully to create a family group or a herd. As our picture of a Sumatran rhinoceros shows, he could bring together in the same picture two animals which had never met; even trick photography could not produce a more satisfactory illusion of togetherness. In the nineteenth century Joseph Wolf had no peer; and although the twentieth has produced wildlife artists who display a wonderful ability to present wild animals in all their moods and in every conceivable setting, they all owe something to him, for he showed them the way.

Most of the prints reproduced in this book have been chosen because they are aesthetically pleasing; a few have been included because of some oddity or special charm. Inevitably, most of the mammals portrayed are large and attractive, whereas most mammal species are small and inconspicuous: so it is important to be able to see the selected subjects in relation to the rest of the mammalian world. A few statistics will help to put things into perspective.

About 4231 mammal species are now living or have recently become extinct. Carnivores, which provide us with the subjects of some of our most compelling illustrations, such as bears, big cats, dogs and seals, account for about 266 of them. What are known as the even-toed ungulates, comprising such well known animals as deer, cattle, antelopes, camels, pigs, giraffes and hippopotamus, account for about 192 species. The primates, including lemurs, baboons, monkeys, great apes and ourselves, comprise at most a further 181 species. These groups, well represented in our 60 illustrative plates, make up roughly a seventh of the world total. Most of the remainder are small and inconspicuous animals.

The rodents, for example, number about 1738 species. Of these about 1120 comprise the *Muridae*, the family containing mice, rats, voles and their allies; this book includes only one member of this family, a rat, but it may claim to be the world's largest rat. When hunting for pictures suitable for inclusion in this book it seemed that those of squirrels (which are rodents) and their allies outnumbered all others. As there are about 255 different kinds on several continents, many of them widespread and abundant, it is not surprising that there should have been so many illustrations of them in the earlier natural history books. Because they are monotonously similar and often drab they do not figure largely in our selection. Unexpectedly, perhaps, there are almost a thousand species of bats in the world. Bats, too, all look much the same as each other and only one, an Australian flying fox, finds a place here. Mice and rats, squirrels and bats, all have their place in nature, but in this book they have had to make way for those mammals which are large, impressive, historically interesting or simply odd.

Sometimes the oddness is less evident in the mammals themselves than in the artists' portraits of them. John James Audubon often dramatised his pictures of birds and mammals to emphasise the harsh realities of nature, red in tooth and claw, but his illustration of the eastern chipmunk shows a little fellow with its mouth full of nuts looking as though it has escaped from an animated cartoon.

Oddest of all in our selection are the two colour printed engravings taken from *The Instructive Picture Book* by an unknown author, dating from 1860. One is meant to show figures of pale-throated sloths, while the other supposedly shows us figures of the red howler monkey. But the sloths have the beguiling faces of displaced nuns and the monkeys are acting the parts of Adam and Eve! Such pictorial curiosities, whatever hidden meanings may lurk behind them, deserve to be rescued from oblivion if only to show us how an unknown artist's vision differed from ours.

Among the more memorable images in this small gallery of mammal pictures is the first credible group portrait of the lowland gorilla, one of Wolf's most sensitive studies. Here, too, is the first published illustration of the giant panda, a remarkable achievement as it was almost certainly based upon a preserved skin of a specimen taken to Paris shortly after its discovery in central China by the missionary Père David. Even more remarkable is P. J. Smit's fine 1902 lithograph of the okapi, the first published figure of a creature which was then a new and exciting discovery. Although it gives the impression of being a portrait of the living animal it was actually a reconstruction based on a skin and some other fragmentary remains which had been brought to London from the Congo. Of importance in a different context are the three lithographs taken from David Low's authoritative book, *The Breeds of the Domestic Animals of the British Islands*. Had Low not taken the trouble to publish such pictures in 1842 it would now be difficult or impossible to reconstruct the appearance of some of these breeds.

The pictures reproduced here and many others like them provide invaluable evidence of the appearance of mammals as they were (or were supposed to be) many years ago: but they are more than factual records. They allow us to view a vanished part of the natural world as if through the eyes of the artists who made the pictures, although this may require some effort on our part. We should realise, for instance, that artists did not always see mammals and other animals as we do now. Seldom, for instance, did they represent their subjects other than broadside on, James Wilson's capybara stands out as a rare exception. For many years, too, they often failed to inject life into their subjects. The studies published by Audubon and Bachman, however, occasionally inject too much of it.

Most artists must have some kind of training if they are to succeed as artists. Those who executed the pictures reproduced here received a very different training to that given to artists now. Their models were usually static and they were seldom encouraged to express their own individualism. As often as not the animals they drew or painted were dead; sometimes they were literally no more than skin and bones.

Today's wildlife artists would not accept such constraints. The material and educational advantages such artists now enjoy should not be taken for granted; they are better equipped than their predecessors in almost every way. In one respect, however, they are at a distinct disadvantage. Some of the animals they would like to have seen in the wild or even in captivity, such as one or two of those portrayed in our selection, are now no more. We should be grateful for the pictorial legacy bequeathed to us by yesterday's wildlife artists. Some of their work, by any standard, was excellent, some of it pedestrian; but it was all worthwhile.

Knowing that some of the animals portrayed by these artists will never be seen alive again has helped us to understand that the animals which remain mean a great deal to us. We may not realise it, but we are close in spirit to the image-makers of Lascaux.

European Hedgehog

PETIT HERISSON (now European Hedgehog, *Erinaceus europaeus*) and other Hedgehogs. Hand coloured engraving by P. Tanjé, pl. 49 from Vol. 1 of A. Seba's *Locupletissimi Rerum Naturalium Thesauri Accurata Descriptio &c*, 1734–65. Size of plate 17¼″ × 11″.

At the beginning of the eighteenth century the Amsterdam apothecary, Albert Seba, assembled a large collection of dried plants, stuffed animals, shells, insects and other natural curiosities. He sold it to Peter the Great of Russia in 1717 and then assembled another, even larger collection which he kept. Seba often acquired exotic specimens from seamen newly arrived from distant lands as payment for his professional services, but he did not disdain to add to his stores specimens of the commoner animals of Europe, such as the European hedgehog (illustrated by the two figures at the top of this plate). The white hedgehog in the centre of the plate was said to have been sent to Seba from Surinam in South America and to have been regarded by the 'Indians' there as 'delicious to eat'. As hedgehogs are not native to South America this white hedgehog must have originated elsewhere.

Although the European hedgehog is host to many different kinds of parasite, such as fleas and ticks, it was formerly esteemed a delicacy among country folk. In a fourteenth-century German treatise about natural history, Konrad von Megengerg wrote, 'the flesh of the hedgehog is wholesome for the stomach and strengthens the same. Likewise it hath a power of drying and relieving the stomach. It deals with the water of dropsy and is of great help to such as are inclined to the sickness called elephantiasis'. Its own sense of taste is well developed: given a choice, it prefers food with a characteristic flavour. An ancient fable would have us believe that it will roll on to windfall apples, impale them on its spines and carry them off to its nest. Although this extraordinary notion still receives an occasional airing it is not supported by any well attested proof.

TAB. IX.

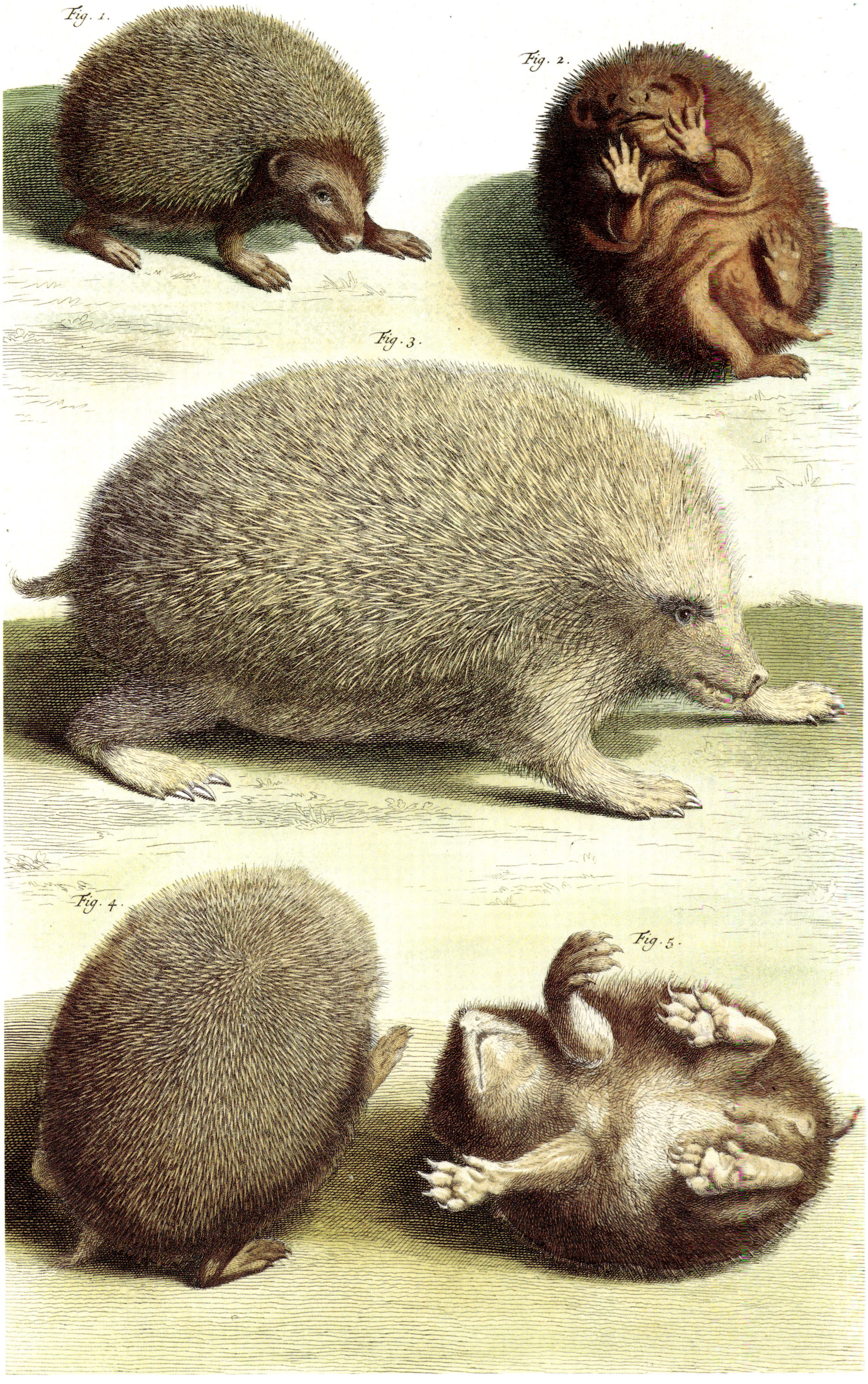

Moose

Elk, *Cervus alces* (now Moose, *Alces alces*). Hand coloured engraving by J. F. Miller, pl. 10 from his *Icones Animalium* (or *Various Subjects of Natural History*, 1776–85. Size of plate 17½″ × 11½″.

This engraving is from one of the rarest of eighteenth-century natural history books. Most of the few surviving copies of John Frederick Miller's *Icones Animalium* are incomplete and all are inaccessible to the general public; even now bibliographers disagree about the book's contents and publication dates. Fortunately the engravings included in it were re-issued in 1796, together with an explanatory text, under the title *Cimelia Physica*. Miller, who worked for Sir Joseph Banks, was more at home with plants than animals, so there is a naive quality about this representation of the largest living deer.

The scientific (genus) name of this bulky animal, *Alces*, is from the Greek word for elk, the name by which the moose is known in Europe. Widespread in northern North America, the moose varies considerably in size, the Alaskan form standing over six feet at the shoulder, weighing up to 1200 pounds or more and sporting enormous, spoon-shaped antlers. By comparison, the antlers of the European forms are much smaller and more flattened. The moose is usually a solitary animal and in summer feeds in low-lying swampy districts and at lakesides. In winter it moves into wooded areas and feeds on leaves, shoots and tender branches. The long, coarse hair provides a coat which helps to insulate the moose against the bitterly cold temperatures of the northern winters. Its great size makes it an easy target for hunters, but it has managed to survive over a considerable part of the northern hemisphere.

TAB. X.

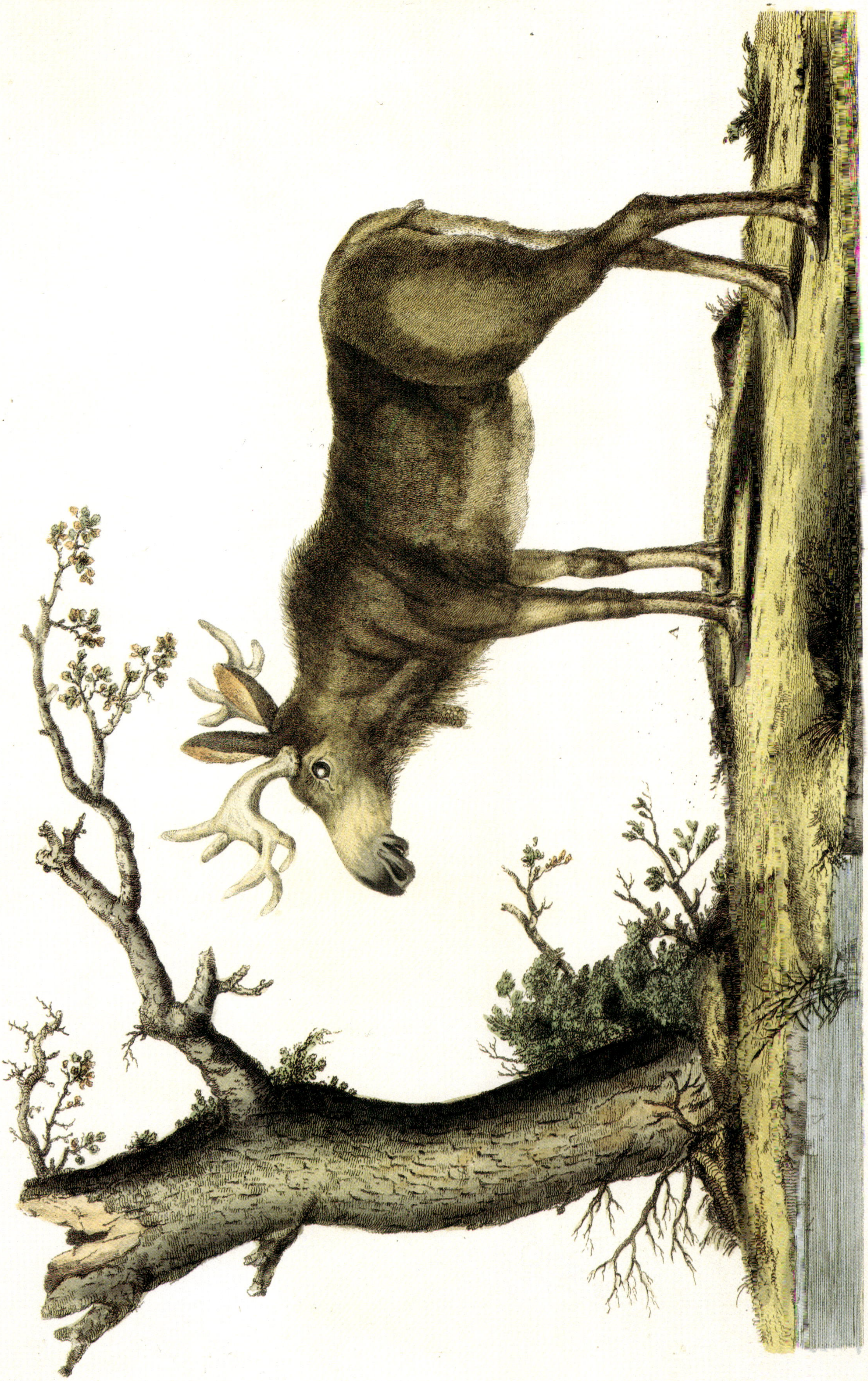

Ring-tailed Lemur

Le Mococo, *Lemur catta* (now Ring-tailed Lemur, *Lemur catta*). Colour printed engraving by J. B. Audebert, pl. 4 (of *Makis*) from his *Histoire Naturelle des Singes et des Makis*, 1799–1800. Size of plate 20″ × 13″.

Jean Baptiste Audebert was one of several outstanding French artists whose illustrations signalled a new and splendid epoch in the history of animal portraiture at the beginning of the nineteenth century. The attitude of the tail in this study of a ring-tailed lemur is so characteristic of the animal that Audebert probably drew from a captive specimen, not from a preserved skin.

Madagascar is the natural home of nearly all the lemurs, most of which live in trees. Audebert correctly shows his ring-tailed lemur on the ground where it lives amongst rocks in the southern part of the island, the black and white rings on its tail distinguishing it from all other lemurs. When not looking for its food, which consists of various kinds of fruit, birds' eggs and insects, it spends most of its time cleaning and licking the fur of other members of its own species. It is usual for the young to cling tightly to the underside of their mother for the first three weeks; afterwards they ride about on her back. When disturbed or worried it will adopt a crouching posture with its tail covering its breast and in this position will run its tail repeatedly through its arms. At the same time it spreads onto its tail secretions from scent glands on its wrists and shoulder region. It is still common in the wild and is the most familiar species of its family in captivity.

Pl. 4

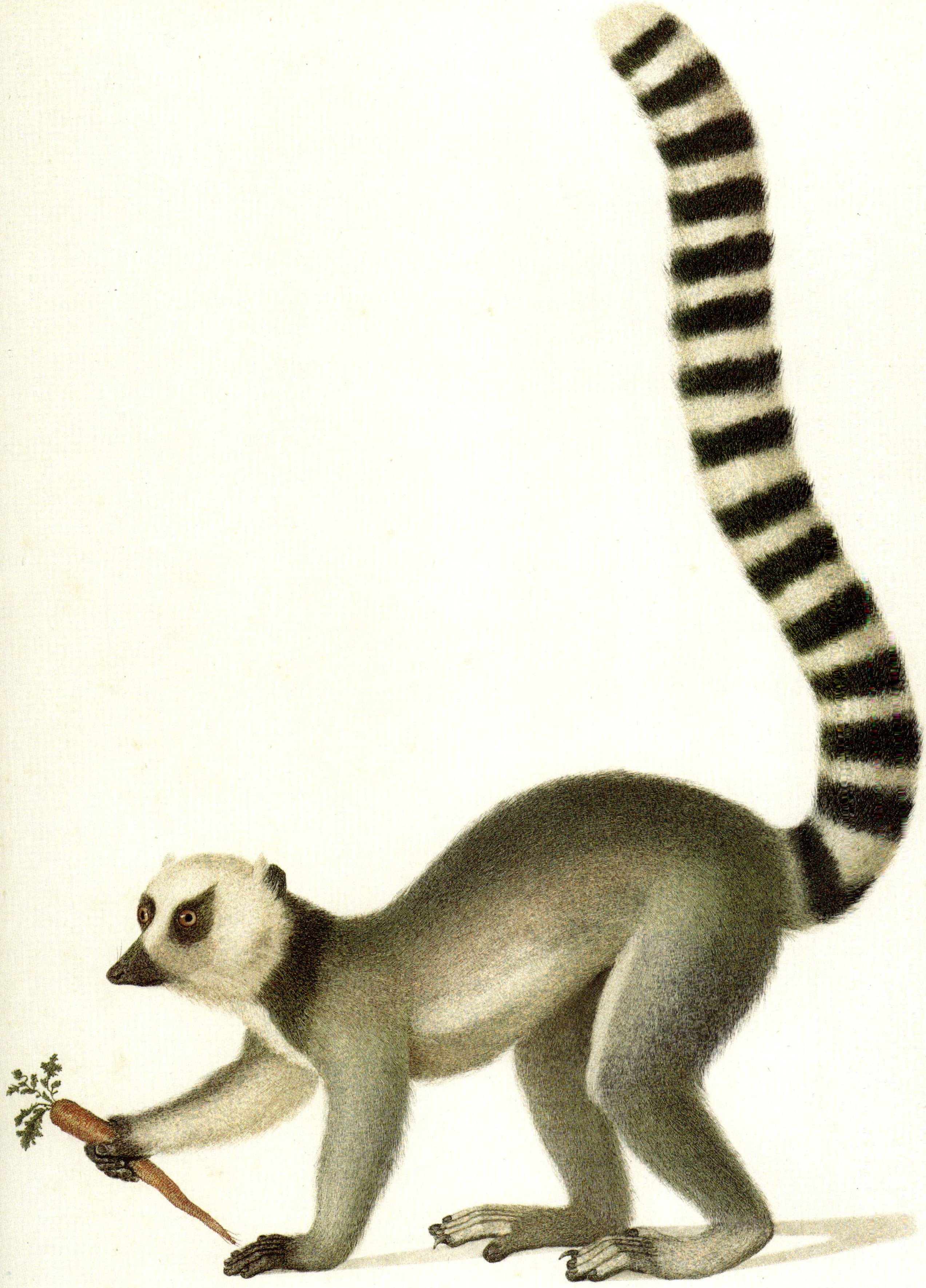

Le Mococo. Buff.

Audebert pinx.t et sculp.t — Lemur Catta. Linn. — *Finot Imp.t*

Indian Rhinoceros

RHINOCEROS UNICORN (now Indian Rhinoceros, *Rhinoceros unicornis*). Hand coloured engraving, unnumbered plate from Vol. 1 of E.G. Saint-Hilaire and G. F. Cuvier's *Histoire Naturelle des Mammifères*, 1819. Size of plate 20″ × 13″.

There are five different species of rhinoceros living today. The largest of the three Asiatic species, and the best known, is the Indian rhinoceros, which is now restricted to grassy areas and jungles in Bengal, Assam, and Nepal. Weighing in at more than two tons, standing six feet at the shoulder and fourteen feet long, the male Indian rhinoceros is not to be trifled with (although its vital statistics are exceeded by those of the white rhinoceros of Africa which is normally larger and has tipped the scales at five tons).

Unlike the African rhinos it has only one horn, present in both sexes and rather short and blunt. Compensating for the inadequacy of its horn as a weapon there is a pair of sharp-edged incisor tusks in the lower jaw, with which it slashes at a potential enemy. It is peace-loving, retiring and solitary by nature and so is unlikely to attack unless provoked.

This view of the Indian rhinoceros displays its characteristically folded and knobbly hide. These features are emphasised in the earliest published illustration of the animal by a western artist, Albert Dürer, which was based on a sketch of a living animal seen and sketched at Lisbon in 1515. Not only did he represent the hide as though it were armour plating, he also gave the Lisbon beast a tiny extra horn on its back behind the head, an embellishment usually reserved for representations of the fabulous unicorn. Nevertheless, Dürer's fanciful picture has been reproduced countless times since his day and is still a popular image of the Indian rhinoceros; such is the power of a great artist.

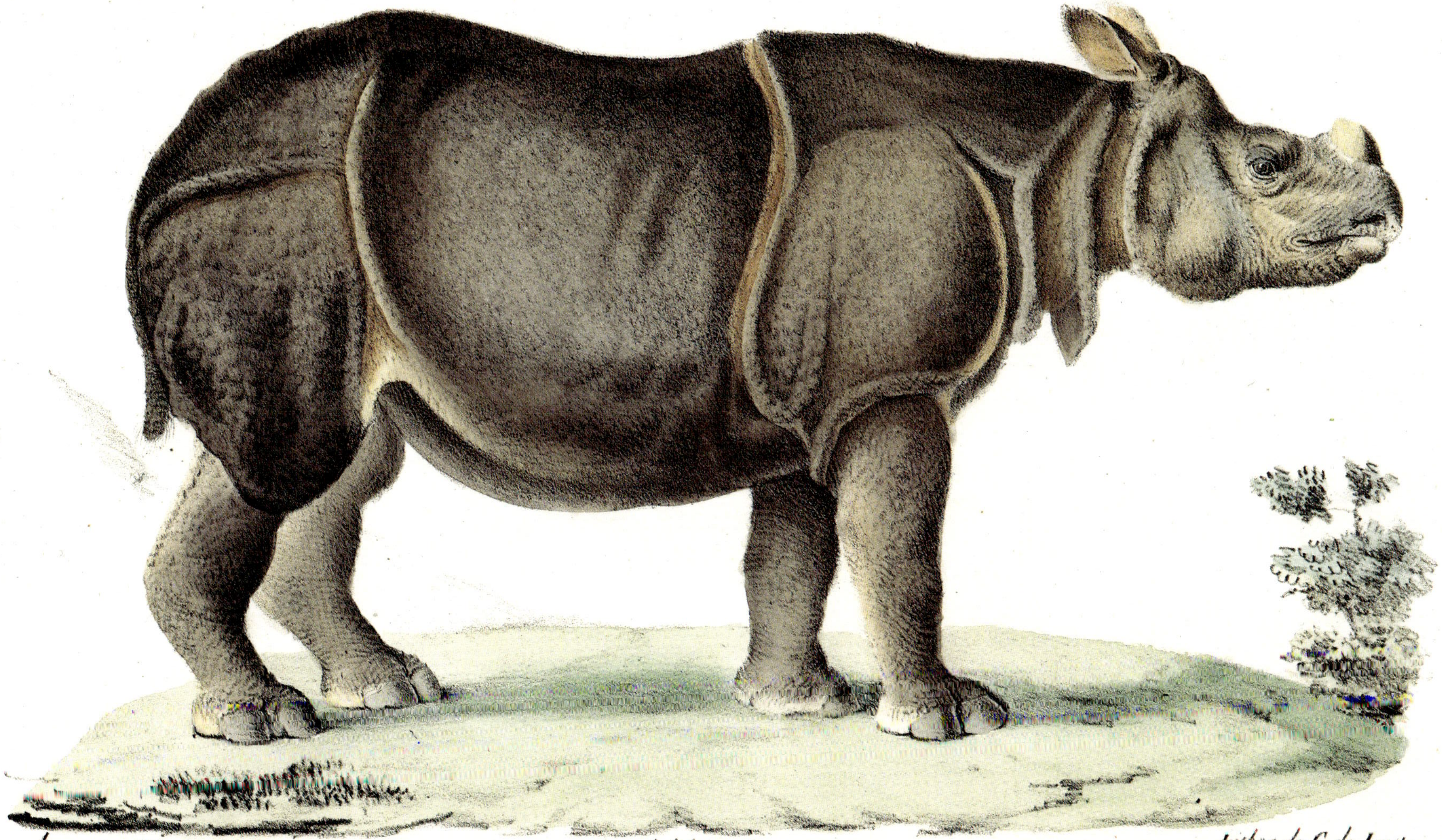

Huet pinx. Werner del. 1/13 de la grand nat. Lithog. de C. de Last.

Rhinocéros unicorne.

Golden-headed Tamarin

Le Sahui Noir, *Hapale chrysomelas* (now Golden-headed Tamarin, *Leontopithecus chrysomelas*). Hand coloured engraving, pl. 9 from Part 2 of Prince Maximilian Alexander Philipp of Wied-Neuwied's *Recueil de Planches Coloriées d'Animaux du Brésil*, 1822–31. Size of plate 10½″ × 9″.

This engraving contrasts strangely with modern illustrations of the golden-headed tamarin, a small South American primate. The tamarins are noted for the mane of long, silky fur around their shoulders but it does not stand up so dramatically as this picture suggests. As this was one of the first, if not the first, published illustration of it and was probably an artist's reconstruction based on a preserved skin we should not be too critical. A small animal, it travels in small groups and leaps from branch to branch with great agility. It shelters in hollow trees and crevices and feeds upon fruit, insects, lizards and probably birds' eggs.

Prince Maximilian led an expedition into the interior of Brazil in the early nineteenth century and said in his published report that this creature often provided him and his colleagues with a meal. He also said that if it could survive the rigours of a voyage to Europe it would 'truly be an ornament in our rooms'; in other words it would make an amusing pet for those in fashionable society. It is not likely to make a pet in our own day because, like the other two golden tamarins of eastern Brazil, it is in danger of being exterminated. In 1981 the total population was estimated at less than 200 specimens. As the destruction of its habitat continues and collectors hunt it to stock zoos there is little likelihood of it surviving for very long in the wild.

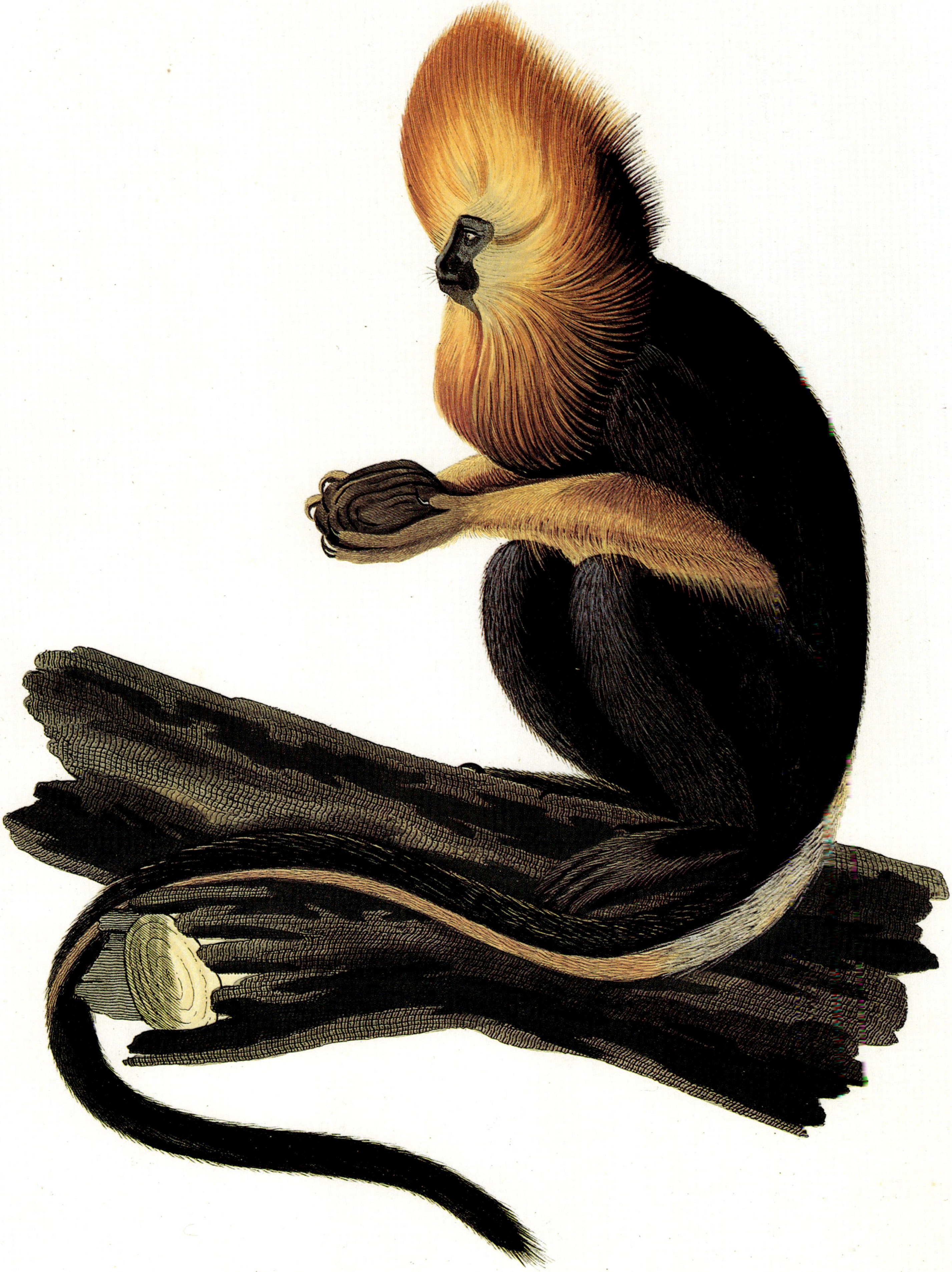

Hapale chrysomelas.

9

Bactrian Camel

LE CHAMEAU DE LA BACTRIANE, *Camelus bactrianus* (now Bactrian Camel, *Camelus bactrianus*). Hand coloured lithograph by C. de Last from an original drawing by Werner, unnumbered plate in Part 29, Vol. 2 of E. G. Saint-Hilaire and G.F. Cuvier's *Histoire Naturelle des Mammifères*, 1824. Size of plate 20″ × 13″.

In the early nineteenth century the Bactrian camel may have been less familiar to Europeans than the Arabian camel, *Camelus dromedarius*. This picture of it is probably better than any published earlier, although it tends to idealise the appearance of a creature which loses its thick, brown winter coat in patches. The twin humps, which immediately distinguish it from the single-humped Arabian camel, have no supporting bony structure and are fat storage organs enabling it to survive when food is scarce. The Bactrian camel is the slower of the two and is used primarily as a beast of burden, often travelling in great caravans across the inhospitable, stony deserts and snow-bound wastes of central Asia.

Its popular name is derived from Bactria, the name of an ancient kingdom of eastern Persia which covered an area corresponding roughly to the modern province of Balkh in Afghanistan. The reliefs decorating the walls of Xerxes' palace at Persepolis show tribute bearers leading Bactrian camels, proof enough that these hardy animals have been domesticated for a very long time. Very few truly wild Bactrian camels are alive today.

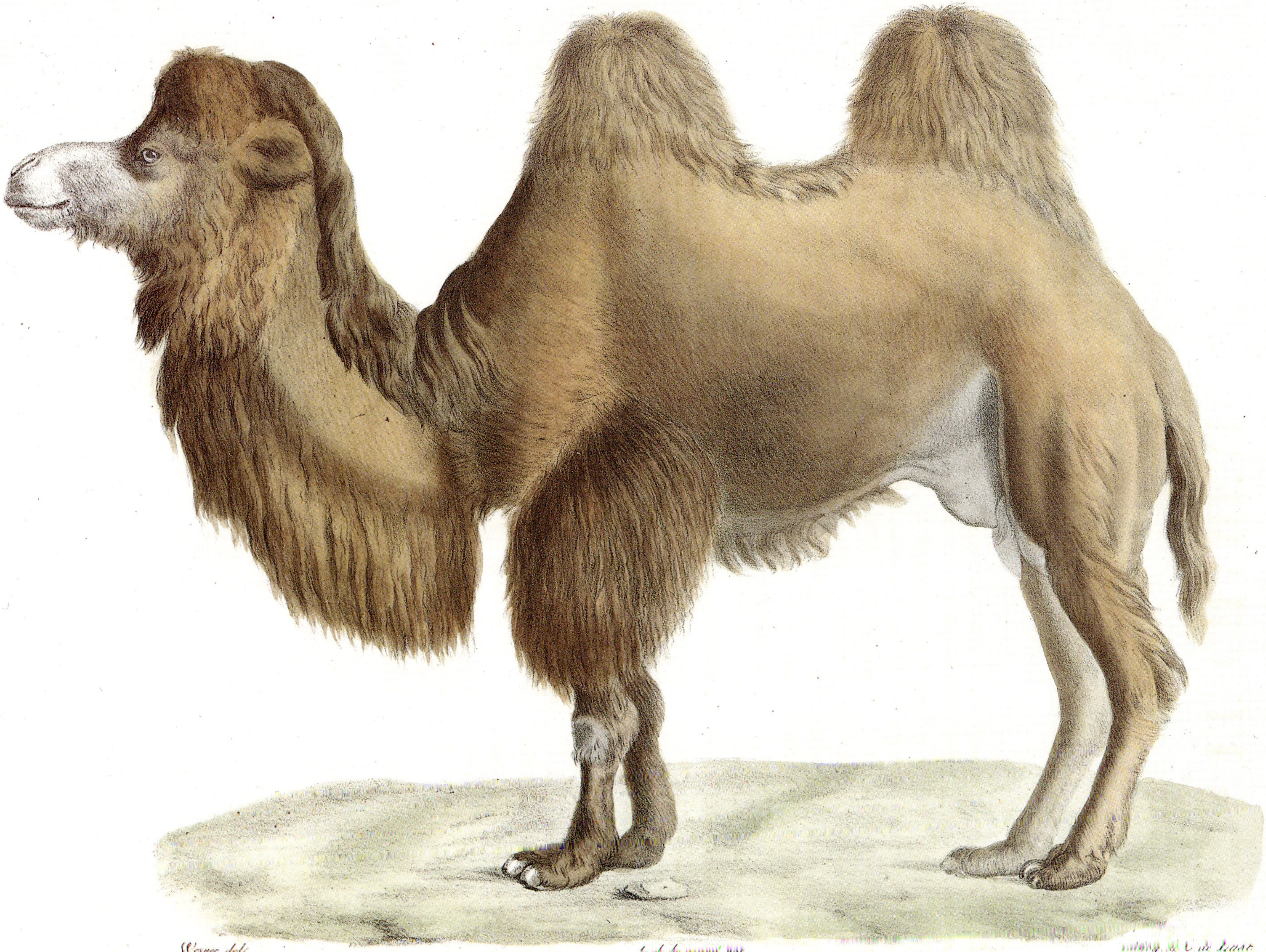

Werner del. 1/10 de la grand. nat. Lithog. de C. de Last

Chameau de la Bactriane.

Quagga

Le Couagga, *Equus quagga* (now Quagga, *Equus quagga*). Hand coloured lithograph by C. de Last from an original drawing by Werner (an error for Maréchal?), unnumbered plate in Part 30, Vol. 2 of E. G. Saint-Hilaire and G.F. Cuvier's *Histoire Naturelle des Mammifères*, 1824. Size of plate 20″ × 13″.

The quagga has been extinct since 1883 when the last one, an old mare, died at the Amsterdam Zoo. Measuring about four and a half feet high at the shoulder it was one of the smallest of the zebras and resembled a horse more closely than did the others because its stripes did not extend much farther back than the base of its mane. It is sometimes aptly described as having had the rear end of a horse and the front end of a zebra. It did not neigh like a horse, however, the name quagga being derived from its barking noise.

Formerly plentiful on the plains of the southern parts of South Africa, its fate was sealed when the Boers began slaughtering it for its meat and hide. The individual illustrated here lived in the Jardin des Plantes at Paris and died there in 1793. In that year Nicolas Maréchal, an artist who specialised in portrayals of natural history subjects, made a brilliant painting of it on parchment. His painting, now preserved in the National Museum of Natural History in Paris, is evidently the original of this lithograph. At the foot of the lithograph the original painting is attributed to Werner. As Jean Charles Werner was not born until long after the animal depicted had died this attribution must be erroneous.

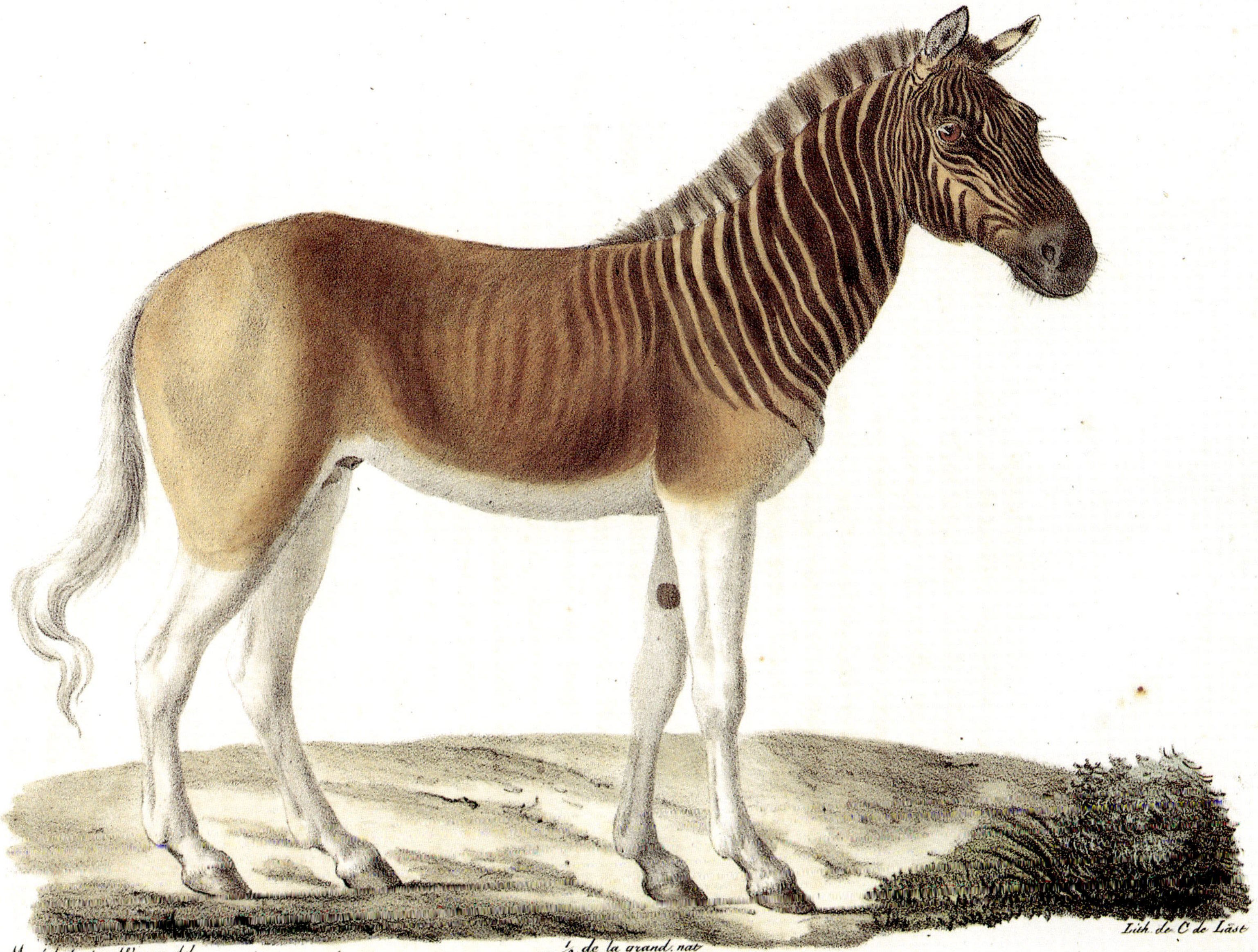

Maréchal pinx Werner del   1/8 de la grand. nat   Lith. de C. de Lâst

Couagga

Spotted Cuscus

PHALANGER TACHETÉ, *Phalangista maculata* (now Spotted Cuscus, *Phalanger maculatus*). Hand coloured engraving by Coutant from an original drawing by Prévost, pl. 7 from the *Atlas* to J. R. C. Quoy and J. P. Gaimard's *Zoologie* (in M. L. de Freycinet's *Voyage autour du Monde . . . sur . . . l'Uranie et la Physicienne*), 1824–26. Size of plate 12½″ × 9½″.

From 1817 to 1820 the French exploring vessels *Uranie* and *Physicienne* went around the world and visited several islands in the Pacific, including Waigeou off the north-western tip of New Guinea. Among the many unusual creatures observed on this tropical island was the spotted cuscus, a tree-living marsupial the size of a domestic cat. At least one example was brought back to Paris to be studied and, eventually, to be immortalised in this rather formal portrait published in the scientific report of the expedition. It is most unlikely that any living examples were taken back to France because the stress involved in capturing and transporting these animals ensures that few survive a long voyage or captivity.

Early travellers would sometimes mistake it for a monkey, partly because it is mainly nocturnal and partly because of their ignorance of marsupials. With its thick, curly coat, furry, prehensile tail and roundish head with large, red-rimmed eyes it would have presented an unusual sight to a traveller seeing it for the first time as it stared out through the thick greenery of its humid forest. It moves about lazily at night, feeding upon leaves and fruit, birds and their eggs or fledglings. During the day it mostly sleeps in the hollows of trees or merely clutches boughs. Of the several colour variants the spotted one seen here is the commonest. Abundant in New Guinea the spotted cuscus is one of the rarer Australian marsupials, being found only in the forests of Cape York Peninsula at the north-eastern extremity of the continent.

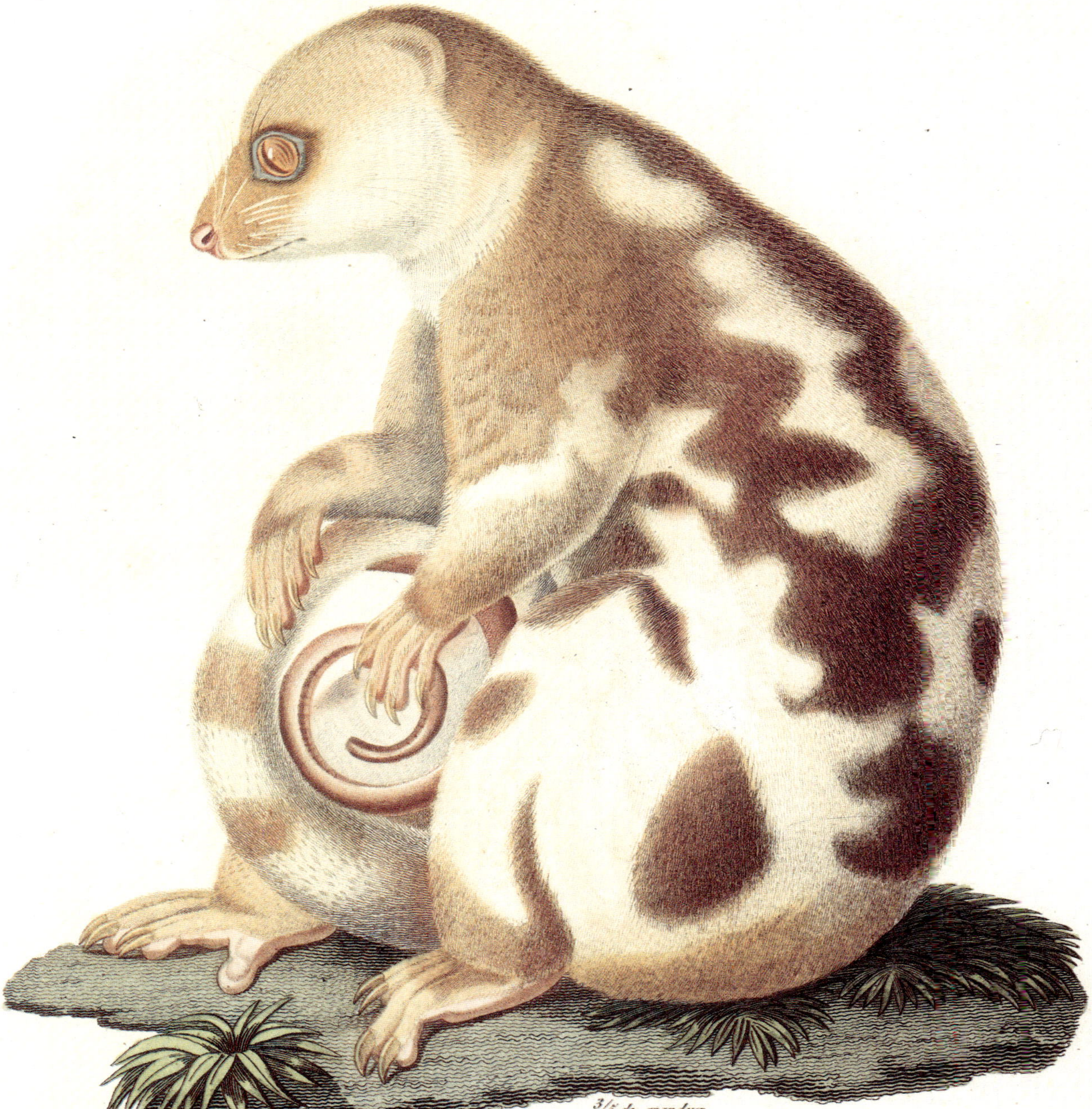

3/5 de grandeur.

A. Prévost pinx.t Contant sculp.

PHALANGER TACHETÉ: (*PHALANGISTA MACULATA*. Geoff.)

Nubian Ibex

Capra sinaitica (now Nubian Ibex, *Capra nubiana*). Hand coloured engraving, pl. 18 from Christian Gottfried Ehrenberg's *Symbolae Physicae. Pars Zoologica, Mammalia*, 1828. Size of plate 19″ × 13″.

This sensitive study captures the noble character of the Nubian ibex and shows that it is a creature of mountainous districts. Virtually a mountain-dwelling wild goat, it displays incredible agility and grace as it bounds from crag to crag, leaps over chasms, and ascends the apparently smooth sides of precipitous slopes. It lives at altitudes of between 600 and 6000 feet above sea level, and is at home in arid, desert country where bare mountains alternate with steep-sided valleys and where rocky outcrops abound; country such as that found in Israel, the Sudan, Sinai, Upper Egypt and Arabia, its collective area of distribution. Apparently impervious to the harshest weather conditions, it never leaves the mountains, finding enough sustenance in the grasses and bushes which constitute the impoverished flora of such an environment.

Although blessed with sharp eyesight and a highly developed sense of smell the Nubian ibex, like the walia ibex, has suffered greatly from the depredations of man, perhaps its only effective enemy. Already of economic importance to the native peoples living in its range (they have always valued it for its flesh, hide, woolly underfur and coarse hair) it has been hunted almost to extinction in recent years. Only a rigorous protection policy will give it a chance to survive. Its fine horns provide hunters with an irresistible incentive to kill it. The horns are not massive but they are longer than those of the walia ibex, measuring more than 40 inches, and are bevelled on the outer front edge, resulting in a narrow front surface. Unfortunately, these majestic ornaments help to make it a conspicuous target.

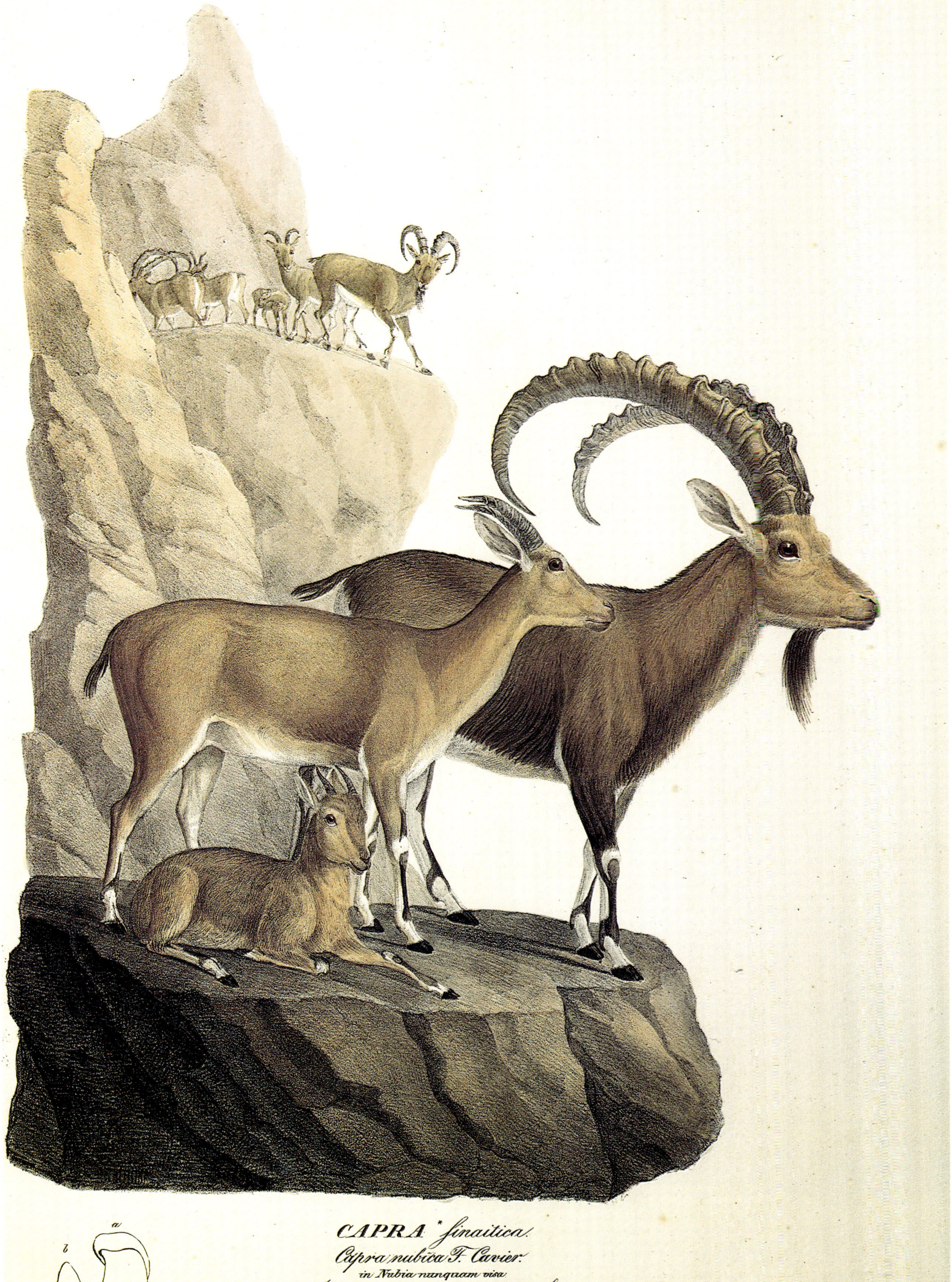

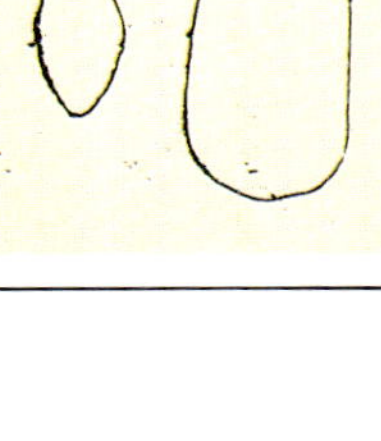

CAPRA* *sinaitica.*

Capra nubica F. Cuvier.

in Nubia nunquam visa

ex Aegypto superiore et e montibus sinaiticis.

Mas. adultus, femina adulta et femina juvenis.

F. Bürde fecit.

Puma

PUMA OR AMERICAN LION, *Felis concolor.* Hand coloured engraving by W. H. Lizars, pl. 1 from J. Wilson's *Illustrations of Zoology*, 1831. Size of plate 16″ × 12″.

In October 1826 a frigate from Brazil arrived at Portsmouth, England. On board was a young puma, intended for Robert Jameson's Natural History Museum in the University of Edinburgh. It escaped during a stopover in London but a night watchman recaptured it and it returned to its quarters peaceably. On 8 January 1827 it reached Edinburgh where, after taking a little time to adjust to the climate, it settled down and began to enjoy its new surroundings – a lumber room under the Library of Edinburgh University! Here it became a great attraction for several months, especially to James Wilson who observed it closely.

'It rejoices greatly in the society of those to whose company it is accustomed', he writes, in the text to this plate, 'lies down upon its back between their feet, and plays with the skirts of their garments, entirely after the manner of a kitten. When let loose, it exhibits the most extraordinary feats of activity, springing about in a large lumber room, and assuming an infinite variety of elegant and picturesque positions. It shows a great predilection for water, and frequently jumps into and out of a large tub, rolling itself about, and seeming greatly pleased with the refreshment.' Wilson points out that 'the only animals which have fallen victims to its rapacity, were a mallard drake and a cock pheasant, both of which inadvertently approached within the circle of its spring, and were each killed by a blow of its forepaw' – which at least sounds more like the normal behaviour of a puma.

Traces of the blackish-brown spots which characterise young individuals of this species may still be seen in this portrait, which was obviously done from life. The curious convolutions of the tail were especially noted by Wilson and have been observed in other captive pumas. It seems that this playful animal did not become a stuffed exhibit in Professor Jameson's Museum but may have ended its days quietly in a menagerie elsewhere in Edinburgh, a fitting conclusion to a curiously unconventional life.

PLATE I.

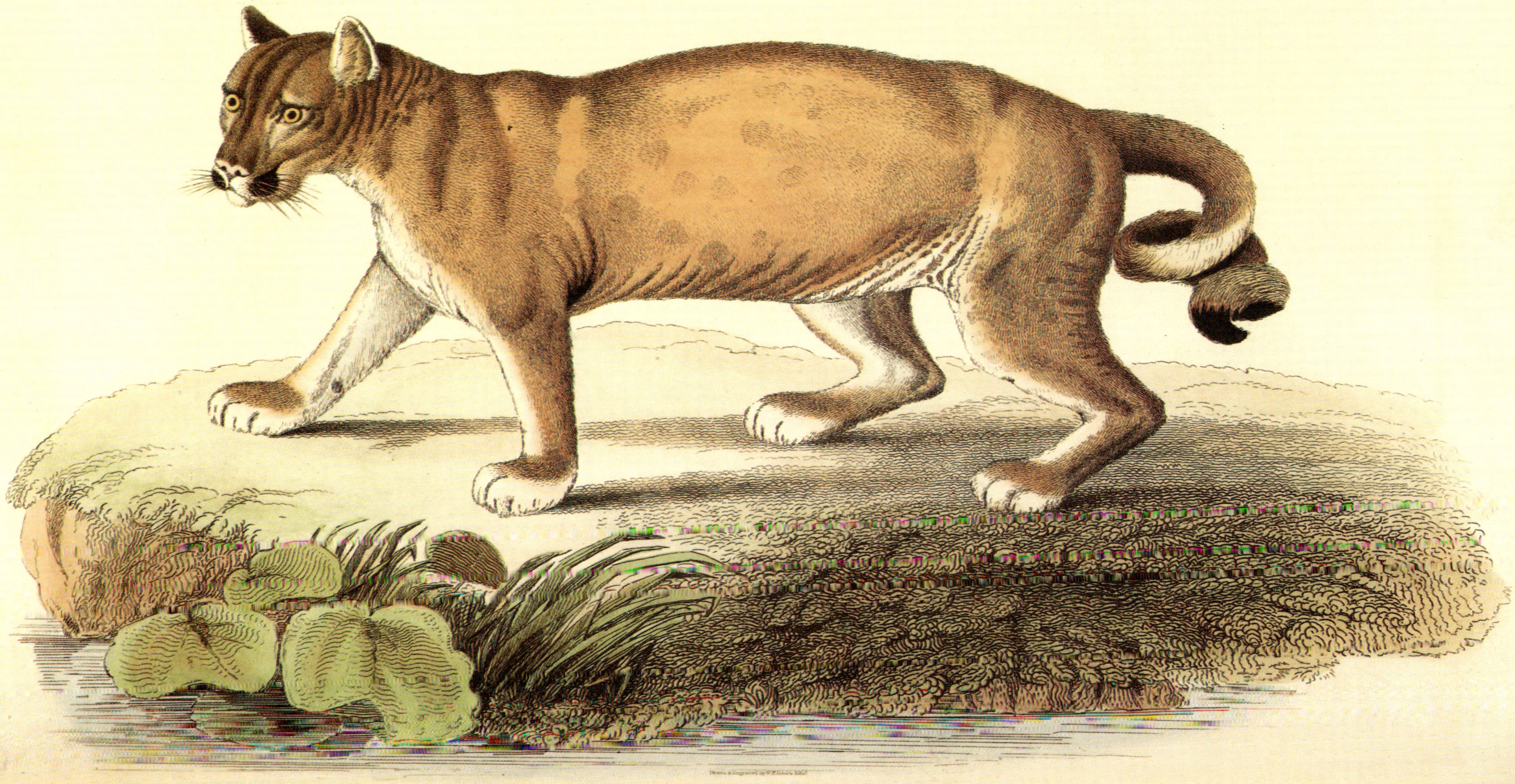

Drawn & Engraved by W.H. Lizars Edin.

The Puma or American Lion

Capybara

Capybara or Water-Hog, *Hydrochaerus capybara* (now Capybara, *Hydrochoerus hydrochaeris*). Hand coloured engraving by W. H. Lizars from an original drawing by A. Mosses, pl. 13 from J. Wilson's *Illustrations of Zoology*, 1831. Size of plate 16″ × 12″.

The adult capybara, largest of living rodents, is about four feet long, stands about 21 inches tall at the shoulder and may weigh more than 100 pounds. At home in the river networks of South America it grazes on river-bank vegetation and aquatic plants. Although attached to water it may come on to dry land in fine weather to rest and to enjoy the sunshine. It adapts readily to life in captivity and may become very friendly with its captors.

James Wilson, commenting on the figures of the capybara reproduced here, said that they 'were drawn by Mr Mosses of Liverpool, from a full grown female capybara which lived for some months in that town'. He added some curious information about its habits in captivity. 'Its voice was plaintive', he said, 'not unlike that of a newly dropped lamb, and seemed very feeble for so large an animal. It loved human society, and frequently hopped up stairs, and entered the bed-rooms in search of the children of the family, whom it readily followed. The length of its hind legs rendered hopping its easiest motion, and it was capable of considerable bounds. It had the power of erecting all its hair after the manner of the hedge-hog, and its black, scaly skin then became distinctly visible through the thinly set fur. It ate grass, and all sorts of vegetable matters, but seemed to prefer wheaten bread to other diet. When taken to the water, it swam and dived admirably, remained a long time beneath the surface, and quitted its favourite element with reluctance.'

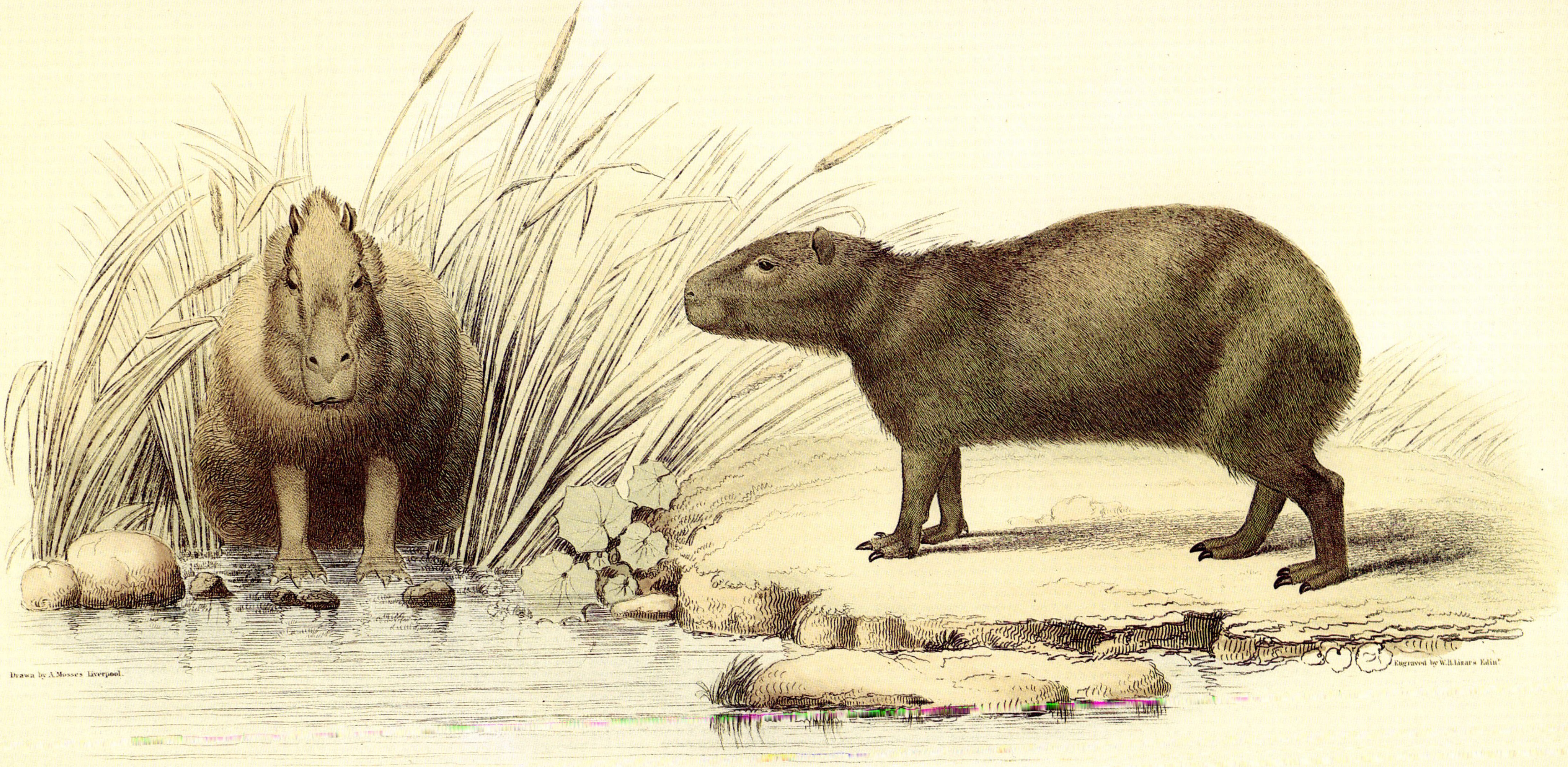

Drawn by A. Mosses Liverpool. Engraved by W.H. Lizars Edin^r.

The Capybara, or Water Hog.

HYDROCHŒRUS CAPIBARA. ERXLEB.

White Whale

BELUGA OR GREAT WHITE DOLPHIN, *Delphinapterus beluga* (now White Whale, *Delphinapterus leucas).* Hand coloured engraving by W. H. Lizars from an original drawing by Patrick Syme, pl. 16 from J. Wilson's *Illustrations of Zoology*, 1831. Size of plate 16″ × 12″.

The reason this strange looking creature found its way into James Wilson's *Illustrations of Zoology* is probably because, for about three months in the spring of 1815, it became a talking point among the intelligentsia of Edinburgh, where Wilson worked. Wilson tells us that it 'was observed to inhabit the Firth of Forth, passing upwards almost every day with the tide, and returning again with the ebbing of the waters. It excited great attention by the purity of its colour, and frequent attempts were made to slay or secure it, but without effect, till the 7th of June, when it was killed in the river near Stirling, by means of spears and fire arms. It was purchased by Mr Robert Bald of Alloa, and kindly transmitted by him to Professor Jameson, and on examination was found to be the Beluga of naturalists.' It measured 14 feet 4 inches from the tip of the jaw to the end of the tail, so it was a youngster; this pure white, gentle creature may grow to almost twice this length.

Normally white whales frequent coasts bordering the Arctic Ocean where their white bodies are not easily seen against the ice and snow. Occasionally, however, young examples will swim far up rivers and have even been reported 700 miles up the River Yukon. This gives fishermen a chance to trap and kill them and explains the presence of one in a river near Stirling in Scotland. But how can the presence of an iceberg in the background of Wilson's picture be explained, bearing in mind the geographical position of Stirling? The answer is simple. In 1820, eleven years before Wilson's book was published, William Scoresby had published at Edinburgh *An Account of the Arctic Regions, with a History and Description of the Northern Whale-Fishery*; it includes an engraving of the white whale, complete with iceberg, almost identical with Wilson's. The one Wilson wrote about was not the same as the one he illustrated, but that may have seemed unimportant in 1831.

PLATE XVI.

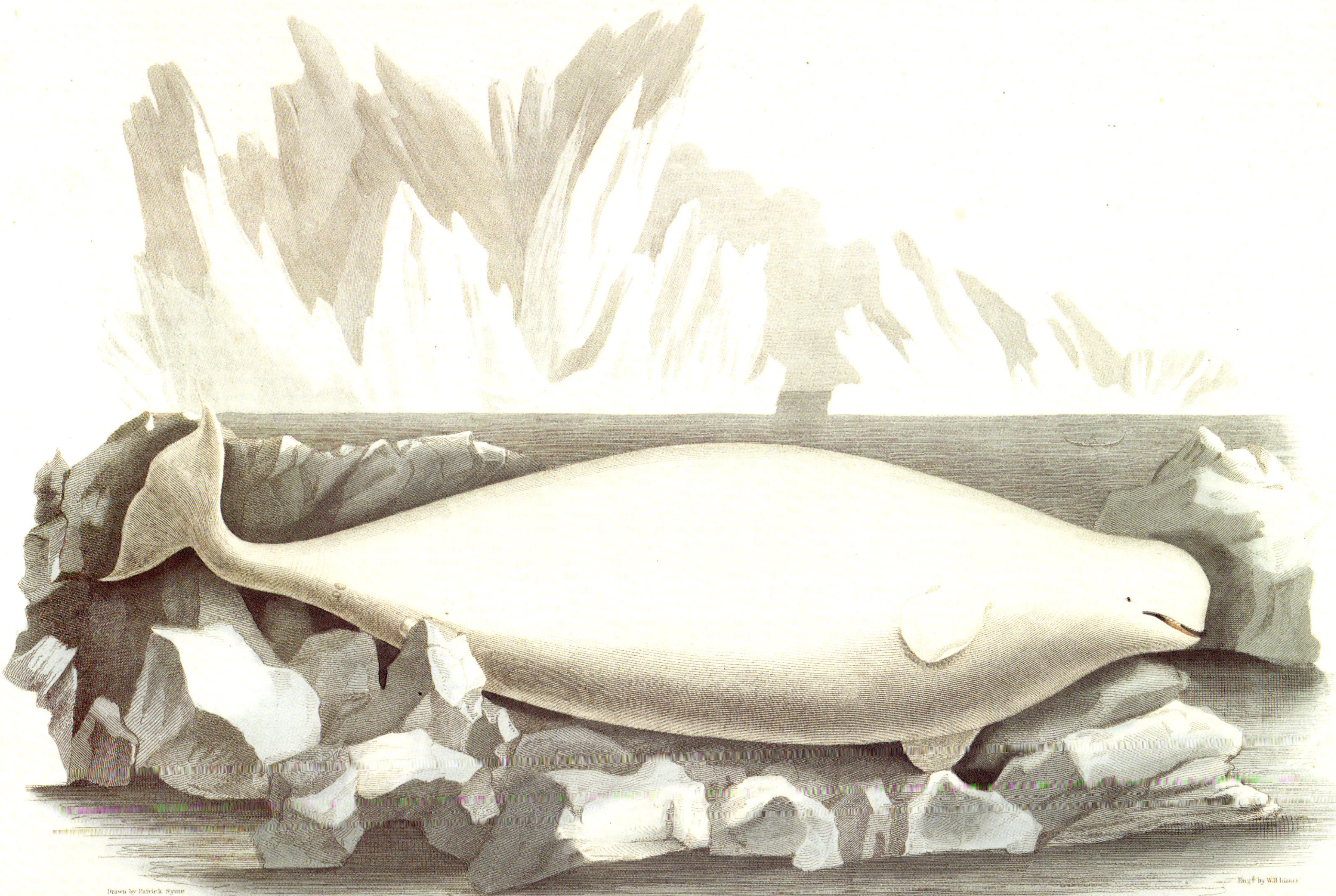

Drawn by Patrick Syme

Engd. by Wm. Lizars

The Beluga, or Great White Dolphin.

DELPHINAPTERUS BELUGA. LACEPEDE.

Wild Cat

Chat Sauvage, *Felis catus* (now Wild Cat, *Felis silvestris*). Hand coloured engraving by François from an original drawing by Werner, pl. 1A from I. G. Saint-Hilaire's *Mammifères et Oiseaux* (in the *Atlas* to Bory de Saint-Vincent's *Expédition Scientifique de Morée*), 1832–36. Size of plate 18½″ × 11½″.

This is a very unusual representation of the wild cat. It looks less like the untamable savage creature we know it to be than an overfed domestic cat caught in the act of timidly climbing a tree. The stiff pose is due to the artist having had only a skin or a poorly mounted specimen as a model. Bory de Saint-Vincent, the leader of the French expedition to Morea in southern Greece, shot the specimen illustrated. Representations of the larger animals in French natural history publications of the early nineteenth century have formal and somewhat wooden poses with minimal background scenery. The animals are depicted with great attention to detail but are seldom imbued with life. Illustrations such as this were primarily adjuncts to scientific descriptions and were not intended to be appreciated as works of art with a separate existence.

In the text to this engraving Isidore Geoffroy Saint-Hilaire said there were minor differences between this form of the wild cat and that typical of other parts of Europe. In particular it had more marked rings around its tail. It was said to be very common on Morea and habitually rested for long periods in trees.

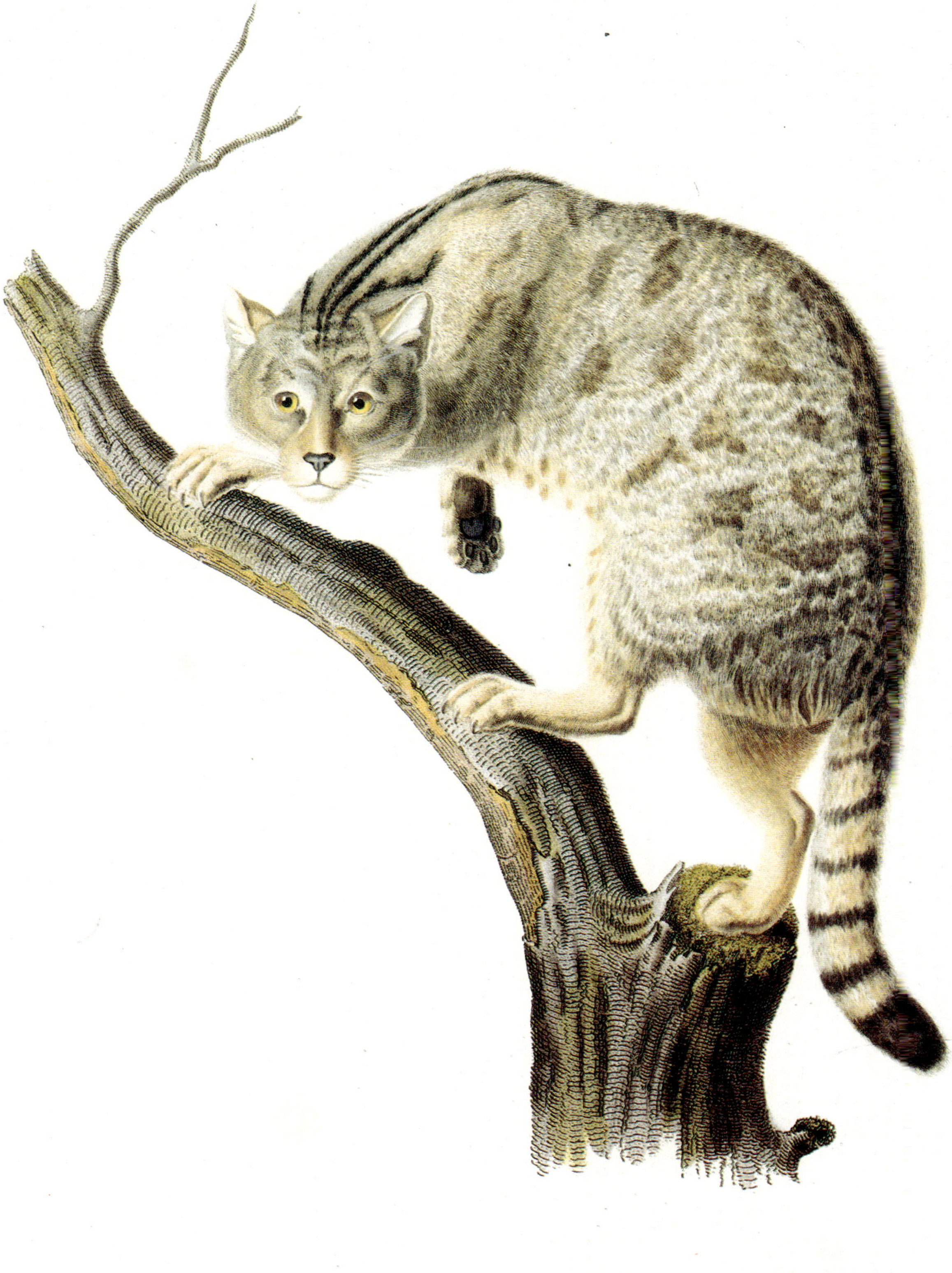

Numbat

Marsupial Anteater, *Myrmecobius fasciatus* (now Numbat, *Myrmecobius fasciatus*). Hand coloured lithograph by W. Dickes, pl. 27 from George R. Waterhouse's *Description of the new genus of mammiferous animals from Australia* (in *Transactions of the Zoological Society of London* Vol. 2), 1836. Size of plate 12½″ × 10″.

This curious animal, the size of a large ferret, lives in open wooded districts of south-western Australia, especially where dead eucalyptus branches are lying about. It obtains its food, principally termites, at or just under the surface and from under fallen branches, using its sticky, four-inch-long tongue.

George Waterhouse, who first brought this distinctively marked marsupial to the attention of the scientific world in 1836, tells us in the text to this illustration that the first example was found by a Lieutenant Dale of Liverpool while accompanying a party exploring the interior of the country at the Swan River Settlement about 90 miles north of the Swan River. Information he had received from Dale about this and another example make interesting reading. 'Two of these animals', said Dale, 'were seen within a few miles of each other; they were first observed on the ground, and on being pursued, both directed their flight to some hollow trees which were near. We succeeded in capturing one of them; the other was unfortunately burnt to death in our endeavour to dislodge it by fumigating the hollow tree in which it had taken refuge. The country in which they were found, abounded in decayed trees and ant-hills. The second individual, I am informed, was found in Van Diemen's Land [Tasmania]; and others, similar to it have been seen in the act of burrowing or digging at the roots of trees in search of insects. The favourite haunts are stated to be in those situations in which the Port Jackson willow abounds.' As no other specimen has ever been recorded from Tasmania it is likely that someone had misinformed Waterhouse.

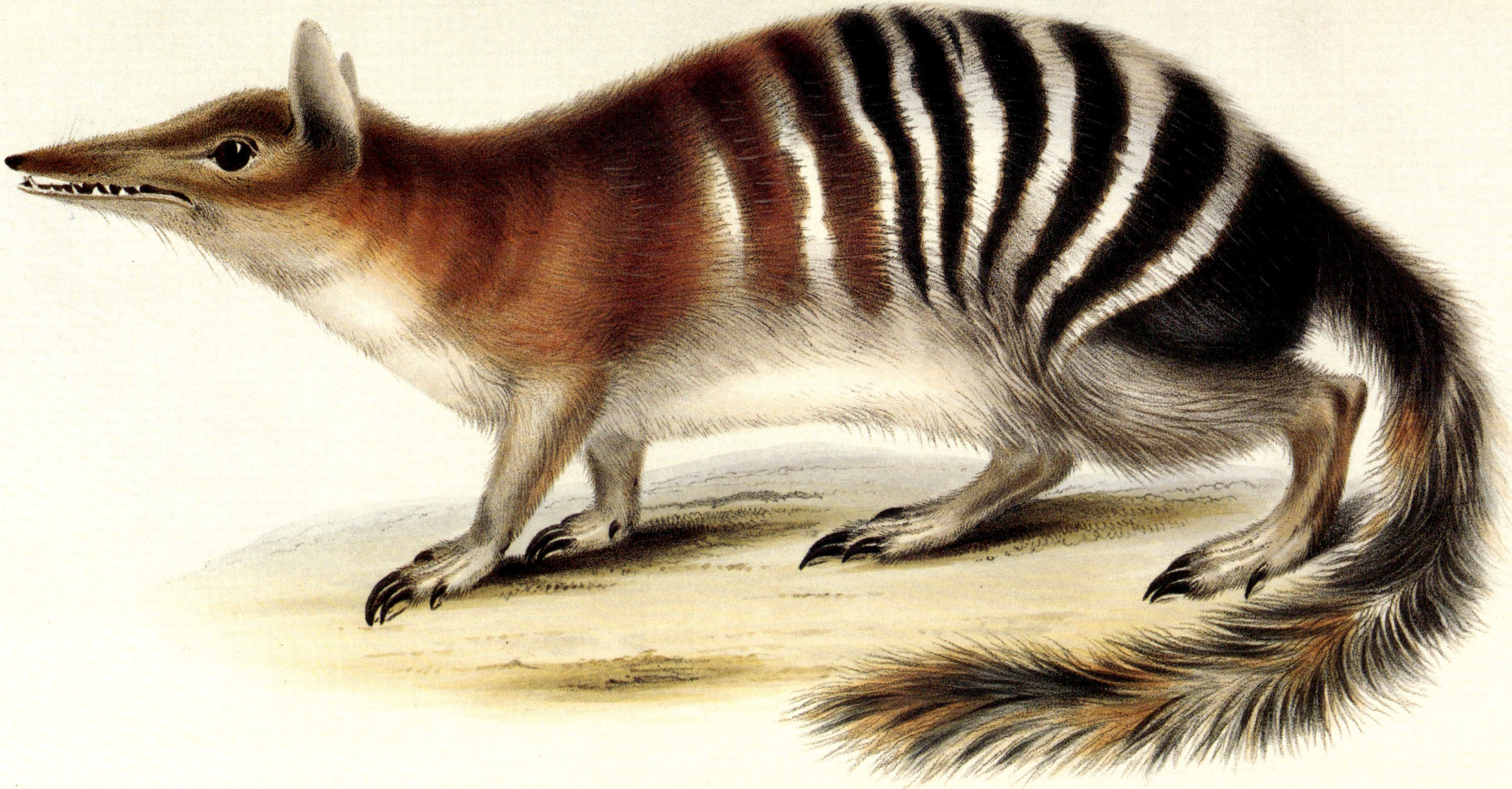

Lithographed from Nature by W. Dickes.

Printed by C. Hullmandel.

Myrmecobius fasciatus

Giraffe

GIRAFFE, *Camelopardalis giraffa* (now Giraffe, *Giraffa camelopardalis*). Hand coloured engraving by W. Warwick after an original drawing by Captain Thomas Brown, pl. 52 from Part B of *The Edinburgh Journal of Natural History*, 1836–37. Size of plate 13½″ × 9″.

When this excellent engraving was published it was sufficient to call a giraffe a giraffe. Now as many as twelve different races are recognised, the visible differences between them, apart from size, being their dissimilar colours and colour patterns – although the differences are often subtle. Captain Brown would appear to have drawn the Nubian giraffe, distinguished by its white legs and broad, geometrical dark patches separated by thick white lines. This race, which occurs in the Sudan, was the first to be described.

The tallest animal in the world, the giraffe's statistics are impressive. Its height at the shoulder is 10–12 feet, at the top of the head 14–18 feet; its tongue is 7 inches long; and it weighs well over 2000 pounds. Both sexes have short horns covered with hair. A giraffe has a fair turn of speed, timed at up to 35 m.p.h. When galloping it swings the hind feet forwards and to the outside of the forefeet; both sets of legs move together, unlike those of a horse, which move diagonally.

The giraffe is a browser and the main advantage of its great height is to make available sources of food which other browsers cannot reach. But its height has the disadvantage of making it visible from a considerable distance; a giraffe cannot hide easily. So it falls prey to the lion, especially when drinking or when feeding at ground level. It is not defenceless, however, and can deliver a kick which may disable or kill even the King of Beasts.

LII.

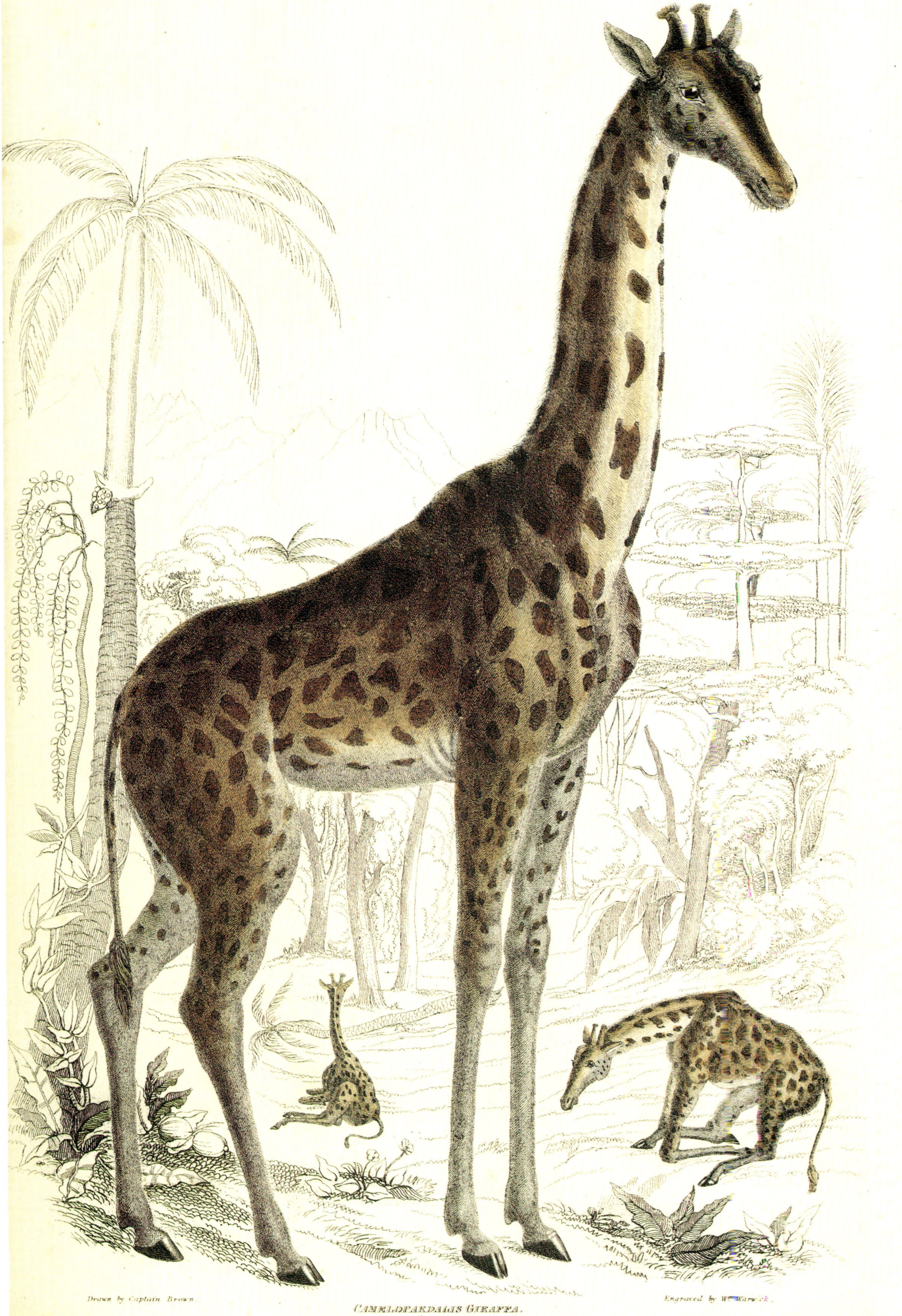

Drawn by Captain Brown. Engraved by Wm. Warwick.

CAMELOPARDALIS GIRAFFA.
THE GIRAFFE.

Asiatic Elephant and African Elephant

INDIAN ELEPHANT, *Elephas indicus* (now Asiatic Elephant, *Elephas maximus*) (top), African Elephant, *Elephas africanus* (now African Elephant, *Loxodonta africana*) (bottom). Hand coloured engraving by S. Milne, pl. 39 from *The Edinburgh Journal of Natural History*, 1837. Size of plate 13½″ × 9″.

This plate is a mixture of fact and fable: the top figure is a tolerably accurate representation of the Asiatic elephant, the bottom little more than a caricature of the African elephant. The principal differences between the two species, though subtle, are well within the capacity of a competent artist to delineate. The African elephant, much the bigger animal, has considerably larger ears and the ridge of its back has a concave curve. It has three nails on each hind foot to the Asiatic elephant's four; and its trunk has two 'fingers' at its tip, the Asiatic elephant having only one. By at least some of these criteria the top figure represents an Asiatic elephant. The bottom figure, by almost any criterion, does not represent the African elephant.

As the distinguishing characteristics of the two animals were well known in 1837, when this picture was published, it is puzzling to see the African elephant portrayed here so inaccurately. But there may be a simple explanation: plagiarism. It was a common practice throughout the eighteenth century and well into the nineteenth for engravings to be copied without acknowledgment. This picture of the African elephant, so called, is almost certainly a copy or a near copy of one published earlier, possibly much earlier. Very similar pictures occur in several eighteenth-century publications. No elephant resembling this one has been at large anywhere outside an artist's imagination.

XXXIX.

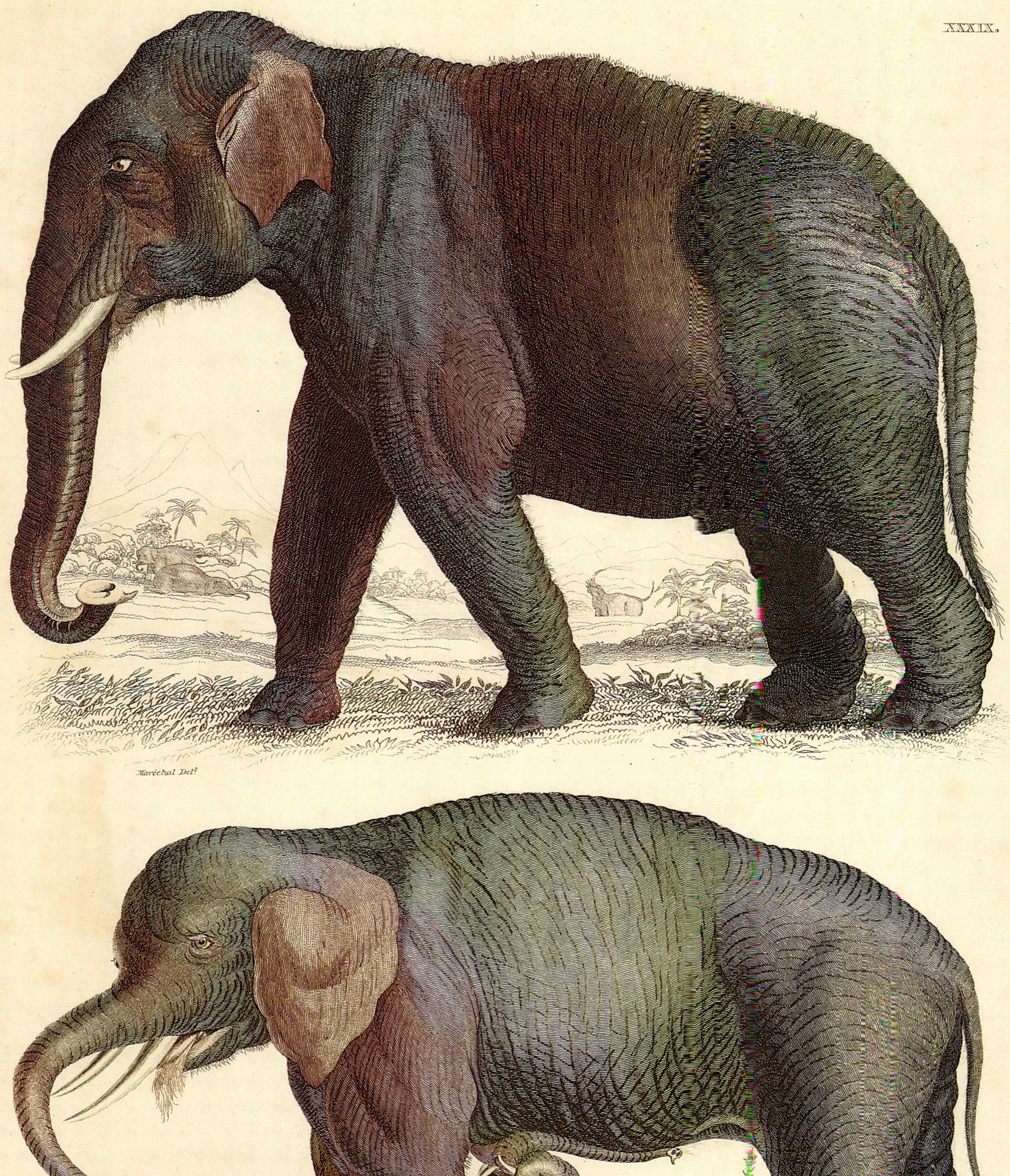

Marechal Del.t

ELEPHAS. ELEPHANTS.
1st Indian   E. Indicus.
2nd African   _Africanus. Fem.

Engraved by S. Milne

Greater Kudu

KOODOO, *Damalis (Strepsiceros) capensis* (now Greater Kudu, *Tragelaphus strepsiceros*). Hand coloured lithograph, pl. 42 from Vol. 1 of A. Smith's *Illustrations of the Zoology of South Africa*, 1838–50. Size of plate 11¾″ × 9¼″.

'When the southern parts of Africa were first colonised', says Andrew Smith in his monumental study of the fauna of South Africa, 'Koodoos were frequently discovered even in the vicinity of the locality where Cape Town now stands. The efficient weapons of the European hunters, however, soon diminished the number, and now specimens are rarely to be found within the Colony . . . The Koodoo is an animal naturally shy and timid, and on being disturbed in its retreats, immediately takes to flight . . . Its gait is elegant, its pace a moderately swift gallop, and while progressing it often springs over distances with great agility, and its bounds are frequently very expansive.'

This illustration shows two of the features distinguishing the male of the greater from the male of the lesser kudu: the white chevron between the eyes and the more developed, more widely divergent horns which spread in two to three open spirals. A fully grown greater kudu, one of the larger antelopes, stands five feet high at the shoulder and the horns themselves may be more than five feet long when measured along the spiral turns. The females of the greater kudu lack horns and are much smaller than the males. No antelope makes a louder sound than the deep bellow of this noble creature. Andrew Smith would not be surprised to know that the greater kudu, an easy target for a man with a gun, is no longer to be seen in the wild in the southern part of South Africa.

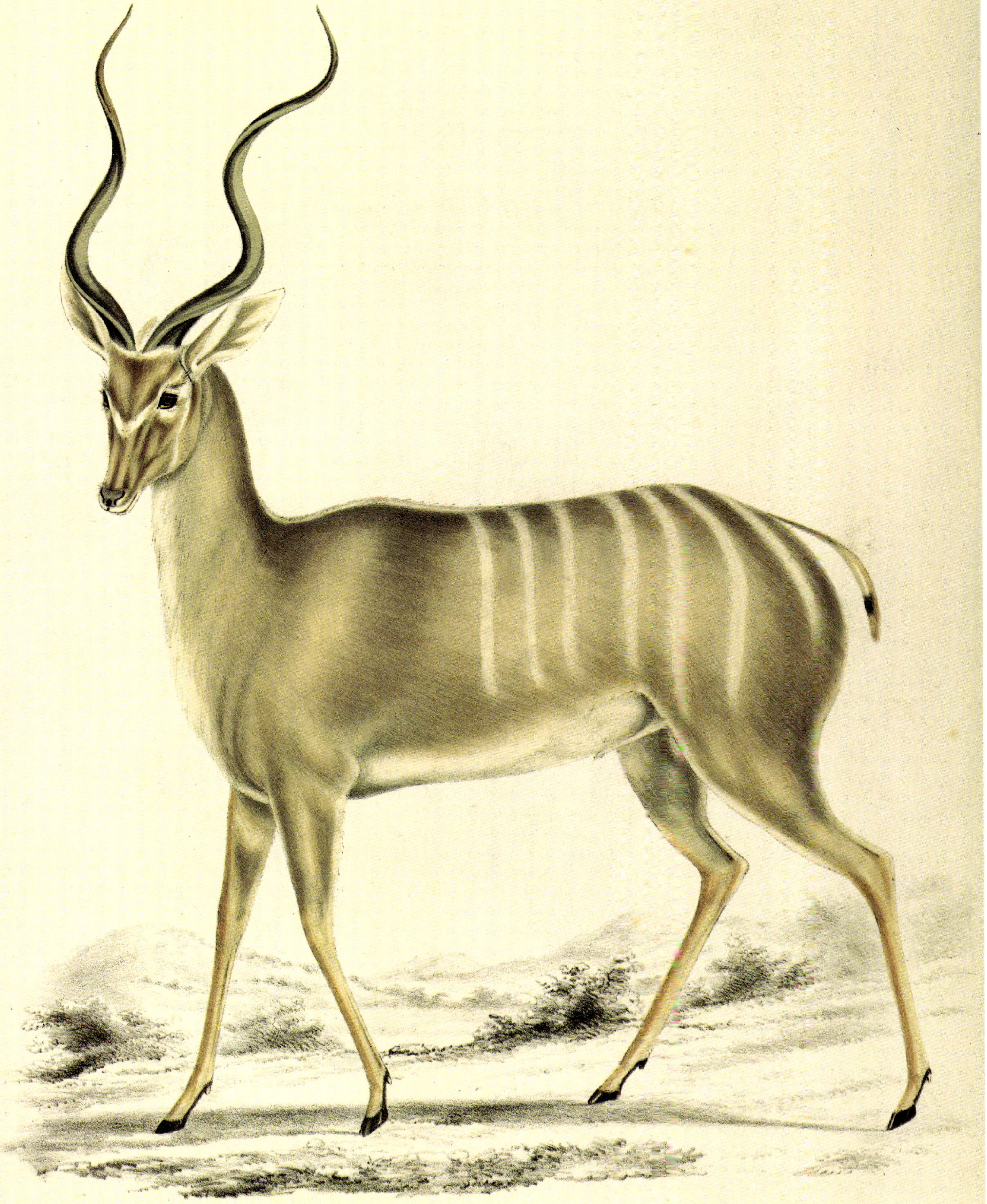

DAMALIS (Strepsiceros) CAPENSIS.
(Mammalia — Plate 42. Male)

Gemsbok

GEMSBOK, *Oryx capensis* (now *Oryx gazella*). Hand coloured lithograph by Frank Howard from an original drawing by Captain W. Cornwallis Harris, pl. 9 from Harris's *Portraits of the Game and Wild Animals of Southern Africa Delineated from Life in their Native Haunts*, 1840. Size of plate 21¼″ × 14¼″.

Captain Cornwallis Harris probably chose to represent the gemsbok in profile partly to show off the tuft of black hair at its throat. This feature, together with its black facial and flank markings, distinguishes it from other species of oryx. The sandy ground colour broken up by the black markings make this large antelope almost invisible in the African veldt.

Like most antelopes the gemsbok's horns are its crowning glory, measuring up to 44 inches in length and projecting straight upwards and backwards from the head, the longest and most impressive horns of all the oryx. Although shy by nature and a fast runner, it will turn and fight if pursued closely by a predator, and can use its horns with deadly effect. A pack of hounds is no match for it and it is believed to have killed lions with its well aimed rapier thrusts.

Gemsbok usually travel in herds of 30–40 head, but they are sometimes seen in hundreds. As they frequent arid regions they must be able to withstand long periods without water. They travel long distances to get at a water supply but, in times of drought, they supplement their diet of grasses with succulent wild fruits, such as melons and cucumbers.

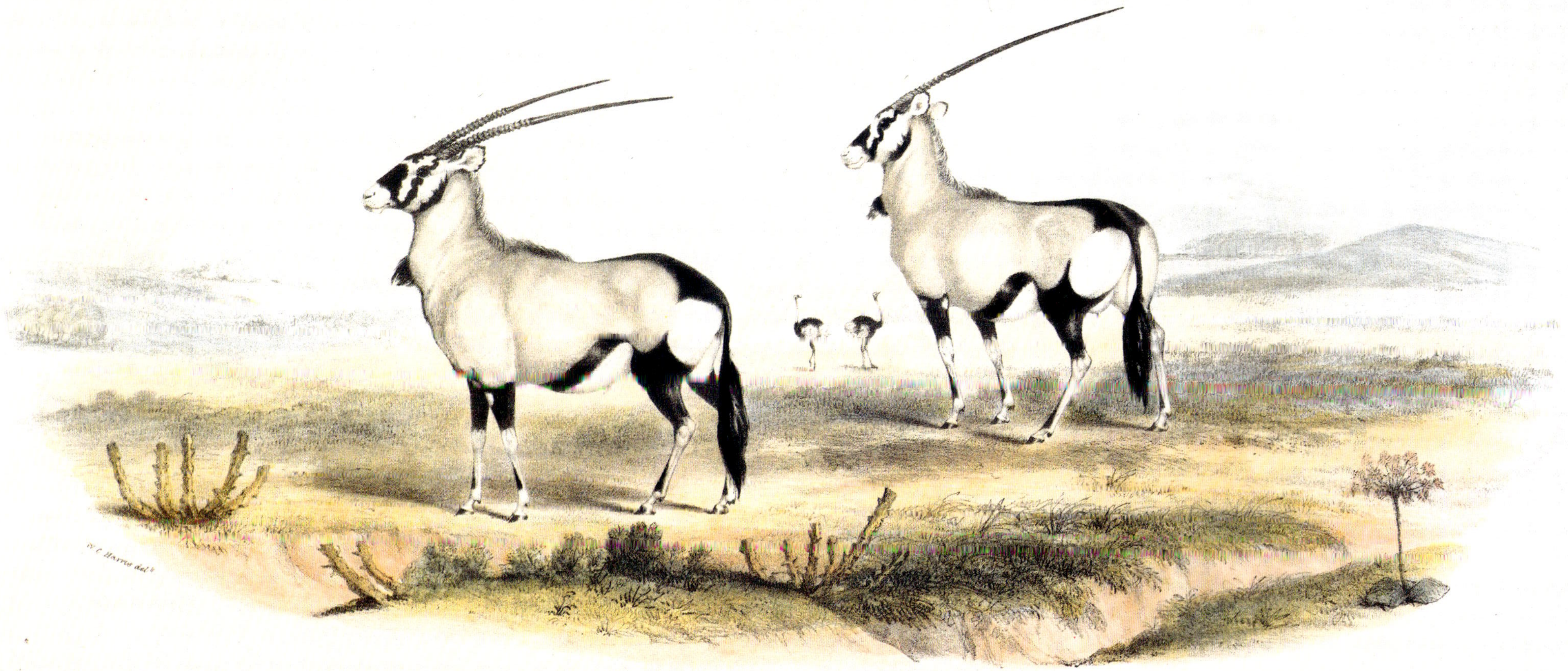

IX. ORYX CAPENSIS.—THE GEMSBOK.

African Buffalo

AFRICAN BUFFALO, *Bubalus caffer* (now African Buffalo, *Synceros caffer*). Hand coloured lithograph by Frank Howard from an original drawing by Captain W. Cornwallis Harris, pl. 13 from Harris's *Portraits of the Game and Wild Animals of Southern Africa Delineated from Life in their Native Haunts*, 1840. Size of plate 21¼″ × 14¼″.

Who can doubt that, for Captain Harris, the most important feature of this animal was its horns? They seem to dominate the entire composition, just as a fine pair of them may have dominated the wall over the Captain's own mantelpiece at home, for this is one of the most respected and most coveted of all game animals. More like an ox than a buffalo, it varies so much in size, shape, and colour that several different forms have been described, that portrayed in this lithograph being the distinctive Cape buffalo from open habitats in southern Africa. This form is much larger, heavier built, and blacker than the other well defined form, the dwarf forest buffalo from the forests of West and Central Africa. Neither form is found very far from water.

The horns of the Cape buffalo are very large, measuring up to a daunting 64 inches maximum width, and contribute significantly to the animal's total weight, which may exceed 1500 pounds. Normally of a peaceful temperament it can become very dangerous when wounded or cornered and many hunters have accused it of deliberate savagery – an accusation which may reasonably be levelled against the hunters themselves.

Apart from its human persecutors the African buffalo, in all its forms, has one principal enemy, the lion, which marks out cows or calves as they become separated from the herd. The crocodile will also prey on them when they are crossing rivers. Towards the close of the nineteenth century the African buffalo was decimated by outbreaks of rinderpest and in some districts has not regained its former population levels. Elsewhere, particularly in East Africa, it is more abundant now than formerly, one of Nature's success stories.

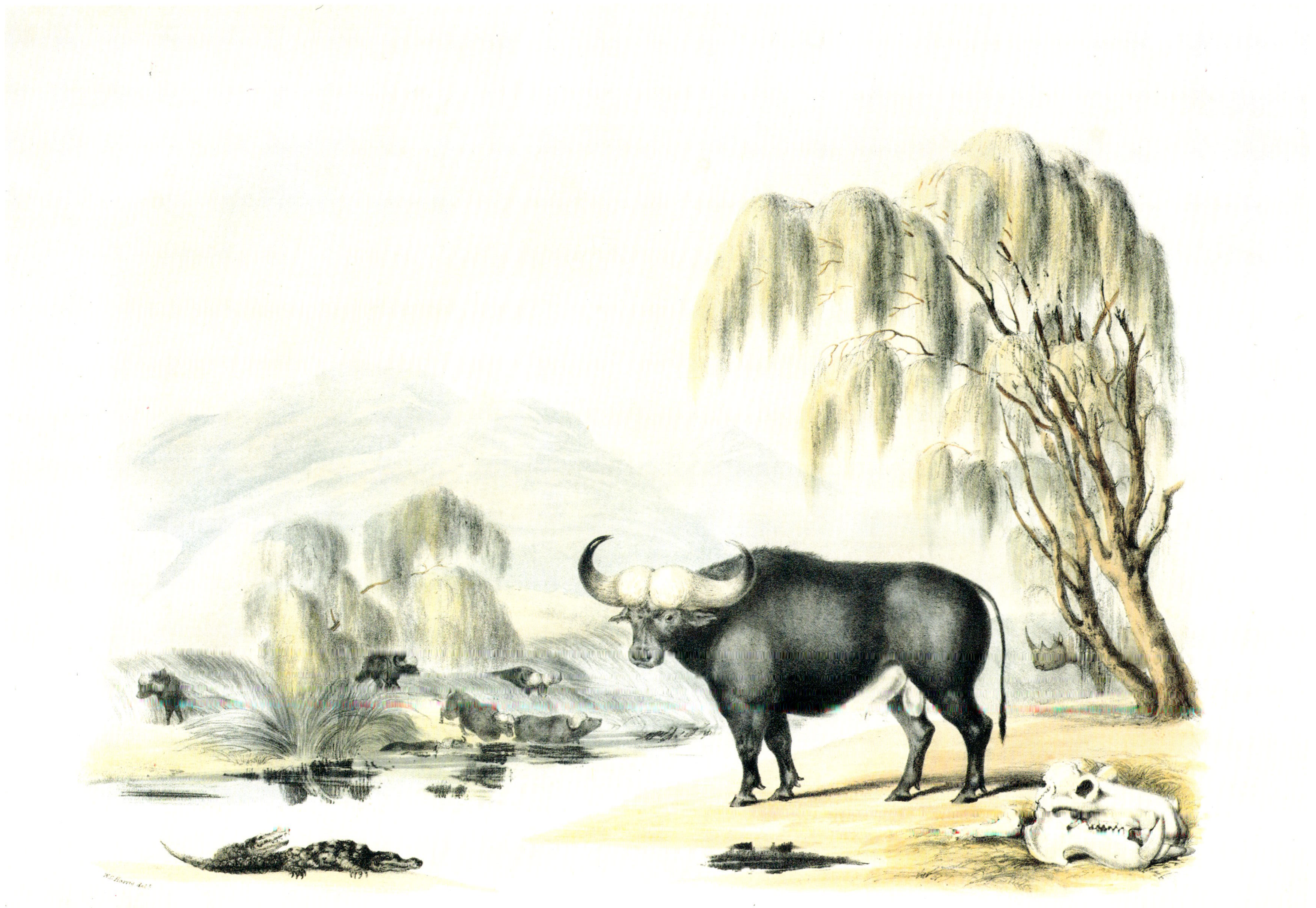

XIII. BUBALUS CAFFER. – THE AFRICAN BUFFALO.

Brown Bear

OURS BRUN, *Ursus arctos* (now Brown Bear, *Ursus arctos*). Hand coloured engraving by A. Dumenil from an original drawing by Werner, pl. 4 from I. G. Saint-Hilaire's *Mammiferès* (in *Atlas, Zoologie* to A. Du Petit-Thouars's *Voyage autour du Monde sur . . . la Vénus*), 1840–64. Size of plate 16″ × 10¾″.

The text to this engraving says that the animal depicted was collected alive by members of the *Vénus* expedition. It had been eating a salmon when captured by the seashore at the southern extremity of the Kamchatka Peninsula, close to Petropavlovsk. When installed in the menagerie of the Jardin des Plantes at Paris in September 1837 it was reckoned to be about four years old. Werner made this drawing of it when it was still alive.

Formerly the brown bear was widely distributed over much of the northern hemisphere and used to be common in Europe, where now only a few isolated populations survive. It is still a familiar sight in North America but only in parts of Russia is it still plentiful in the wild. Many different subspecies of the brown bear have been described, including the Kodiak form from Alaska, which may weigh up to three-quarters of a ton, but it is now agreed that all represent variations within a single species. It is omnivorous, has few natural enemies and is solitary. Fortunately for its continued survival it also breeds more freely in captivity than any other kind of bear.

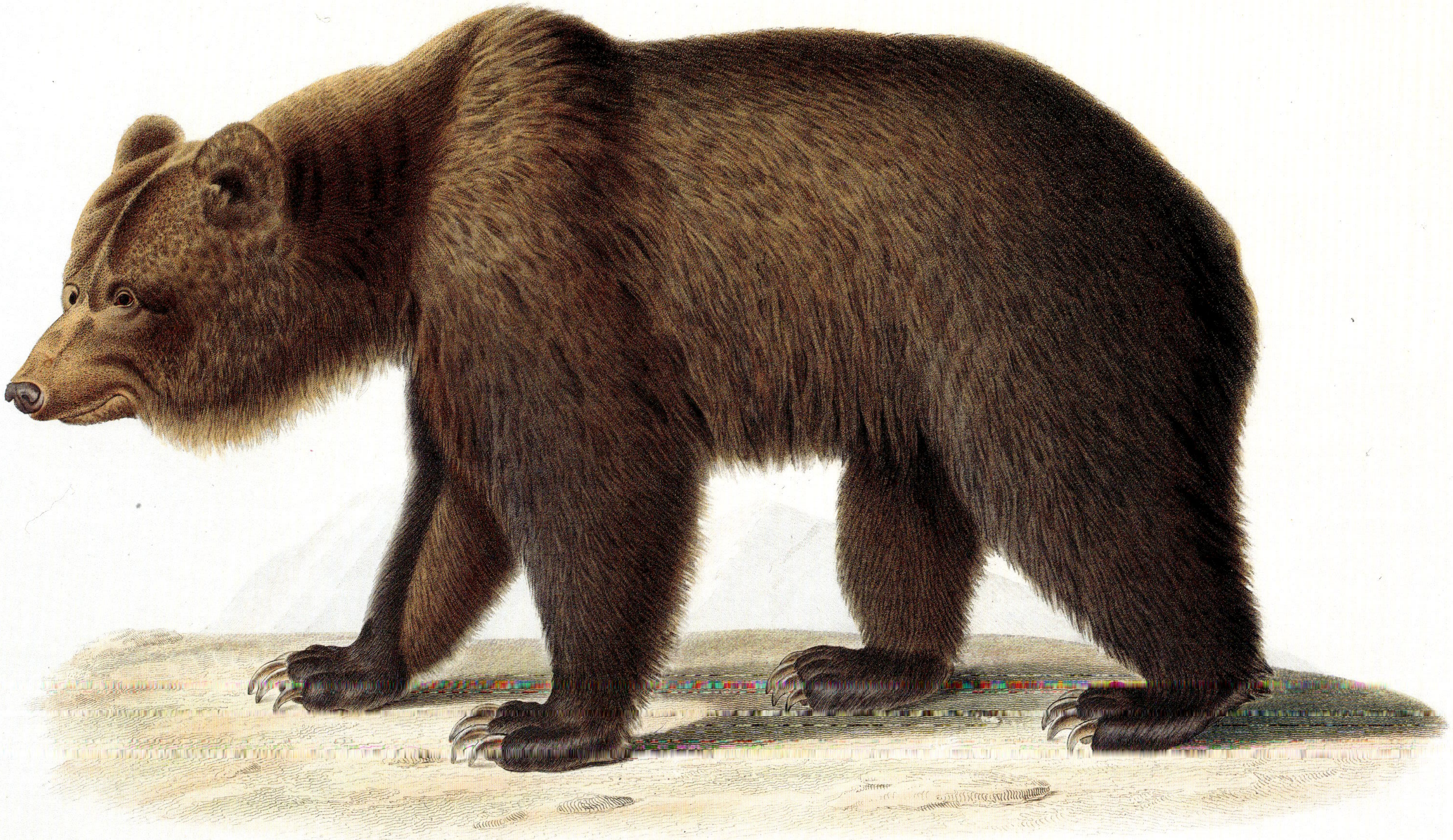

1/4

Peint par Werner. Dirigé par Borromée. Gravé par A. Dumenil.

OURS BRUN, *URSUS ARCTOS*, L.; Var. du Kamtschatka.

Gide Editeur. Impr. de Bougeard.

Slender-tailed Cloud Rat

PHLOEMYS DE CUMING, *Phloemys cumingi* (now Slender-tailed Cloud Rat, *Phloemys cumingi*). Hand coloured engraving by Annedouche from an original drawing by Werner, pl. 8 from the *Atlas* to J. F. T. Eydoux and L. F. A. Souleyet's *Zoologie* (in *Voyage autour du Monde . . . sur . . . la Bonite*), 1841–42. Size of plate 12¾″ × 9½″.

This is an early illustration of one of the largest rats in the world and is based on a specimen collected during the global voyage of the *Bonite* between 1836 and 1837, one of several voyages of discovery and exploration sent out by the French government during the first half of the nineteenth century. The head and body together measure about nineteen inches, to which should be added a tail length of about eleven or twelve inches, making the animal the size of a very large domestic cat. It has rough fur, paler underneath than above, and its feet are adapted to a tree-living existence.

The slender-tailed cloud rat is found only in mountainous districts on the island of Luzon in the Philippines where it was first collected in the late 1830s by an Englishman, Hugh Cuming, whence it was brought to England and described as new to science. Cuming spent four years in the Philippines, spending all his time collecting animals and plants. He was mainly interested in marine and non-marine molluscs, hundreds of those he collected proving to be new to science, but he brought many other previously unknown animals to the attention of scientists, who often named them after their discoverer. This rat, one of his more significant mammalian discoveries, is scarce throughout its range and may not be much better known now than it was in his day.

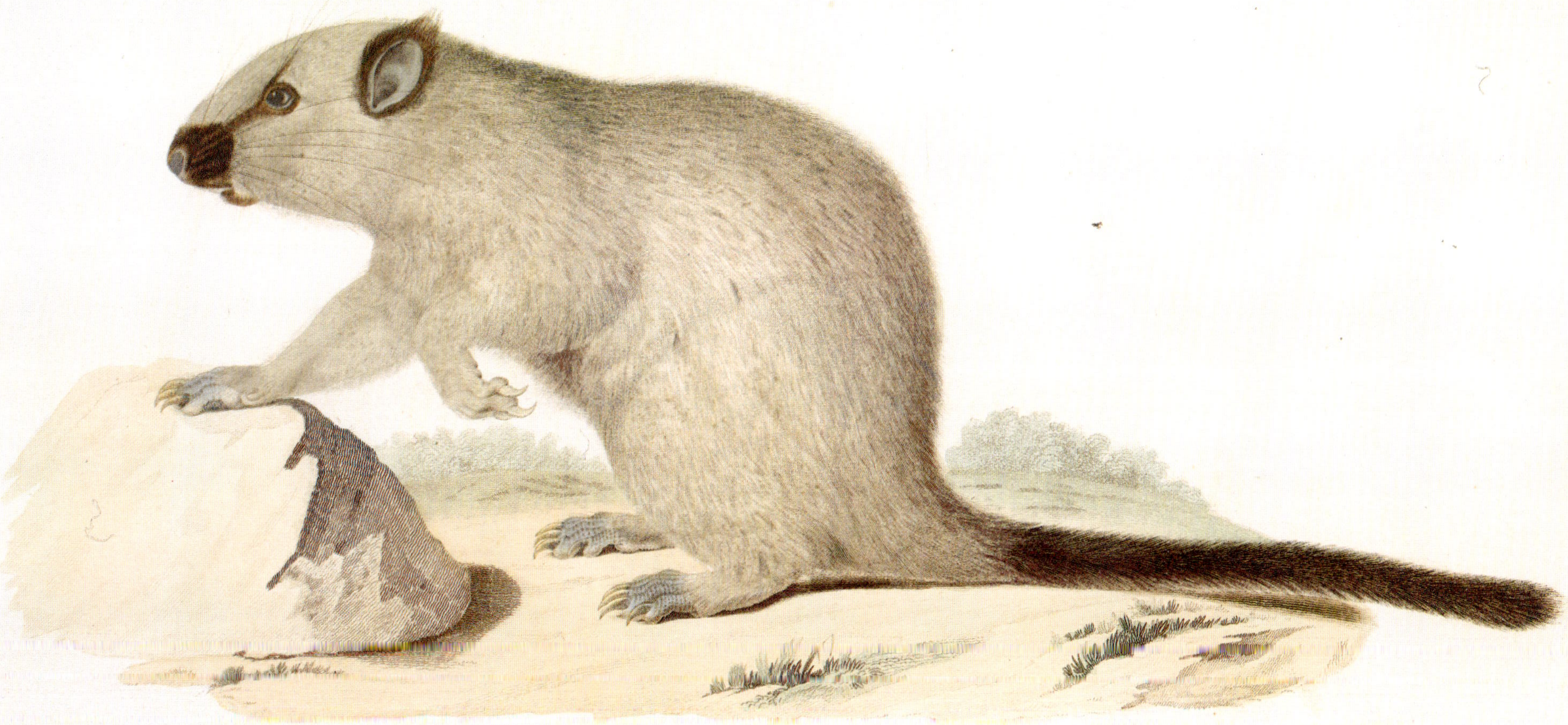

PHLŒOMYS DE CUMING. Waterhouse

Werner del.

Arthus Bertrand Editeur

N. Rémond imp.

Annedouche sc.

Arab Horse

ARABIAN HORSE (now Arab Horse, *Equus caballus*). Hand coloured lithograph from a drawing by W. Nicholson after a painting by W. Shiels, pl. 1 from Vol. 1 of D. Low's *The Breeds of the Domestic Animals of the British Islands*, 1842. Size of plate 17″ × 13″.

David Low has an interesting story to tell about the horse in this picture which, like all the animals portrayed in his excellent book, was originally the subject of a painting by William Shiels, a painter from Berwickshire. 'The figure in the Plate represents correctly the form of the genuine Arab', says Low. 'The horse here represented was taken in an attack by an Arab tribe on a party of the Royal Family of Persia, when journeying on a pilgrimage. The Arab chief who headed the attacking party was killed, and his charger, running into the Persian ranks, was taken. A ransom, enormous for so poor a tribe, was subsequently offered by the Arabs for their noble horse, but refused; and he was brought to England by Sir John M'Neill. He stands fourteen and a half hands high. He is gentle in the highest degree, and so thoroughly trained to that kind of exercise which the Arabs are careful to teach their horses, that he may be galloped around the narrowest circle. When his portrait was in the course of being painted, he was languid from the cold of the weather. It was wished to rouse him for a little, and the idea occurred of trying the effect of some tones of simple music. The sounds no sooner struck his ear than his whole frame was agitated; his heart throbbed so violently as to be seen beating; and so great was his excitement, that it was necessary instantly to stop the music. Some chord of feeling, it seems, had been struck: perchance he was reminded for a moment of his desert home, and of the friends from whom he had been so rudely severed.'

The Arab, often considered to be the principal ancestor of most breeds of light horse (but actually descended from a northern African type) is noted for its elegance and its intelligence. It is rightly held in great esteem by Bedouin horsemen but its small size has prevented it from achieving great popularity among western nations where it is not considered enough for a horse to be elegant and intelligent.

Plate I

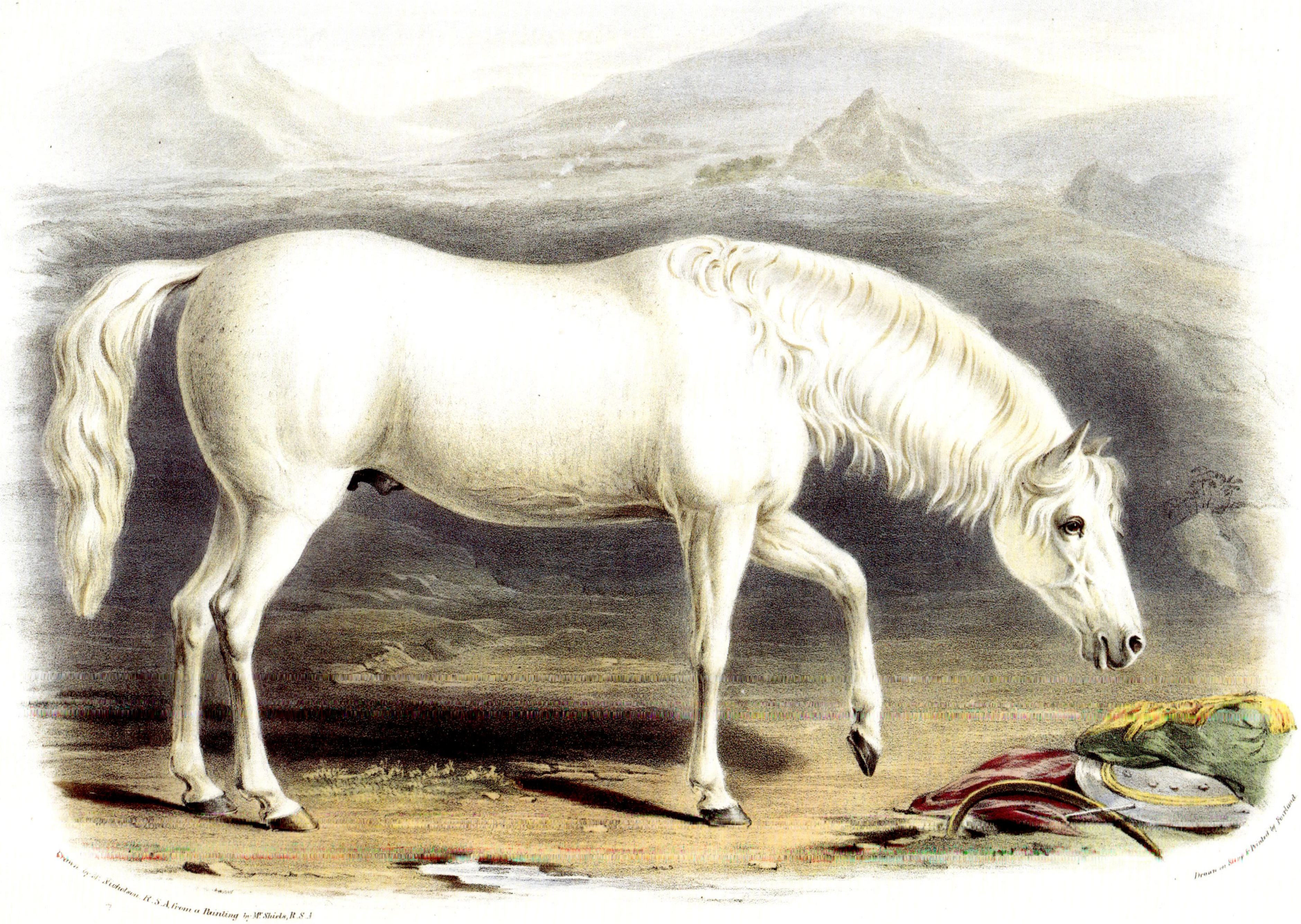

THE ARABIAN.

Stallion, taken in a skirmish with an Arab Tribe, brought to England by Sir John Mc Neill, British Ambassador at the Court of Persia.

PROFESSOR LOW'S ILLUSTRATIONS OF THE BREEDS OF THE DOMESTIC ANIMALS.

Hereford Cattle

HEREFORD BREED (now Hereford Cattle, *Bos taurus*). Hand coloured lithograph from a drawing by W. Nicholson after a painting by W. Shiels, pl. 17 from Vol. 1 of D. Low's *The Breeds of the Domestic Animals of the British Islands*, 1842. Size of plate 17″ × 13″.

This picture may puzzle some of those acquainted with today's breed of Hereford cattle. Many Herefords now lack horns, for instance, and also differ in other characteristics. Selective breeding has altered the breed considerably since William Shiels painted this picture, though the white face is still a Hereford hallmark. Even in Low's time, however, the breed was of long ancestry and mixed characters. His text is a historical document of interest both to cattle breeders and to those who merely gaze at cattle from over farm fences.

The cow in the foreground was the property of the Earl of Talbot and was descended from the stock of Benjamin Tomkins of King's Pyon in Herefordshire, a gentleman who influenced the characters of the breed profoundly. 'About the year 1769', says Low, 'the late Mr Benjamin Tomkins began a system of breeding, which ultimately exercised a great influence on the stock of this part of England. It appears that size, and adaptation to the dairy and the purposes of labour, were than the properties chiefly sought for by the breeders of Herefordshire. Mr Tomkins, when a young man, was in the employment of an individual, afterwards his father-in-law, and had the especial charge of the dairy. Two cows had been brought to this dairy, supposed to have been purchased at the fair of Kington, on the confines of Wales. Tomkins remarked the extraordinary tendency of these animals to become fat. On his marriage he acquired these two cows, and commenced breeding from them on his own account. The one with more of white, he called Pigeon, and the other, of a rich red colour, with a spotted face, he called Mottle; and it is remarkable that the marking of the two cows may be distinguished in their descendants at the present day.' Pigeon and Mottle will probably continue to have a visible impact on the progress of the breed for a long time to come.

Plate XVII.

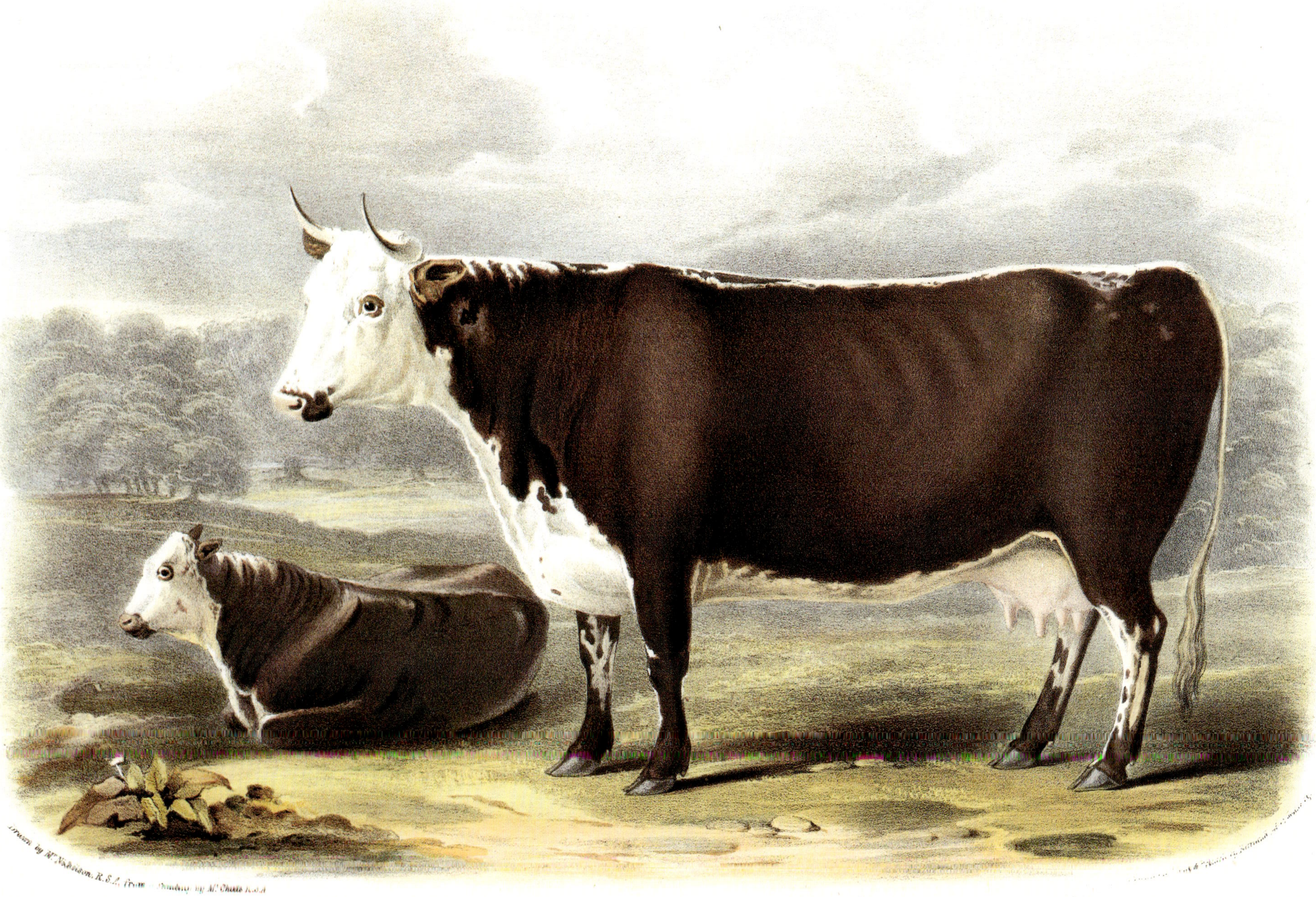

Drawn by W. Nicholson, R.S.A. from a Painting by W. Shiels R.S.A.

THE HEREFORD BREED.

Cow, bred by the Right Honourable the Earl of Talbot; descended from the Stock of Mr. Tomkins of Kingspion, Hereford.

PROFESSOR LOW'S ILLUSTRATIONS OF THE BREEDS OF THE DOMESTIC ANIMALS.

London, Published February 1842, by Longman, Brown, Green & Longmans, Paternoster Row.

Lincoln Longwool Sheep

OLD LINCOLN BREED (now Lincoln Longwool Sheep, *Ovis aries*). Hand coloured lithograph from a drawing by W. Nicholson after a painting by W. Shiels, pl. 16 from Vol. 2 of D. Low's *The Breeds of the Domestic Animals of the British Islands*, 1842. Size of plate 17″ × 13″.

British breeds of sheep comprise longwools and shortwools. The Lincoln represents one of the longwool breeds, some other examples being the English Leicester, the Romney Marsh, the Cotswold, and the Wensleydale, the last being the only horned longwool. According to Low the extraordinary looking animal portrayed here came from a flock which had been maintained perfectly pure, retaining all the essential characters of the ancient race and presenting, perhaps, 'the only living example of the most remarkable breed of sheep which the British Islands have produced'.

Descendants of the original Lincoln Longwool have been much exported, especially to Argentina, so they are commonplace today. As the original reasons for the popularity of the breed may be unfamiliar, the following comments by Low are worth repeating. 'The Old Lincoln Sheep, of which the remnants only now exist, are destitute of horns, are of coarse form, have large limbs and hoofs, hollow flanks, and flat sides. Their long unctuous wool almost hangs to the ground, and they have a large tuft on the forehead. Their fleece weighs from 10 to 12 lb. and in the rams and fattened wethers, often greatly exceeds this weight. They are slow feeders, and consume much food, but are valued by the butchers for their tendency to produce internal fat.'

Plate XVI.

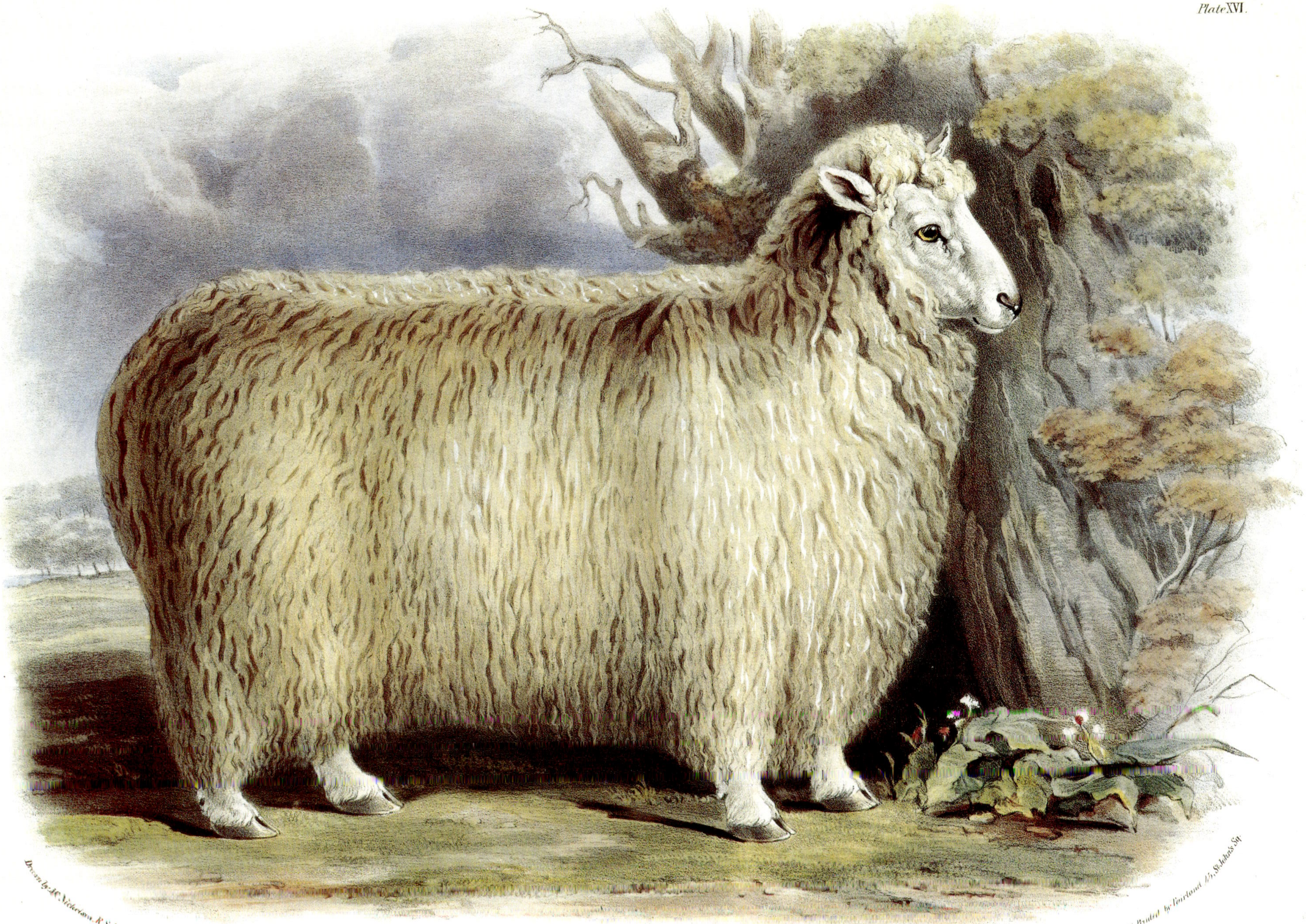

Drawn by J.C. Nicholson, R.S.A. from a Painting by Mr. Shiels, R.S.A.

Drawn on Stone & Printed by Fairland 45, St. John's Sq.

THE OLD LINCOLN BREED.

Ram, bred by Mr. Jex, St. Jermains, near Lynne, County of Norfolk.

PROFESSOR LOW'S ILLUSTRATIONS OF THE BREEDS OF THE DOMESTIC ANIMALS

Published June 1841, by Longman, Orme, Brown, Green & Longmans, Paternoster Row, London

Hog-nosed Skunk

LONG-NOSED SKUNK, *Mephitis nasuta* (now Hog-nosed Skunk, *Conepatus mesoleucus*). Hand coloured lithograph by Charles Couzens, pl. 7 from L. Fraser's *Zoologia Typica*, 1845–49. Size of plate 14½″ × 10½″.

This lithograph from Louis Fraser's little-known *Zoologia Typica* makes the unfortunately-named hog-nosed skunk seem almost glamorous. Skunks are not popular mammals because we associate them with unpleasant smells (though most of us have never smelt one) and because they have an unmusical collective name. But these negative attributes should be measured against the attractiveness of their fur, which is usually glossy and strikingly marked in black and white.

There are seven different types of hog-nosed skunk in the southern United States and South America, each characterised by the pig-like shape of its nose. Measuring about two and a half feet from nose to tail tip the one illustrated here is slow moving and nocturnal in its habits. It uses its snout to root about in the soil for grubs and insects, but it will also eat small mammals and snakes. Living in wooded and open land, sometimes occupying burrows abandoned by other animals, it produces a litter of two to five young. It ranges from the southern United States to Nicaragua and has been hunted occasionally for its fur which, contrary to the impression given by this illustration, is not soft but coarse.

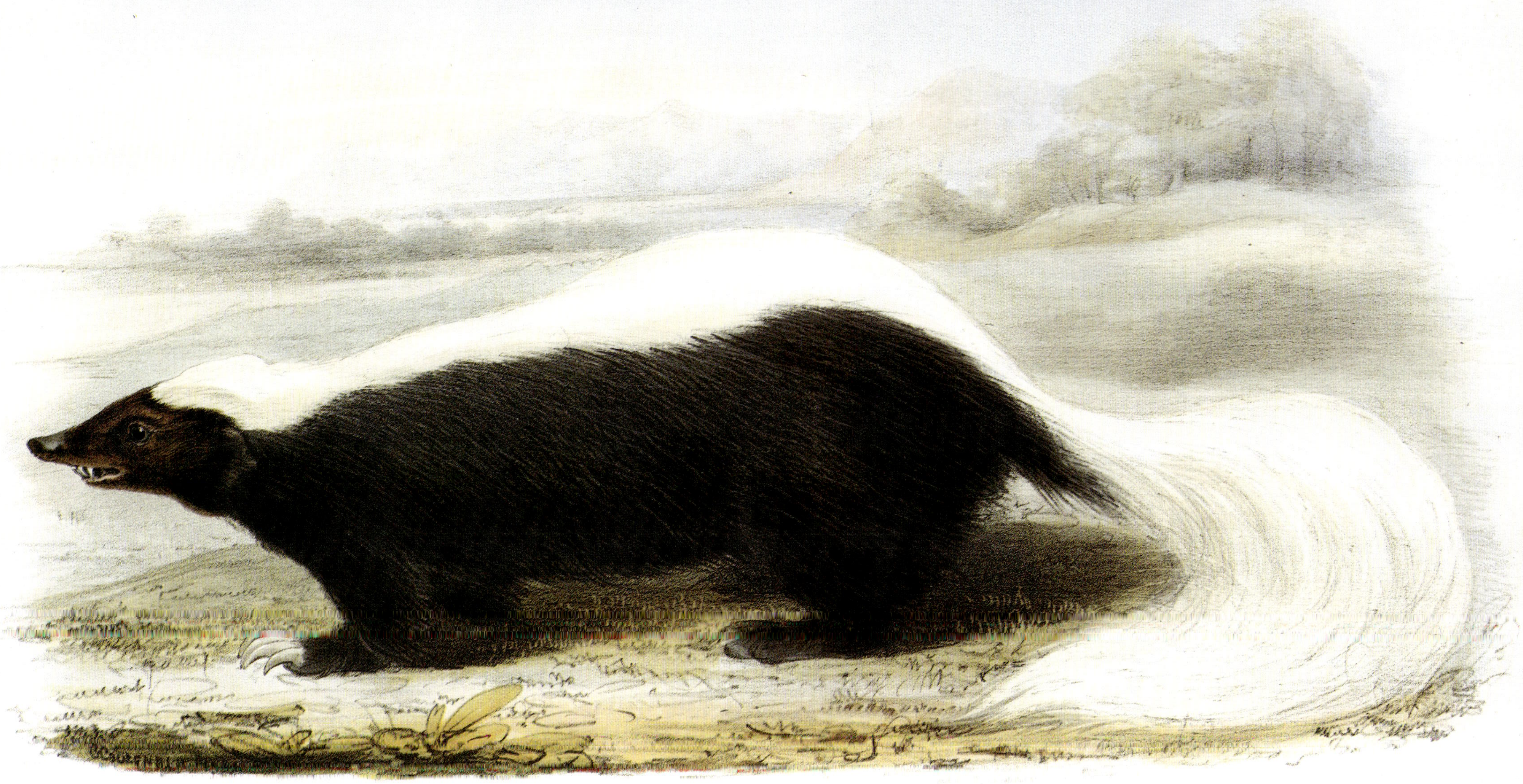

MEPHITIS NASUTA.

Koala

KOALA, *Phascolarctos cinereus*. Hand coloured lithograph by J. Gould and H. C. Richter, pl. 14 from Vol. 1 of J. Gould's *The Mammals of Australia*, 1845–63. Size of plate 21½″ × 14½″.

When you see a koala curled up in the fork of a swaying sapling with a youngster clinging to its back you wonder how it got there and how it stays there. As its hands and feet are specialised climbing organs it has no difficulty installing itself in such a place; and because each of its limbs has two clawed fingers which oppose the other three and provide it with a very firm grip it is not easily dislodged. John Gould often had a vivid demonstration of the koala's reluctance to let go when he was collecting materials for his book about Australian mammals in the late 1830s. In those days the acceptable way to collect mammals, even lethargic and inoffensive ones, was to shoot them, and Gould seems to have considered it necessary to shoot many koalas. 'Those that fell to my gun', he says, 'were most tenacious of life, clinging to the branches until the last spark had fled.' Not surprisingly these endearing creatures suffered an alarming decline in numbers until protective measures were taken, millions having been killed for their fur; epidemic diseases, fires and forest clearances have also taken their toll.

Unlike most mammals the koala feeds almost exclusively upon the leaves of eucalyptus trees, and it requires two or three pounds of such leaves each day to remain healthy. As the leaves must also be of a certain age and must come from only certain species of eucalyptus grown in the right kind of soil it is difficult to feed them in captivity. Under normal conditions eucalyptus leaves provide sufficient water for the koala to disdain drinking.

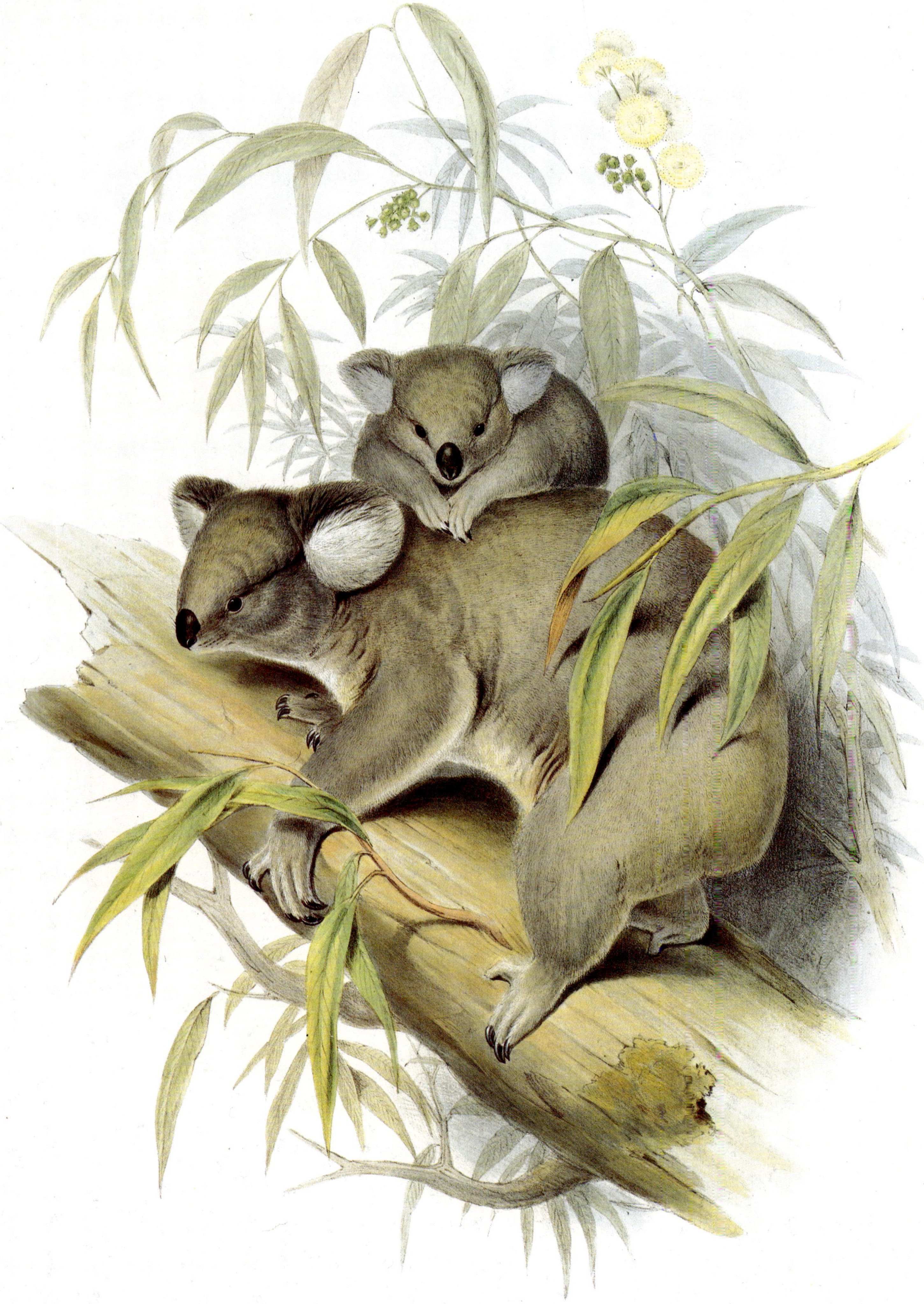

PHASCOLARCTOS CINEREUS.

J. Gould and H.C. Richter del. et lith. *Hullmandel & Walton, Imp.*

Thylacine

THYLACINUS, *Thylacinus cynocephalus* (now Thylacine, *Thylacinus cynocephalus*). Hand coloured lithograph by H. C. Richter, pl. 54 from Vol. 1 of J. Gould's *The Mammals of Australia*, 1845–63. Size of plate 21½″ × 14½″.

The thylacine is an enigmatic creature. It was thought to be related to the oppossums when first described in 1808; the seventeen dark stripes on its back earned it the name Tasmanian tiger; and its dog-like shape, very long incisors and habit of running on its toes earned it the alternative name Tasmanian wolf. Once widespread over much of New Guinea and Australia it survived into modern times only in Tasmania. A wild thylacine was captured in Tasmania in 1933 and survived in captivity until 1936. It has not been sighted positively since then. There is slender evidence to show that one may have entered and escaped from a trap on the west coast in 1961; and a later photograph provides further, equally slender proof that it may not be extinct.

Largest of the carnivorous marsupials, the thylacine fed mostly on kangaroos and wallabies, but the early colonists claimed that it preyed upon their sheep and poultry and waged ceaseless war on it. In the text to this plate John Gould described the early effect of that war: 'The destruction it deals around has, as a matter of course, called forth the enmity of the settler, and hence in all cultivated districts the animal is nearly extirpated; on the other hand, so much of Tasmania still remains in a state of nature, and so much of its forest land yet uncleared, that an abundance of covert still remains in which the animal is secure from the attacks of man; many years must therefore elapse before it can become entirely extinct.' Alas, the many years seem to have elapsed. The only thylacines in existence are probably those on display in museums.

54.

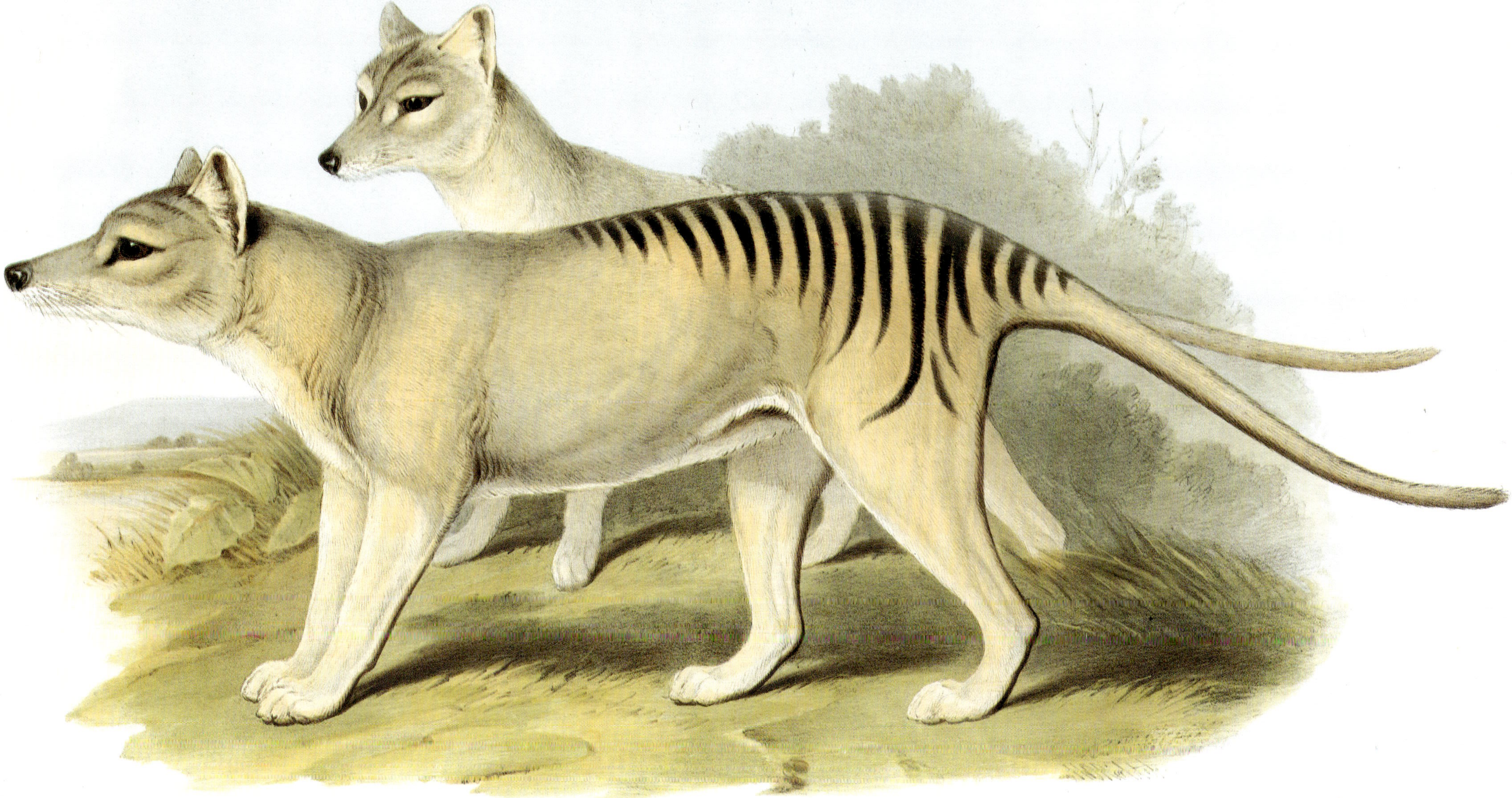

H. C. Richter del. et lith. THYLACINUS CYNOCEPHALUS. Hullmandel & Walton Imp.

Wallaroo

BLACK WALLAROO, *Osphranter robustus* (now Wallaroo, *Macropus robustus*). Hand coloured lithograph by H. C. Richter, pl. 11 from Vol. 2 of J. Gould's *The Mammals of Australia*, 1845–63. Size of plate 21½″ × 14½″.

Participants in Captain Cook's first voyage of exploration to the Pacific may have seen and captured this marsupial in 1770 near the Endeavour River on the east coast of Australia. But it was not until after John Gould returned to England in 1840, with specimens he had obtained near the Liverpool Range in New South Wales, that it was described as a species new to science.

Years later Gould expressed surprise that it was not better known. 'I have in vain requested my numerous friends and correspondents to procure and transmit examples of this large and truly fine animal', he said in the text to this lithograph. 'I believe I was the first scientific man who visited the locality in which it dwells as well as the first who made it known to science; and I may ask, is it not surprising that during the interval of fifteen years which has elapsed since the account of this species was published in my "Monograph of the Kangaroos", no examples besides those I myself brought home should have been procured, and that no attempts to secure living examples of so conspicuous an animal should have been attempted? Indeed, were it not for my visit to its native haunts, it might have remained unknown to us even to the present time. This is the more to be wondered at, since the animal is found within the colony of New South Wales. Surely the exterminating hand of civilized man, so fatal to the animal productions of a new country, cannot have dealt out destruction so unsparingly as to have destroyed the entire race.'

Fortunately the 'exterminating hand' did not eliminate the seven foot long wallaroo, which is still widely distributed in eastern Australia, mainly in mountainous regions. Occasionally it will shelter in caves and it has been known to go without water for two or three months. Evidently it is a survivor.

11.

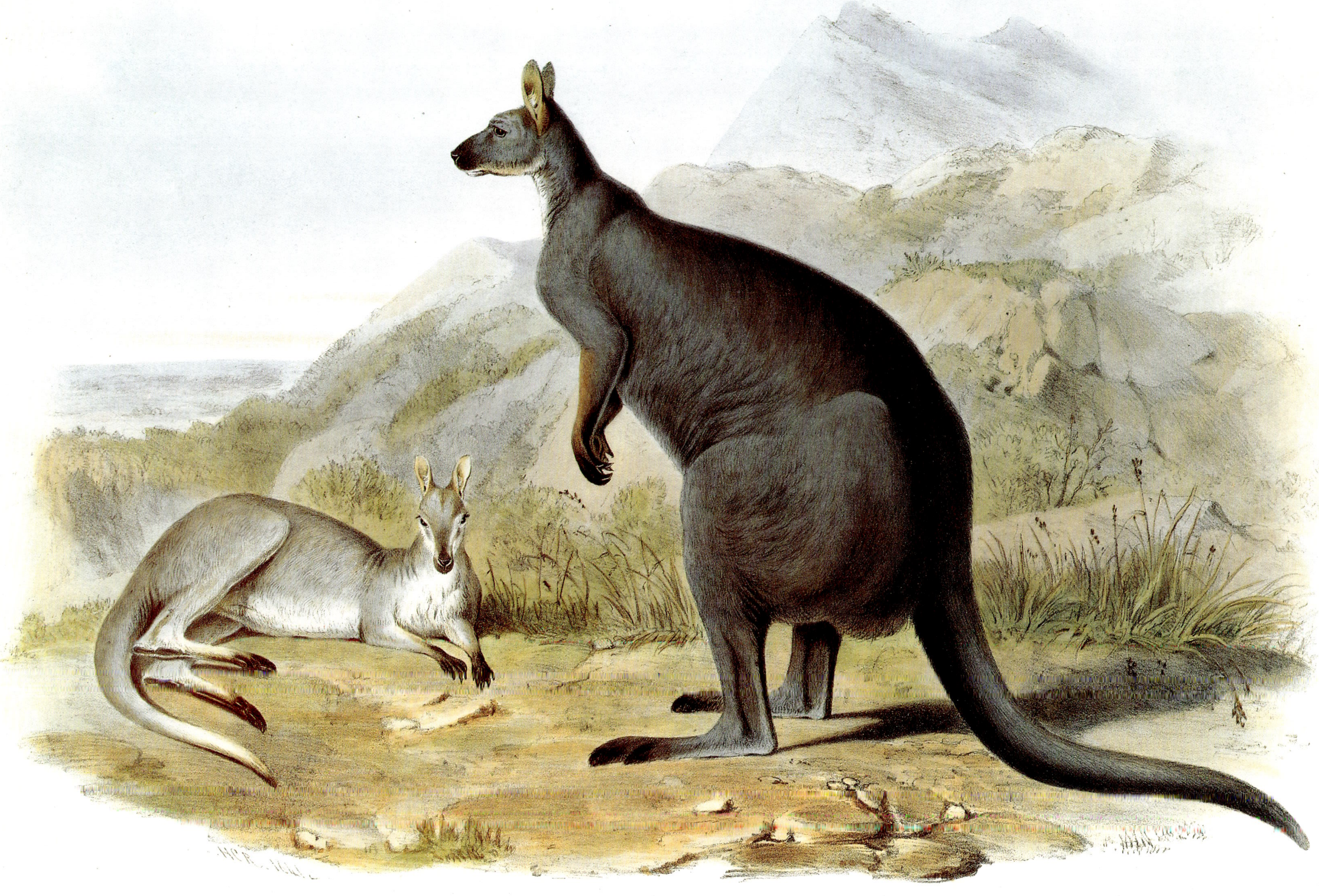

OSPHRANTER ROBUSTUS, *Gould*

Grey-headed Flying Fox

Grey-headed Vampire, *Pteropus poliocephalus* (now Grey-headed Flying Fox). Hand coloured lithograph by J. Gould and H. C. Richter, pl. 28 from Vol. 3 of J. Gould's *The Mammals of Australia*, 1845–63. Size of plate 21½" × 14½".

Flying foxes are widespread on island groups in the Indian and Pacific Oceans and Australia is home to several species. The larger species have wingspans of up to five feet. Unlike many of the smaller bats, which navigate by echo-location, these giants of the bat world have large, functional eyes (they are larger than shown on the right-hand animal in this picture). They differ in other ways: their ears are smooth like those of non-flying mammals; and their noses lack the peculiar processes characteristic of many insect-eating bats. Gould's picture accurately represents the way flying foxes suspend themselves upside down. They feed on soft fruit and may roost in large groups. Many species are endangered because they are easily shot, may be hunted for food and are adversely affected by the destruction of forest habitats.

The grey-headed flying fox comes from eastern Australia where it is still common. It is victimised by fruit growers, who consider it threatens their livelihood, though it does not normally eat cultivated fruit unless its natural food is scarce.

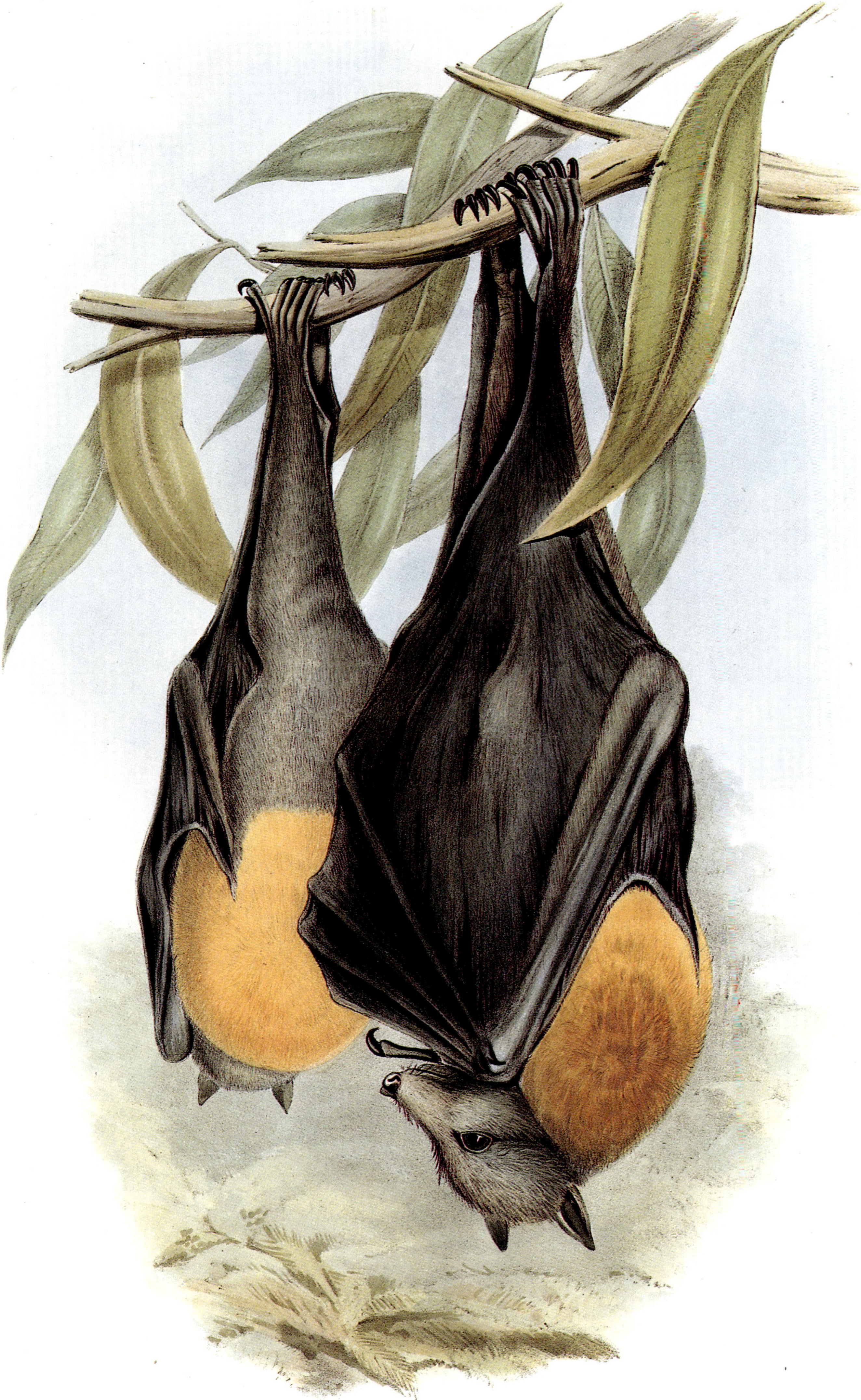

PTEROPUS POLIOCEPHALUS, *Temm.*

Eastern Chipmunk

CHIPPING SQUIRREL, HACKEE, *Tamias lysteri* (now Eastern Chipmunk, *Tamias striatus*). Hand coloured lithograph from an original drawing by J. J. Audubon, pl. 8 from *Atlas*, Vol. 1 of J. J. Audubon and J. Bachman's *The Viviparous Quadrupeds of North America*, 1846–54. Size of plate 27¼″ × 20¾″.

Following the success of his monumental book *The Birds of America*, John James Audubon conceived the idea of writing and illustrating a similar book about the mammals of North America. The Revd John Bachman of Charleston, South Carolina, offered to help him with the writing. A careful and scientific observer of animal life, Bachman became co-author of *Viviparous Quadrupeds of North America* and spent a dozen years researching and writing. Members of Audubon's immediate family also provided much help, his son John Woodhouse Audubon contributing drawings which were lithographed and included in the book.

A caption at the foot of this lithograph says 'Male, female and young first autumn.' The young, presumably, are the skittish ones on the tree trunk. Five black and four pale stripes characterise the eastern chipmunk. A forest dweller in the eastern United States, it digs its own burrow and constructs therein a nest of dry plant material. It was known to Bachman as the 'Chipping Squirrel' because, as he remarked, 'its chucking resembles the chip, chip, chip, of a young chicken'. He wrote of its 'chops distended' by nuts and berries, in which condition Audubon has depicted the creature at bottom right. There are many different kinds of chipmunk, all but one of them confined to North America.

No. 2. PLATE VIII.

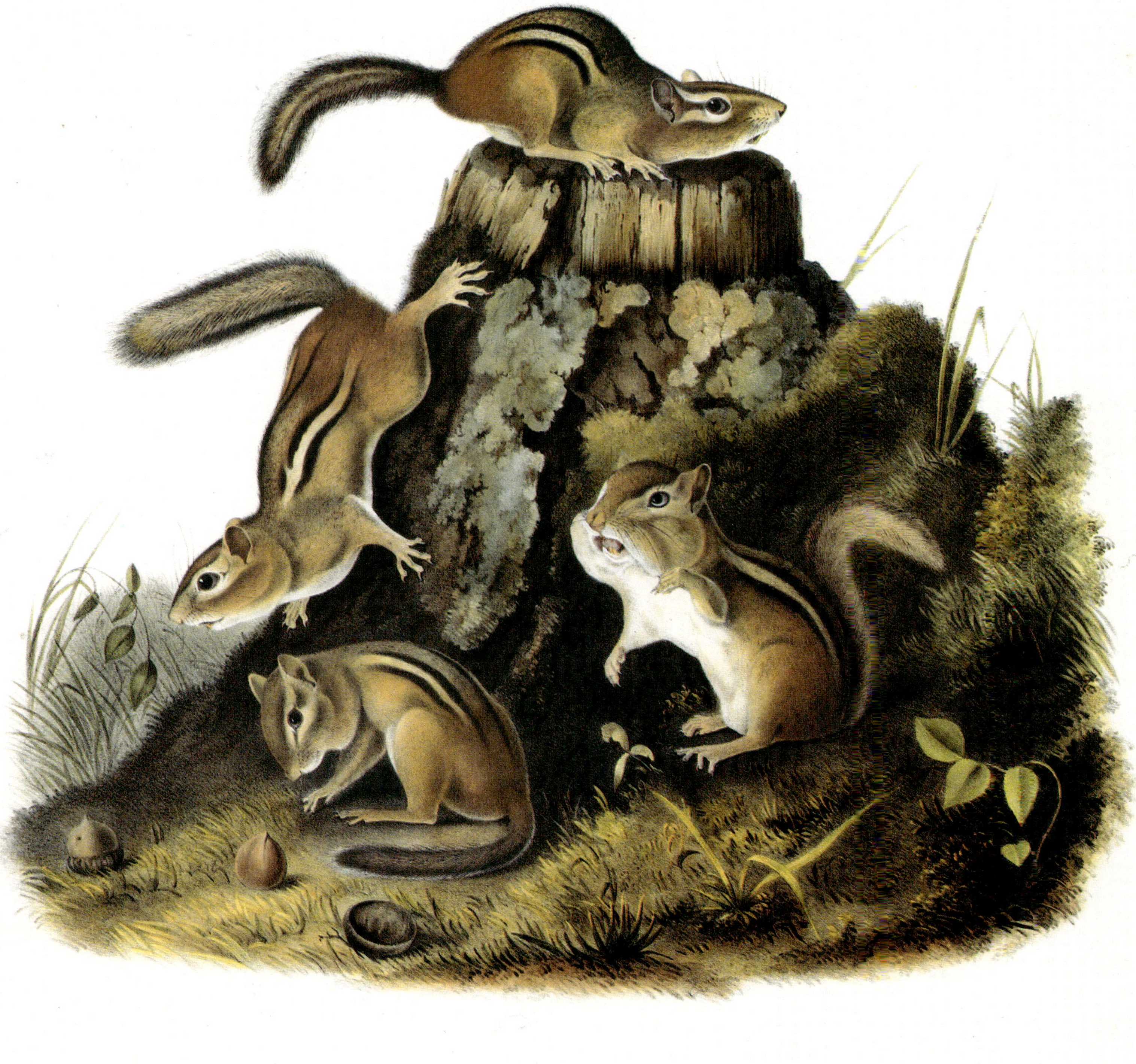

Drawn from Nature by J. J. Audubon F.R.S F.L.S.

Lith. Printed & Col.d by J. T. Bowen, Philad.a

TAMIAS LYSTERI, RAY.

CHIPPING SQUIRREL, HACKEE &c.

Natural Size

MALE, FEMALE AND YOUNG FIRST AUTUMN.

Long-tailed Weasel

Bridled Weasel, *Putorius frenata* (now Long-tailed Weasel, *Mustela frenata*). Hand coloured lithograph from a drawing by J. J. Audubon, pl. 60 from *Atlas*, Vol. 2 of J. J. Audubon and J. Bachman's *The Viviparous Quadrupeds of North America*, 1846–54. Size of plate 27¼″ × 20¾″.

In spite of the enormous efforts put into the production of *The Viviparous Quadrupeds of North America* by John James Audubon, the Revd John Bachman and their respective families, factual and artistic mistakes were inevitable. Even some of the larger mammals were poorly known in their day. But the smaller ones were especially puzzling; specimens of certain species could be difficult to come by, the life histories of most were unknown – and there were so many of them. The treatment of the weasels, for instance, shows an incomplete understanding of their sexual size differences and the different appearances resulting from the seasonal moult, but this is hardly surprising. Bearing in mind the vastness of the North American wilderness, the problems of travel and the imperfect state of contemporary biological knowledge (to say nothing of the difficulty of acquiring that knowledge far from centres of learning) it is remarkable that the Audubons and the Bachmans did not make many more mistakes.

The long-tailed weasel is very variable in appearance and several subspecies occur throughout North and Central America. Northern subspecies are white in winter, other subspecies only a lighter shade of brown than in summer. The tip of the tail is black all year round. This illustration, a lively interpretation of the animal's appearance, has a curious subsidiary feature; the upper surface of the right-hand tree stump mirrors the attitude of the animal standing on it. Whether this effect was fortuitous or intentional we may never know, but it is easy to imagine Audubon smiling over it.

Nº12.

PLATE LX.

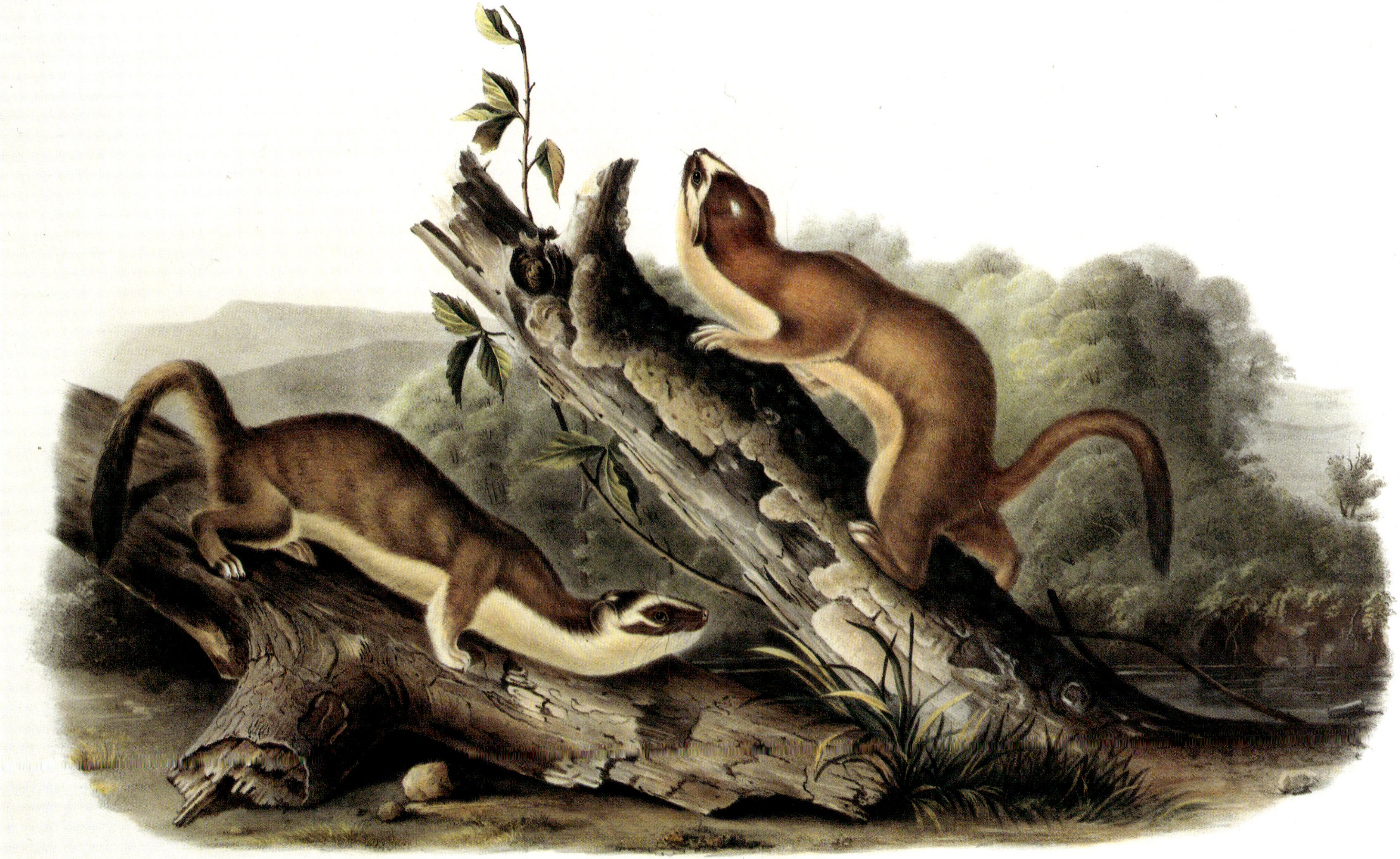

Drawn from Nature by J. J. Audubon F.R.S.F.L.S.

PUTORIUS FRENATA, LICHT.

BRIDLED WEASEL.

MALES.

Natural Size.

Northern Flying Squirrel

SEVERN RIVER FLYING SQUIRREL, *Pteromys sabrinus* (top), Rocky Mountain Flying Squirrel, *Pteromys alpinus* (bottom), (both now Northern Flying Squirrel, *Glaucomys sabrinus*). Hand coloured lithograph from an original drawing by J. J. Audubon, pl. 143 from *Atlas*, Vol. 3 of J. J. Audubon and J. Bachman's *The Viviparous Quadrupeds of North America*, 1846–54. Size of plate 27¼″ × 20¾″.

John James Audubon and the Revd John Bachman considered the two animals shown in this lithograph to be representatives of two different species, but each is a form of the northern flying squirrel, a common inhabitant of evergreen forests in Canada and the western United States. Large eyes give it the sharp vision required to undertake nocturnal flights safely. The upper figure shows how, in flight, it spreads the loose folds of fur-covered skin which extend from each side of its body and between its fore and hind limbs. When the legs are fully extended the stretched skin provides sufficient air resistance to enable it to glide downwards for a distance of well over 200 feet. The figure also shows how the tail is flattened out in flight, thus helping to control the direction in which the animal is travelling and acting as a brake. As soon as the animal lands on a tree trunk it scuttles around to the opposite side and so eludes any predators that may have followed its aerial journey.

Very agile and sure-footed, the northern flying squirrel usually lives in hollow trees in winter and builds an outside nest in summer. There is only one other flying squirrel in the United States, but many more occur in tropical and sub-tropical parts of the world. One of them, from Borneo, is a mere three and a half inches long; some others are up to three feet long.

Nº 29.

PLATE CXLIII.

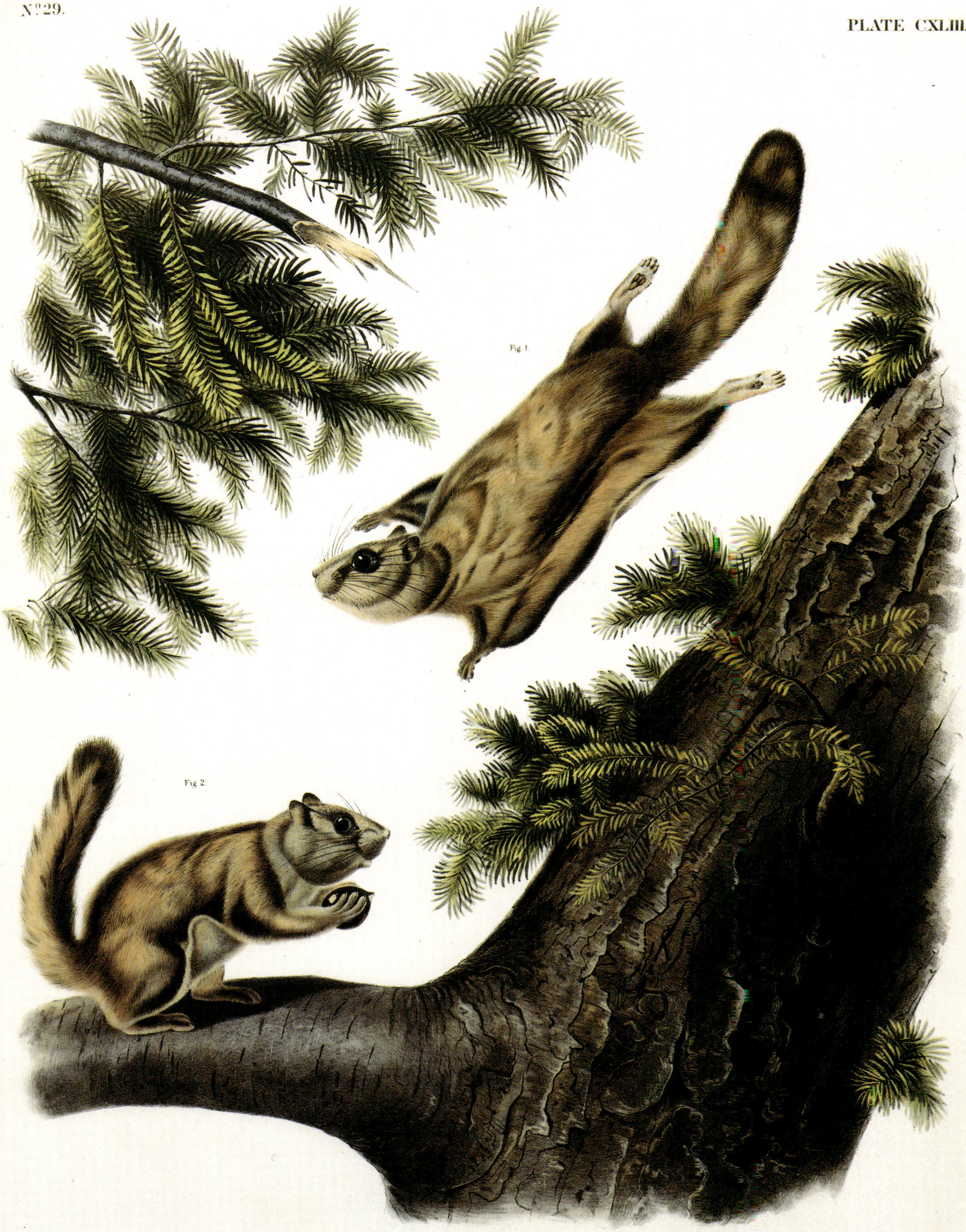

Drawn from Nature by J. W. Audubon

Fig. 1. PTEROMYS SABRINUS, PENNANT. SEVERN RIVER FLYING SQUIRREL | Fig. 2. PTEROMYS ALPINUS, RICH. ROCKY MOUNTAIN FLYING SQUIRREL.

Lith. Printed & Col. by J. T. Bowen, Philad. 1848.

Orang Utan

Ourang Outan or Pongo (now Orang Utan, *Pongo pygmaeus*). Hand coloured lithograph by W. Wing, pl. 1 from J. E. Gray's *Vertebrata* (in A. Adams' *The Zoology of the Voyage of H. M. S. Samarang; under the Command of Captain Sir E. Belcher*), 1848–50. Size of plate 10″ × 8″.

This picture reveals much more about mid-nineteenth-century attitudes and beliefs than it does about the physical appearance of the orang utan (a Malay expression meaning 'man of the forest'). Before 1869, when Alfred Russell Wallace published his personal observations of the animal sometimes called 'the wild man of Borneo', the man-like apes had been represented in popular literature as creatures with distinctly human attributes. The orang utan, then known mostly from hearsay evidence, had usually been illustrated in books standing or sitting; often, as here, it had been given a stick to hold. The idea of 'wild men' existing in remote, thickly forested places had been circulating in Europe for three or four centuries and the orang utan was seized upon eagerly as an embodiment of that idea. This picture, published in a scientific report, shows that the idea was acceptable even to professional natural historians such as the author of the report, John Edward Gray, then Keeper of Zoology at the British Museum.

The orang utan is confined in the wild to the islands of Borneo and Sumatra. Comparable in weight to an average human male, it is never more than four and a half feet tall, though it may have an arm spread of seven and a half feet. Primarily a tree dweller, it swings with slow and graceful movements from branch to branch, apparently testing the branches before trusting them with its weight. On the ground, however, it moves around awkwardly on all fours, as uncomfortable as a fish out of water. Unlike the other great apes, it is solitary by nature. The continued destruction of suitable habitats has reduced its numbers drastically but it exists in large numbers in zoos and breeds regularly in captivity.

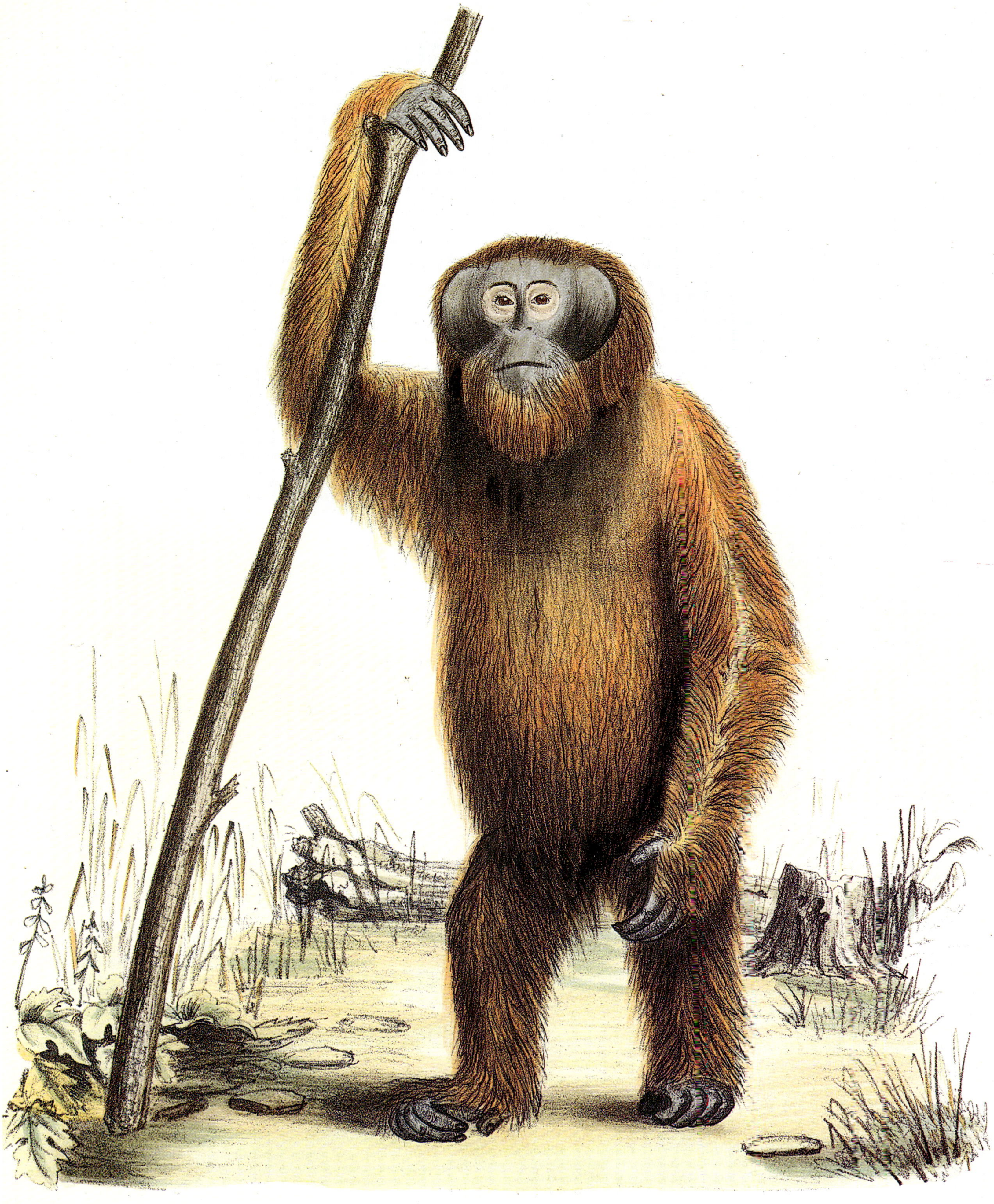

OURANG OUTAN or PONGO.

Simia satyrus.

Eland

IMPOPHOO OR ELAND, *Oreas canna* (now Eland, *Tragelaphus oryx*). Hand coloured lithograph by B. Waterhouse Hawkins, pl. 27 from Vol. 2 of J. E. Gray's *Gleanings from the Knowsley Menagerie and Aviary at Knowsley Hall*, 1850. Size of plate 22″ × 15″.

This massive antelope, measuring almost six feet at the shoulder and weighing up to 2000 pounds, must have been impressive when it was brought to Knowsley Hall near Liverpool. Lord Stanley had spent much money on his collection of exotic mammals and birds by the time this lithograph was published in 1850; a year later his menagerie contained 345 mammals belonging to 94 species. He employed agents throughout the world and financed expeditions to Africa, Central America and elsewhere in his search for rare and unusual species. Transporting a large and powerful animal such as this by sea from South Africa to England would have been no easy matter in those days and the earl must have been relieved to see it installed safely among his other living treasures.

Although rather more ox-like in appearance than this lithograph suggests, the eland does have a certain gracefulness about it and is surprisingly agile, jumping more than its own height with ease. It is timid and easily tamed, occasionally being used as a draught animal. As it also makes excellent eating and is more easily fattened than any other African antelope attempts have been made to domesticate it as though it were a species of cattle, with some success.

Like many antelopes its horns are distinctive. They are massive, about two and a half feet long (the record is 43½ inches), slightly diverging, and have a tight spiral towards the base. Of the several recognised forms of this antelope the one illustrated here is characterised by the absence of stripes in the adult. Other forms have vertical white stripes.

Guanaco

GUANACO, [*Lama huanaca*] (now Guanaco, *Lama guanicoe*). Hand coloured lithograph by B. Waterhouse Hawkins, pl. 50 from Vol. 2 of J. E. Gray's *Gleanings from the Knowsley Menagerie and Aviary at Knowsley Hall*, 1850. Size of plate 22″ × 15″.

The guanaco, an engaging and attractive animal with a well developed sense of curiosity, must have been a welcome addition to the Earl of Derby's menagerie at Knowsley Hall. Measuring about five feet to the top of its head, it is the tallest mammal native to South America. The guanaco is in the same family as the Old World camels although its ears are long and mobile and it lacks a hump. It moves like a camel but except for its long neck it is more like a sheep; the male even bleats like a sheep. It is found along the west coast from Peru southwards to Tierra del Fuego and may ascend as high as 13,000 feet in the rainy season to wander the treeless plains and passes of the Andes.

Guanacos congregate in small herds comprising a male, four to ten females and young ones of various ages; young males, on the other hand, will form themselves into herds of up to fifty strong. It is often said that the llama, *Lama glama*, is a domesticated form of the guanaco, but this ancestry may be disputed because there are striking differences between the behaviour of the two animals.

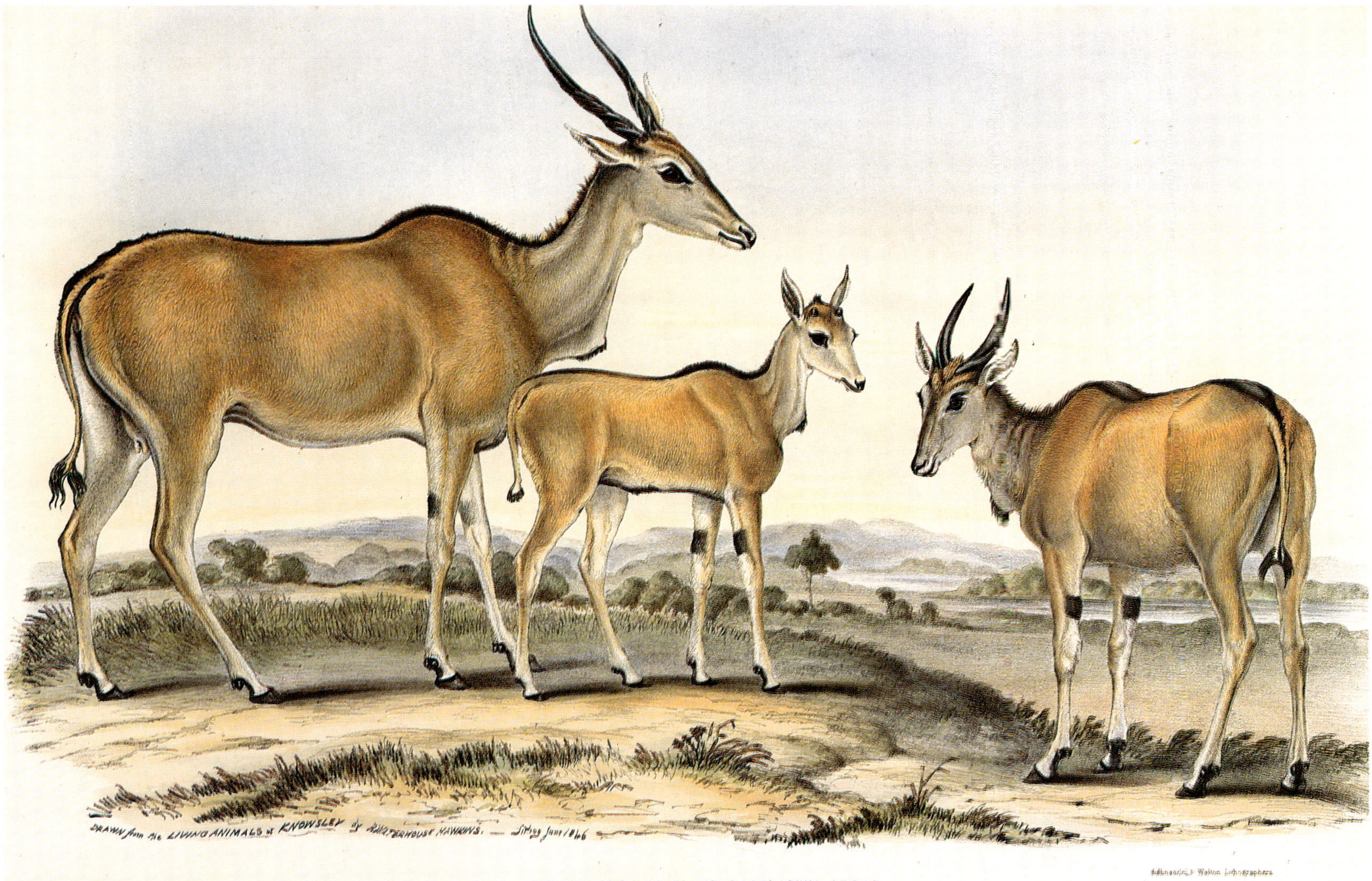

THE IMPOPHOO OR ELAND-BOSELAPHUS OREAS

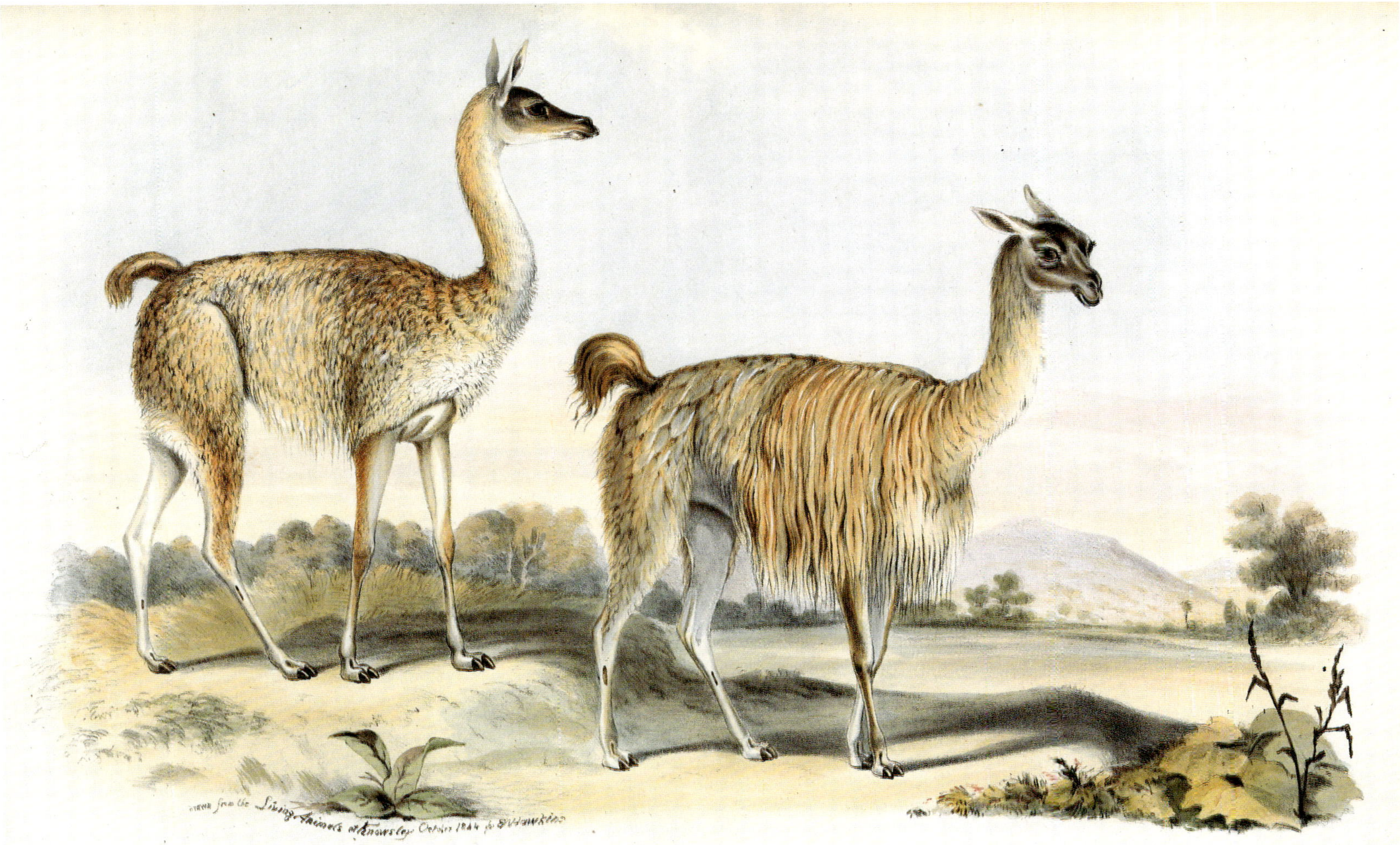

Burchell's Zebra

Burchell's Zebra, *Asinus burchellii* (now *Equus burchelli burchelli*). Hand coloured lithograph by B. Waterhouse Hawkins, pl. 55 from Vol. 2 of J. E. Gray's *Gleanings from the Knowsley Menagerie and Aviary at Knowsley Hall*, 1850. Size of plate 22″ × 15″.

This is not merely a charming and delicately drawn picture; it is also an invaluable scientific record, for the animal pictured here is extinct. John Edward Gray, an eminent zoologist at the British Museum and author of the book containing this lithograph, named and described Burchell's zebra in 1824 when it roamed the wilds of the Bechuanaland and Orange Free State territories of South Africa.

The familiar animals with bold black and white stripes on their hind legs, now occupying territories farther north in Africa, are often named Burchell's zebra but they represent different forms (named after their various discoverers). It seems as though the striping of zebras becomes more vivid and more detailed the farther north they occur, but that observation will not help to bring back the true Burchell's zebra; so this picture provides important evidence of the appearance of an animal future generations will never see. It is melancholy to reflect on the probable causes of the demise of so large and distinctive an animal so soon after William John Burchell brought it to the attention of the scientific world. Fortunately its near cousins are still plentiful both in the wild and in captivity.

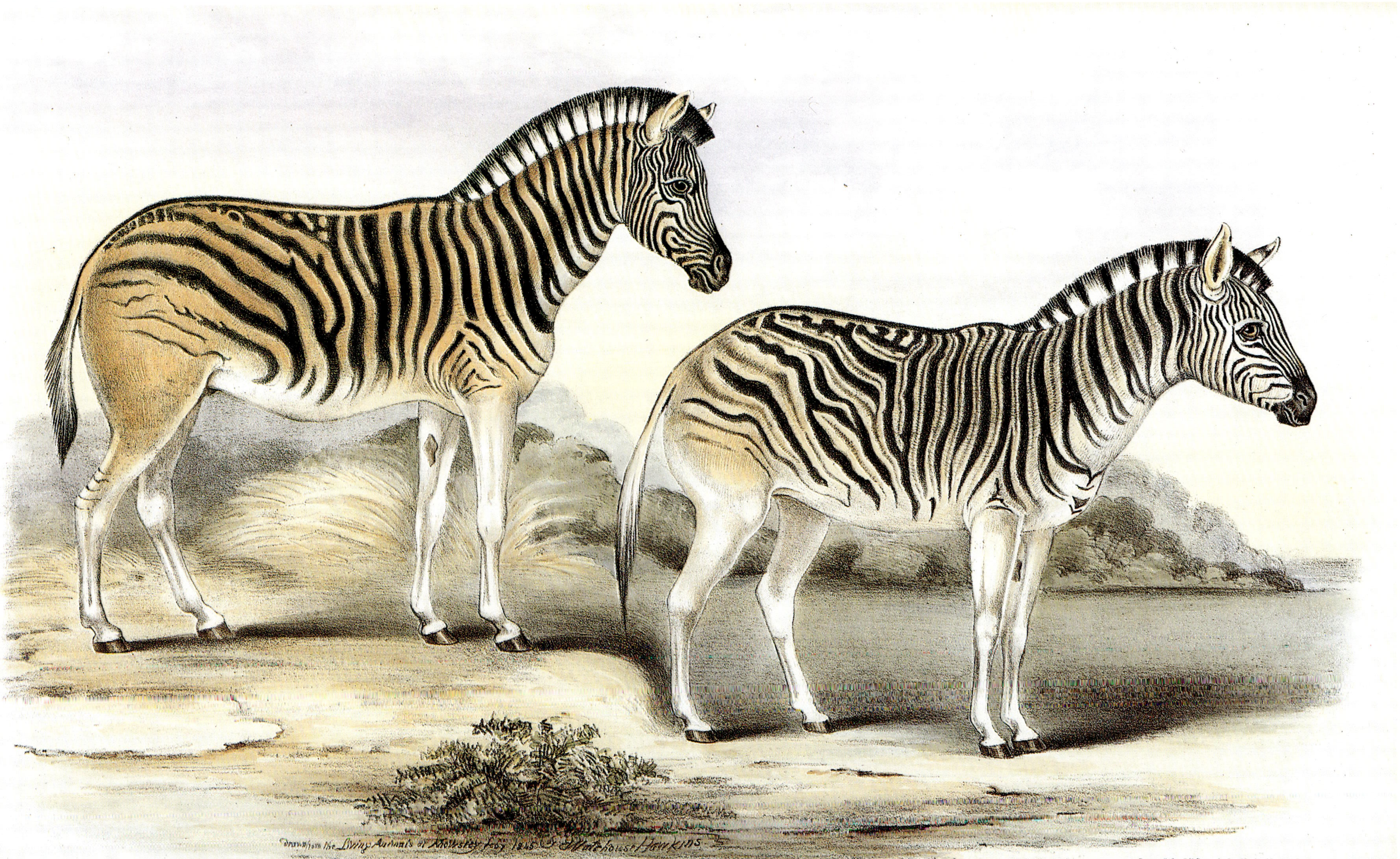

B. Waterhouse Hawkins del. & lith.

Printed by Mc Lean & Co 70 St. Martins Lane

BURCHELLS ZEBRA _ ASSINUS BURCHELLII

Gorilla

Gorilla, *Troglodytes gorilla* (now *Gorilla gorilla*). Hand coloured lithograph by Joseph Wolf, pl. 44 from Richard Owen's *Contributions to the natural history of the anthropoid apes* (in Vol. 5 of the *Transactions of the Zoological Society of London*, No. 8), 1865. Size of plate 12½″ × 10″.

There was only one recognised race of the largest living primate when Joseph Wolf produced this group portrait representing the lowland gorilla, an inhabitant of rain forests in west Central Africa. This form is distinguished by the silvery grey coat developed by the adult male. In 1901, however, a black, long-haired race was discovered on the Congo border, living in forests high up in the mountains. This race, now known as the mountain gorilla, may attain a height of six and a half feet and a weight of more than 500 pounds. The lowland gorilla, although smaller and lighter, is still a formidable creature.

This is one of two lithographs by Wolf which illustrated an article published in 1865 by the famous palaeontologist Richard Owen. Before that date the gorilla had been an almost legendary creature, and proof of its existence in darkest Africa was based mostly on travellers' tales. It was fashionable then to regard the gorilla as a bloodthirsty monster of hideous aspect with no redeeming features. Wolf's tender, even sentimental interpretation of it marked a new departure in our understanding of this gentle giant.

The gorilla is a vegetarian, notwithstanding its intimidating canine teeth. For most of the day it wanders about as part of a family group, nonchalantly munching succulent shoots and other forest produce, and sleeping at night on specially prepared beds of twigs and leaves. Apart from humans a fully grown gorilla has no natural enemies among predatory animals, does not kill except in self defence, and is usually content merely to scare off intruders with a show of noisy bravado. Wolf's picture has a remarkably modern look and must have annoyed those of his contemporaries who wanted to promote the idea of the gorilla as the embodiment of bestiality.

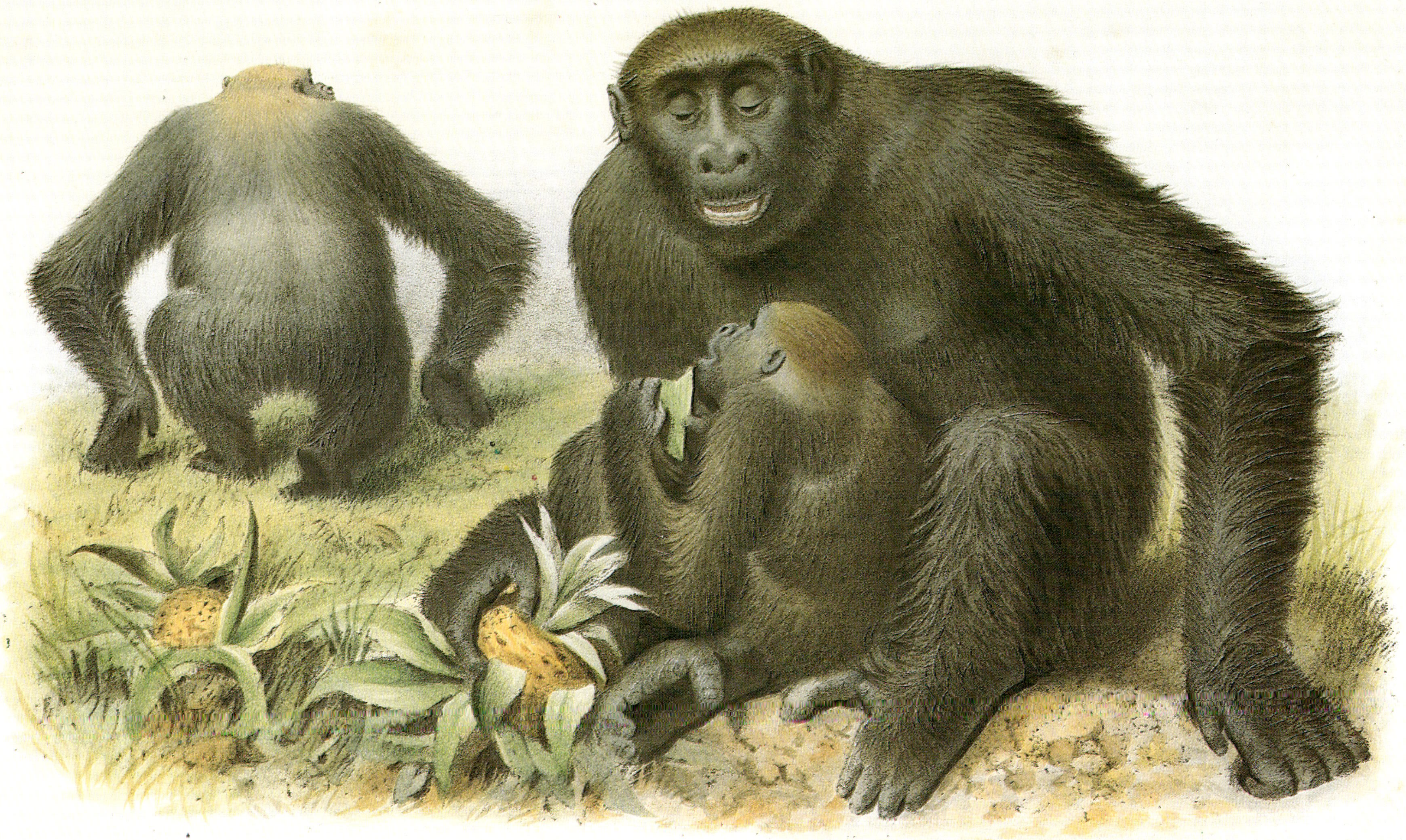

J. Wolf, del. et lith.

M&N Hanhart, Imp.

TROGLODYTES GORILLA. fem et juv.

Maned Wolf

Canis jubatus (now Maned Wolf, *Chrysocyon brachyurus*). Hand coloured lithograph, pl. 21 from C. H. C. Burmeister's *Erlauterungen zur Fauna Brasiliens*, 1856. Size of plate 17½″ × 12″.

The maned wolf comes from northern Argentina, Paraguay and southern Brazil and is the largest member of the dog family in the southern hemisphere. It differs from the true wolves, all from the northern hemisphere, in both appearance and habits. In some ways it looks like a long-legged fox, a resemblance made the more striking by its pointed muzzle and bushy, white-tipped tail. The fur is long and soft, orange-red above the white below. What is not clearly seen in this picture is the mane of slightly longer fur on the neck, but this feature is revealed only when the animal is excited.

Its long legs help it to see over the top of the long vegetation covering the savanna and grasslands through which it roams in search of its food. It pursues wild deer, rats, birds, reptiles and other small animals, usually at night. On occasion it will also eat insects, snails, fruit and sugar cane. It will mate with the domestic dog and the resulting mongrels are said to make good hunting animals. The maned wolf, protected by law in several parts of its range, is exhibited in many of the larger zoos and breeds regularly in captivity.

Taf. XXI.

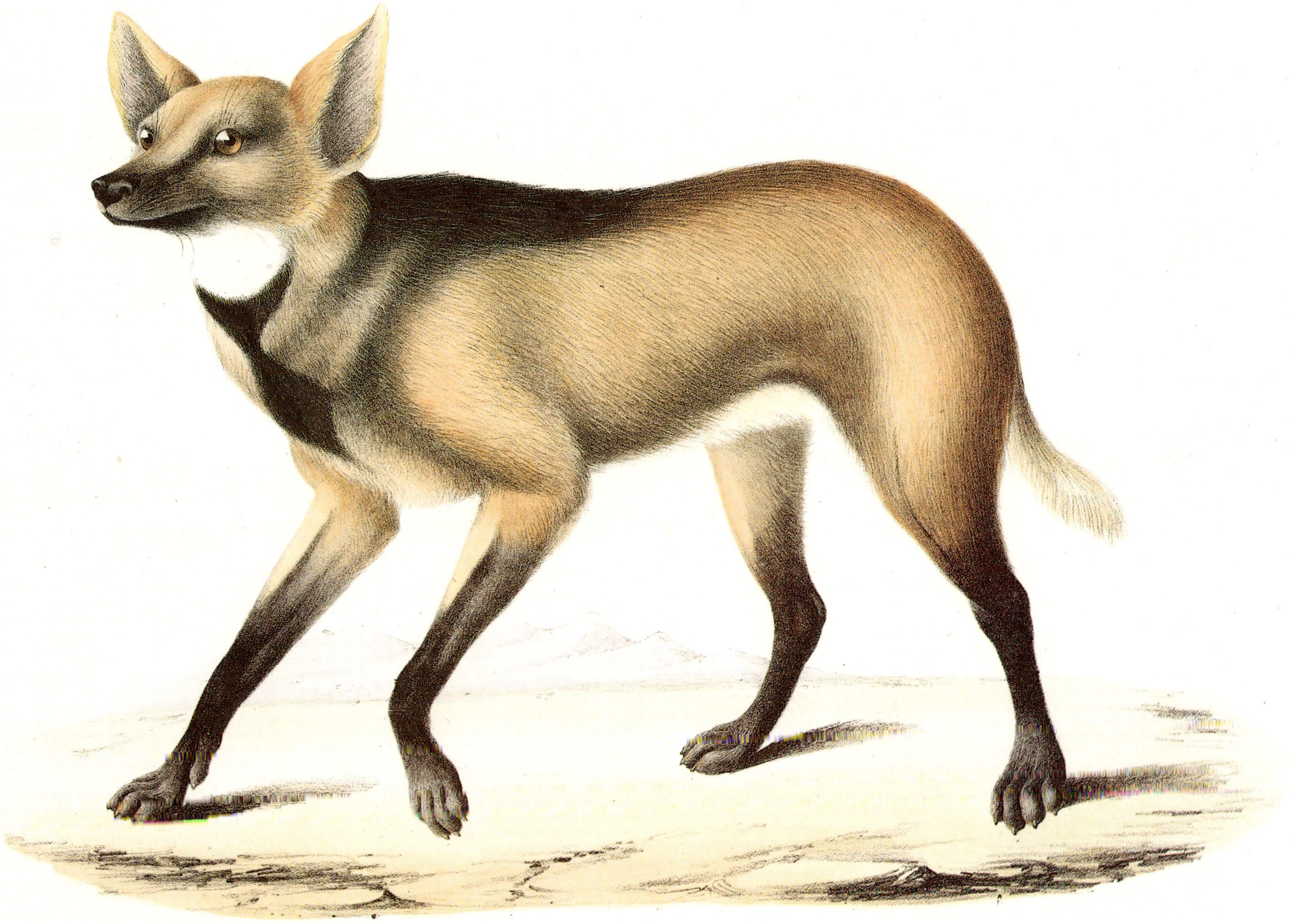

Canis jubatus.

1/4 nat. Gr.

Mule Deer

BLACK-TAILED DEER, *Cervus lewisii* (now Mule Deer, *Odocoileus hemionus*). Hand coloured engraving from an original drawing by T. R. Peale, pl. 11 from the *Atlas* to J. Cassin's *Mammalogy and Ornithology* (in *United States Exploring Expedition . . . Under the Command of C. Wilkes*), 1858. Size of plate 16½″ × 11″.

Between 1838 and 1842 the United States Exploring Expedition investigated remote and little-known parts of the globe and did not ignore the natural history of the United States itself. This engraving, from an original drawing by Titian Rembrandt Peale, a naturalist–artist attached to the expedition, represents a mammal which occurs from southern Alaska to northern Mexico. Standing about three feet high at the shoulder, the mule deer had been described in 1807 in the *Journal* of the explorers Lewis and Clarke. It was well known by the time the Exploring Expedition report was published, but Peale had made some useful notes about it which were included therein. 'The Black-tailed Deer never carries its tail erect when running', he said. 'When on the prairies, in long grass, it has a habit which is somewhat peculiar – that of frequently springing up to a considerable height to get sight of its pursuers.'

There have been many advances in our knowledge of this deer since Peale observed it and several races of it have been described. Undoubtedly, too, it has been illustrated more accurately since this engraving of his drawing was published, but few illustrations published later are more appealing than his. Less a scientist than an artist, it was natural for Peale to make an animal portrait more than a dry factual record. By glamourising his subject he took it out of the realm of science and into that of art – which is why it continues to be worth looking at.

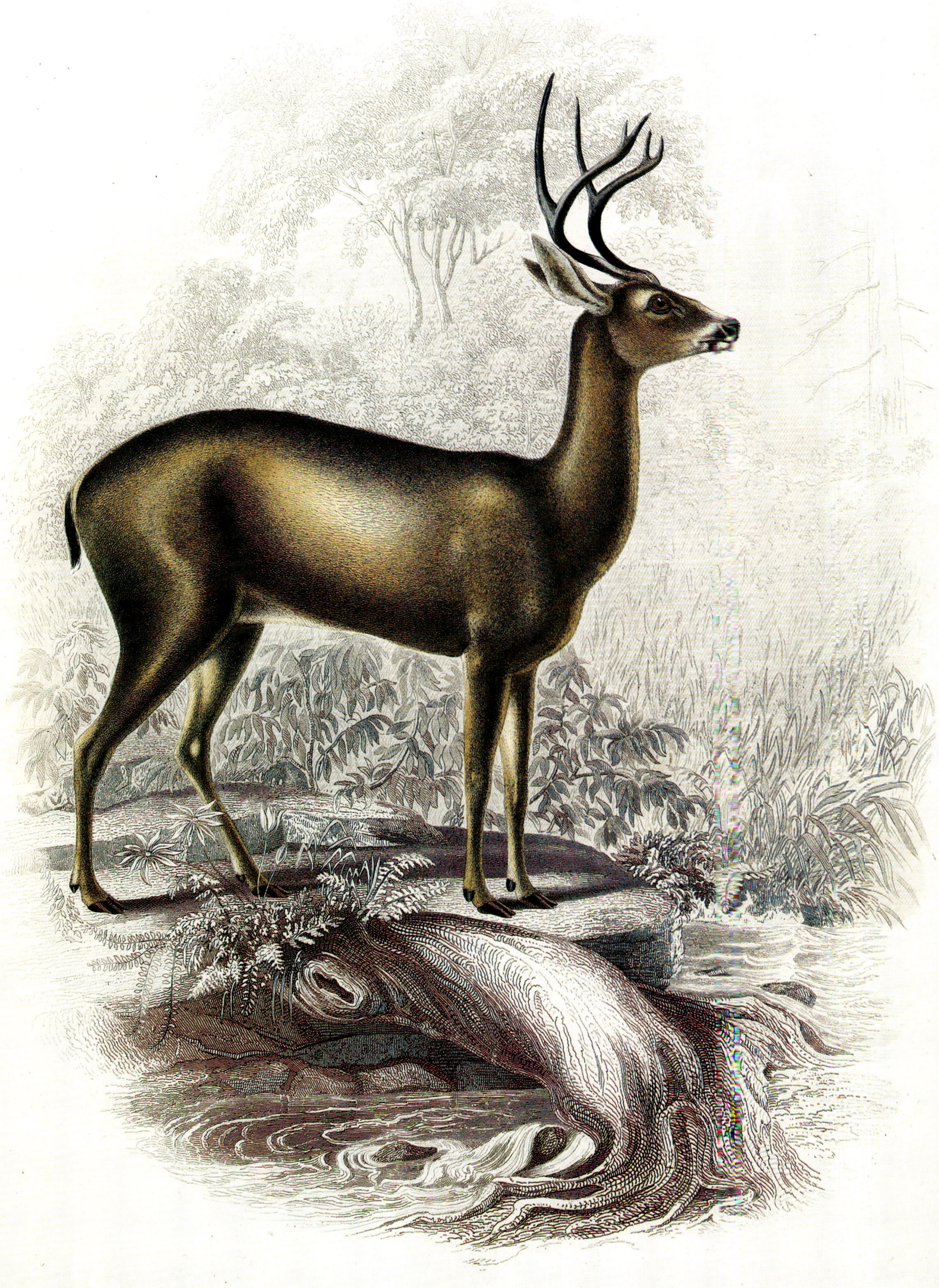

Cervus Lewisii, Peale.

Pale–throated Sloth

YELLOW-THROATED SLOTH, *Bradypus gularis* (now presumably Pale-throated Sloth, *Bradypus tridactylus*). Colour printed engraving, pl. 47 from M. H. H. T.'s *The Instructive Picture Book, Lessons from the Geographical Distribution of Animals*, 1860. Size of plate 10″ × 6¾″.

There are two groups of sloths, those with two claws on each fore limb and those with three on each fore limb (all sloths have three-clawed hind limbs). The pale-throated sloth, the creature supposedly portrayed here, belongs to the latter group and is found in the northern half of South America. Its specialised diet makes it almost impossible to keep in captivity, and as it seems to spend most of its life asleep it is difficult for us to get to know it well. Thus many fanciful notions have accrued around it. One early traveller said it lived on ants and another said it survived on air alone – although those who have observed it, if only briefly, know that it eats leaves. It has been considered incapable of covering more than fifty paces in a day – but some of those who have studied it in the wild have occasionally seen it move rapidly through the branches of forest trees. Those who have kept three-toed sloths as pets know that they are trusting, gentle and fascinating to study, even though they may require at least fifteen hours sleep a day.

This engraving dates from mid-Victorian times when little was known about the habits of sloths and their appearance in life was largely conjectural. But the creatures shown here look more like lively, black-faced nuns playing hide-and-seek in a tree than the shaggy-coated indolent creatures we know them to be. The artist was unable to resist the tendency to turn a little-known animal into a caricature of a familiar kind of human being. This was a common tendency among early animal artists, but it is remarkable to see such a blatant example served up for public consumption in the middle of the nineteenth century.

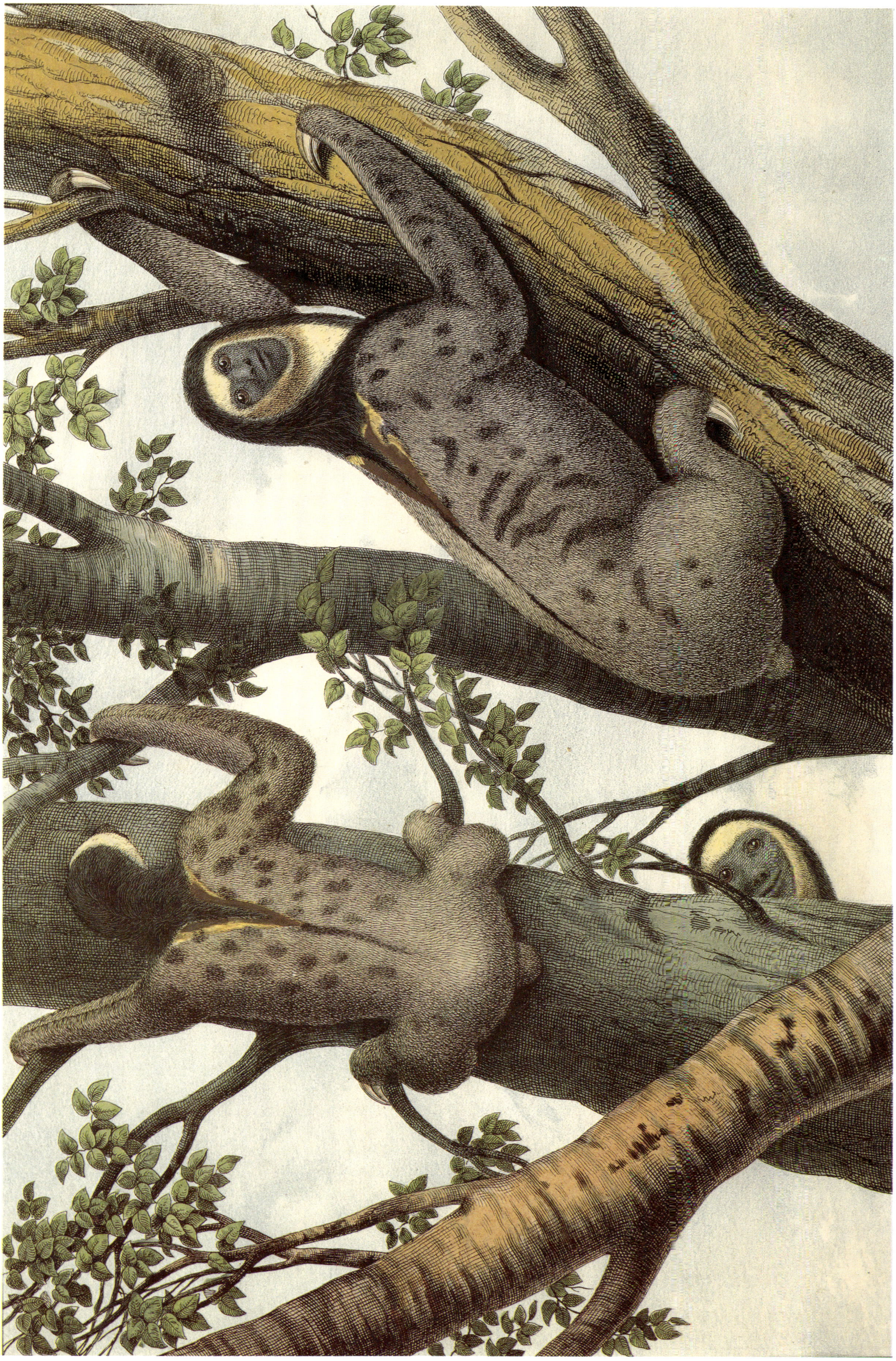

Red Howler

Howling Monkey, *Mycetus ursinus* (now Red Howler, *Alouatta seniculus*). Hand coloured engraving, pl. 50 from M. H. H. T.'s *The Instructive Picture Book, Lessons from the Geographical Distribution of Animals*, 1860. Size of plate 10″ × 7″.

Although this engraving was intended to represent the red howler – an intention singularly unsuccessful in its execution – its principal, though unstated, purpose was to illustrate a story from the Bible. *The Instructive Picture Book* was one of many Victorian publications which tried to popularise natural history while attempting to put across religious messages. Often the text or the illustrations, sometimes both, would 'point a moral'. In this instance the very red apple in the very human hand of the squatting figure leaves us in no doubt that we are looking at Eve offering the fruit to Adam.

The red howler, an improbable actor in the Adam and Eve story, is one of the largest and noisiest of the New World monkeys. The engraving correctly represents the prehensile nature of the long tail – used almost as though it were an extra limb – but fails utterly to give a correct idea of any other part of the creature. No one who has seen a red howler squatting in a tree and has listened to it howling at the top of its voice would ever confuse it with the benign-looking creatures shown here. Evidently the artist did not work from living models. Like many Victorian popularisers of natural history he was guilty of plagiarism. The left-hand figure in this picture is based on a figure published in 1812 in a book describing and illustrating the zoological discoveries of the great German explorer/naturalist, Alexander von Humboldt. In Humboldt's original version the monkey's right hand is empty while its left hand grasps a pod-like vegetable or fruit. In most other respects the two figures are similar. For the right-hand figure the artist who produced the illustrations for *The Instructive Picture Book* seems to have used his own well-developed imagination entirely. Just possibly Adam may have looked like this – but never the red howler!

The coloration of the red howler may or may not resemble that of the engraving, for in captivity its coat may change colour after contact with water, red turning to orange and orange to yellow. If this kind of change is repeated in the wild, as is probable, it would explain why there has been disagreement among observers about its coloration.

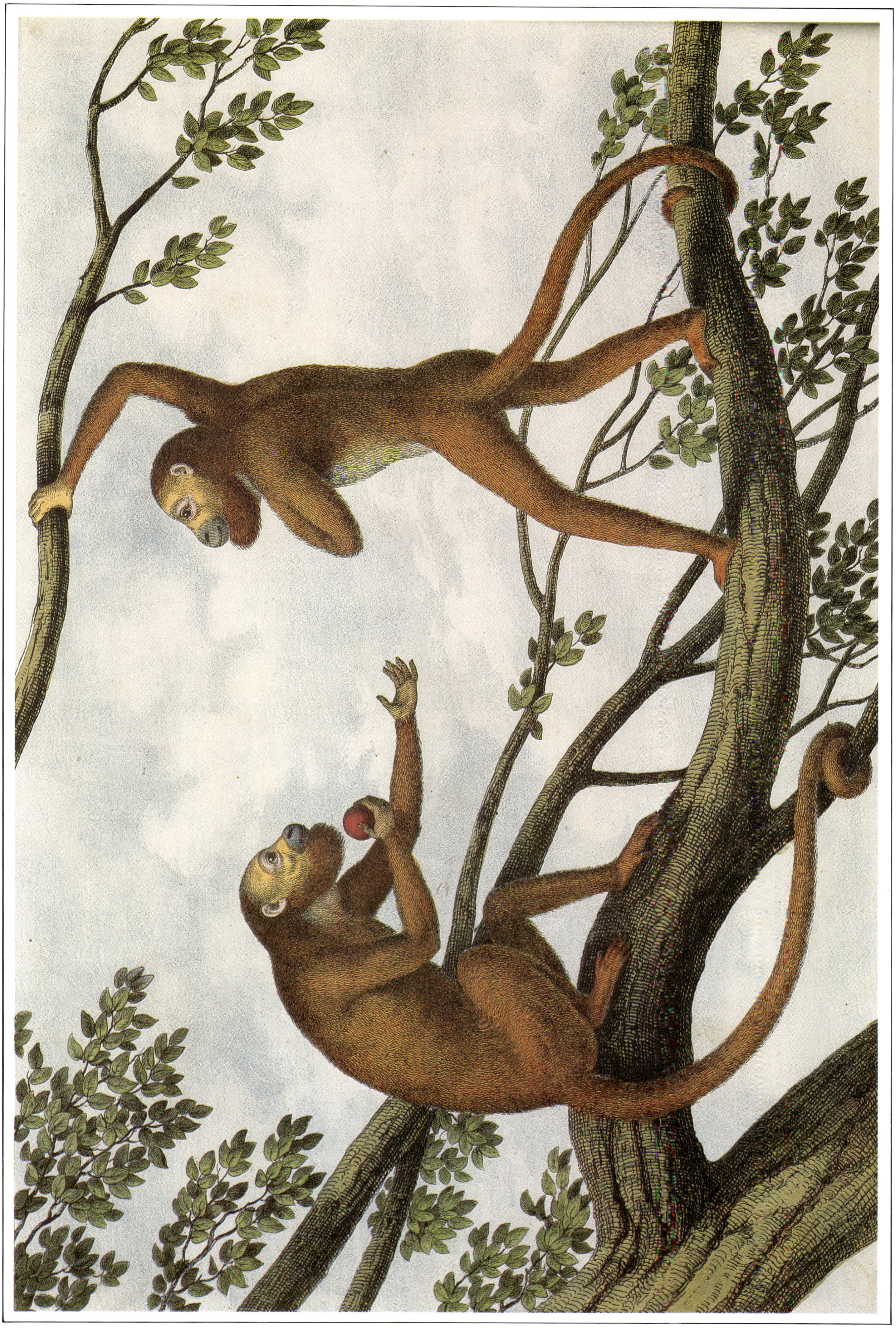

Chimpanzee

CHIMPANZEE, *Troglodytes niger* (now *Pan troglodytes*). Hand coloured lithograph by J. Wolf, pl. 1 from *Zoological Sketches, First Series* (edited by D. W. Mitchell and P. L. Sclater) 1861. Size of plate 13¼″ × 9″.

During the nineteenth century there was little hope of a chimpanzee surviving for long in England or other European countries. The one shown here, for instance, died after a few months' residence at the London Zoo. Philip Lutley Sclater, co-editor of the book in which this sensitive study by Joseph Wolf appeared, had this to say about the fate which awaited many apes snatched from their native forests: 'The efforts made in Europe to preserve the Chimpanzee and other anthropoid Apes in captivity for any length of time, have hitherto proved unavailing. Shut up by itself in a barred den, without companions of its own species, and subjected to the continual changes of climate, which occur in these latitudes, the poor captive soon withers and dies, and is replaced by another, fresh from the warm tropics, certain to undergo a similar fate in its turn.' The captors of this youngster had probably killed its mother first.

Nowadays chimpanzees flourish better in captivity than any other anthropoid ape. They are also the most intelligent of the apes, and their curiosity and manual dexterity are well known, but they are incapable of concentrating on any activity for very long. In the wild they spend most of their time gathering fruit and moving from one feeding site to another.

The true chimpanzee occupies a broad band of country from Sierra Leone on the west to the large lakes east of Zaire. The much smaller pygmy chimpanzee, *Pan paniscus*, is found in a small area in Zaire, south of the Zaire River.

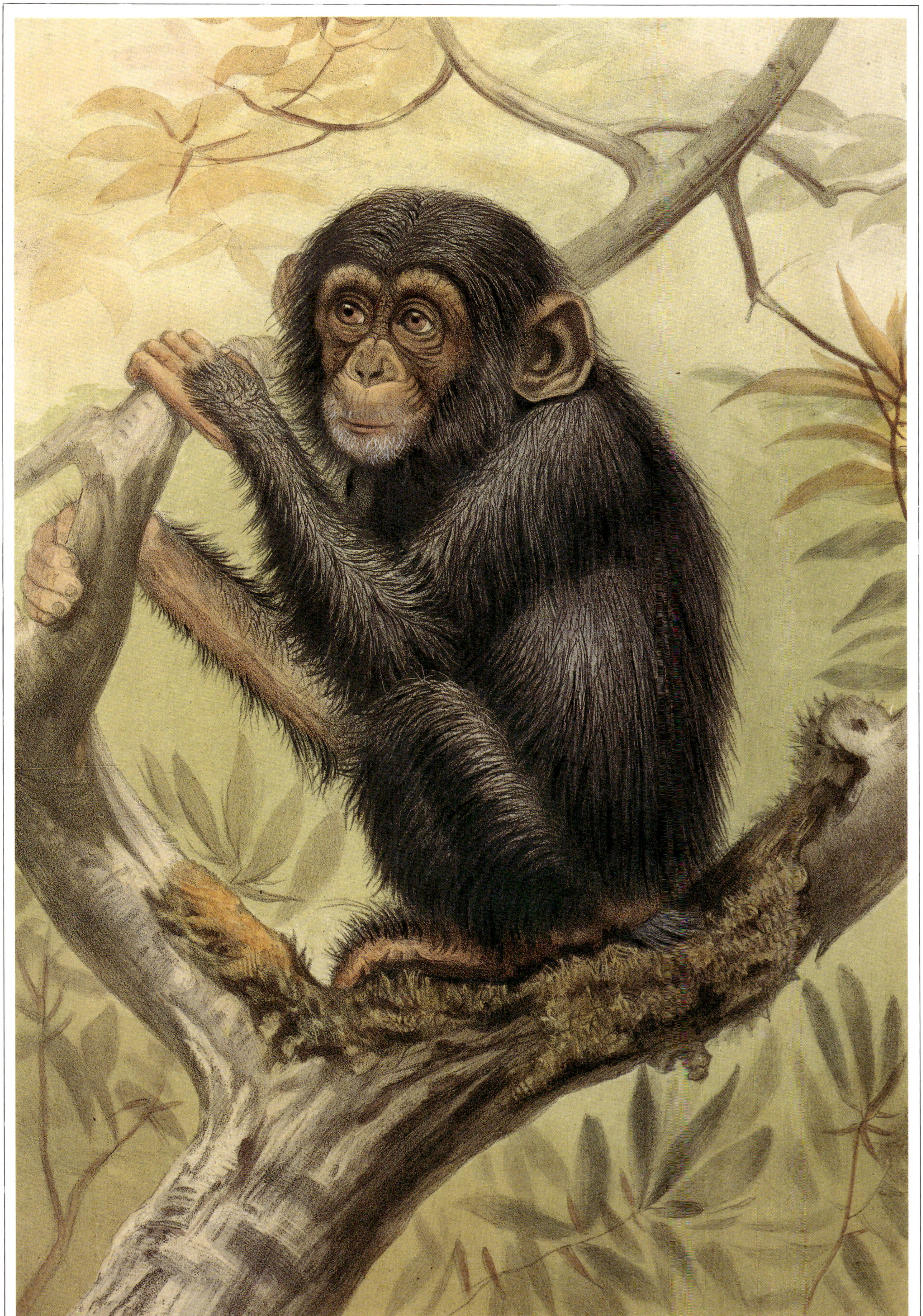

Hippopotamus

HIPPOPOTAMUS, *Hippopotamus amphibius.* Hand coloured lithograph by J. Wolf, pl. 27 from his *Zoological Sketches, First Series* (edited by D. W. Mitchell and P. L. Sclater), 1861. Size of plate 13¼″ × 9″.

The hippopotamus weighs up to four tons and stands about five feet at the shoulder. Formerly widespread over much of tropical Africa it has now disappeared north of the Sahara but is still common in East Africa. When this picture was commissioned the hippopotamus was still a novel sight in Europe. The first one to be seen at the London Zoo, a male, was installed there in 1850. A female was added in 1854, bringing together the first pair to be seen in Europe since Roman times.

The unfriendly disposition of the first of these animals towards certain people was described by Philip Lutley Sclater, Secretary of the Zoological Society of London (the governing body of the London Zoo): 'There are individuals whose appearance always excites his wrath; and certain classes of persons, especially laborers and workmen wearing linen-jackets. The inveterate feeling against the latter is probably traceable to the discomfort he experienced from them at the time his present habitation was in the course of construction; his distinction of individuals is more difficult to account for. The gentleman towards whom he most constantly expresses his displeasure maintains that he never "gave his fat friend any cause of offence whatever, except that he one day addressed to him some expressions in Arabic which were certainly not complimentary."' A usually placid animal, when disturbed the hippopotamus can be aggressive and has killed many humans.

With only these two captive animals as models Joseph Wolf tried to create a realistic picture of hippopotami in the wild. The result, as with most of Wolf's imaginative wildlife scenes, was entirely satisfactory.

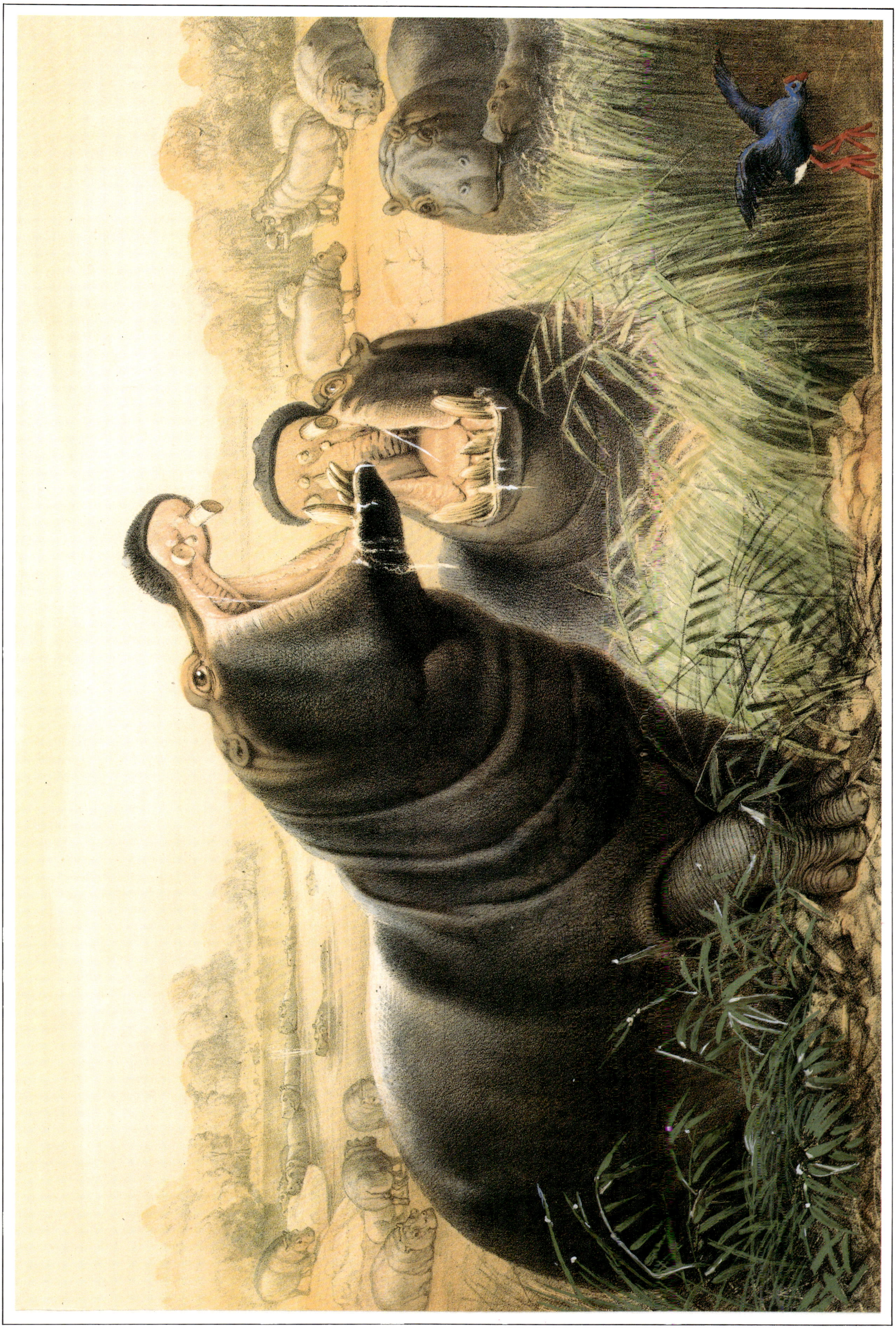

Giant Panda

AILUROPE, *Ailuropus melanoleucus* (now Giant Panda, *Ailuropoda melanoleuca*). Chromolithograph by G. Severeyns after an original drawing by Huet, pl. 50 from Vol. 2 (*Atlas*) of H. H. and A. Milne Edwards's *Recherches pour Servir à l'Histoire Naturelle des Mammifères*, 1868–74. Size of plate 12″ × 9¼″.

Although the giant panda seems always to have been among us it was unknown in the West until 1869 when Alphonse Milne Edwards, a naturalist working in Paris, received a letter from the French missionary Père David describing his discovery of it in the central Chinese province of Szechuan. Père David thought he had discovered a bear but it turned out to be a quite different animal, destined by its striking markings, its friendly disposition, its rarity and its vulnerability to become one of the best known of all the larger mammals. Those familiar with the illustration designed by the late Sir Peter Scott as the logo of the World Wildlife Fund may criticise this picture as being inaccurate. The criticism is justified, but there are extenuating circumstances. It is the first published picture of the giant panda and was probably based upon a preserved skin brought to Paris from Szechuan when transport was difficult and time-consuming: all things considered we should be full of praise for the artist.

The giant panda has been declining in numbers in its native bamboo forests for many years and does not breed readily in captivity. Many of us may go through life without seeing one. As no more than a thousand giant pandas were living in the wild in the early 1980s it is possible that the logo of the World Wildlife Fund, an organisation dedicated to the preservation of endangered species, could represent an extinct animal by the year 2000, less than 150 years after the first picture of it was published.

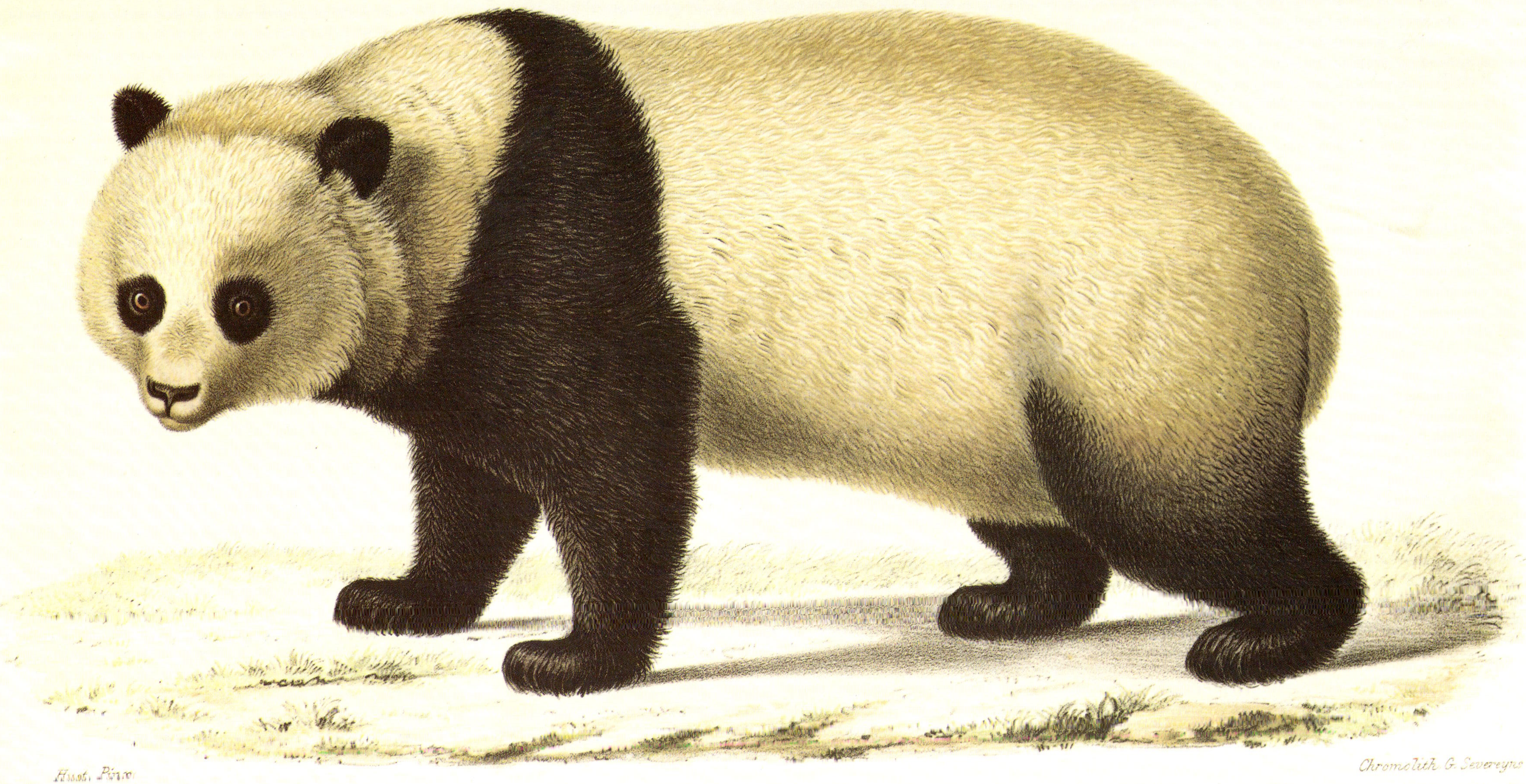

Huet, Pinx. Chromolith. G. Severeyns

Sumatran Rhinoceros

SUMATRAN RHINOCEROS, *Rhinoceros sumatrensis* (now *Dicerorhinus sumatrensis*). Hand coloured lithograph by J. Wolf and J. Smit after a drawing by Wolf, pl. 97 from P. L. Sclater's *On the Rhinoceroses now or lately living in the Society's Menagerie* (in *Transactions of the Zoological Society of London*, Vol. 9 No. 1), 1877. Size of plate 12″ × 9½″.

Philip Lutley Sclater said he wrote his article on the rhinoceroses exhibited at one time or another in the gardens of the Zoological Society of London, 'to illustrate the very beautiful drawings by Mr Wolf'. This drawing was based on sketches made by Wolf of an old female animal purchased for the London Zoo on 2 August 1872 from William Jamrach, a dealer in exotic animals, who received £600 for it. The first Sumatran rhinoceros to be exhibited there, it had been captured in the Sunghi-njong district of Malacca on the western side of the Malayan Peninsula. It died six weeks later and after it had been stuffed it was placed in the British Museum (it is now in the Natural History Museum in London). Jamrach speedily obtained a living replacement for it which he sold to the Zoo for the same amont. Wolf's masterly drawing shows the two animals together although they never met. Under the circumstances even the cleverest use of photography could not have improved upon Wolf's imaginative juxtaposition of the two animals.

This species differs from the Indian rhinoceros in having two horns instead of one and in its smaller stature. Standing only four and a half feet at the shoulder, it is the world's smallest rhinoceros and is easily the lightest, seldom weighing more than a ton. It is also the world's hairiest rhinoceros. In large bulls the front horn may reach a length of about 20 inches, more than twice the length attained by the rear horn. Now an endangered species, the Sumatran rhinoceros lives in thick bamboo forests in Sumatra, the Malay Peninsula and Borneo.

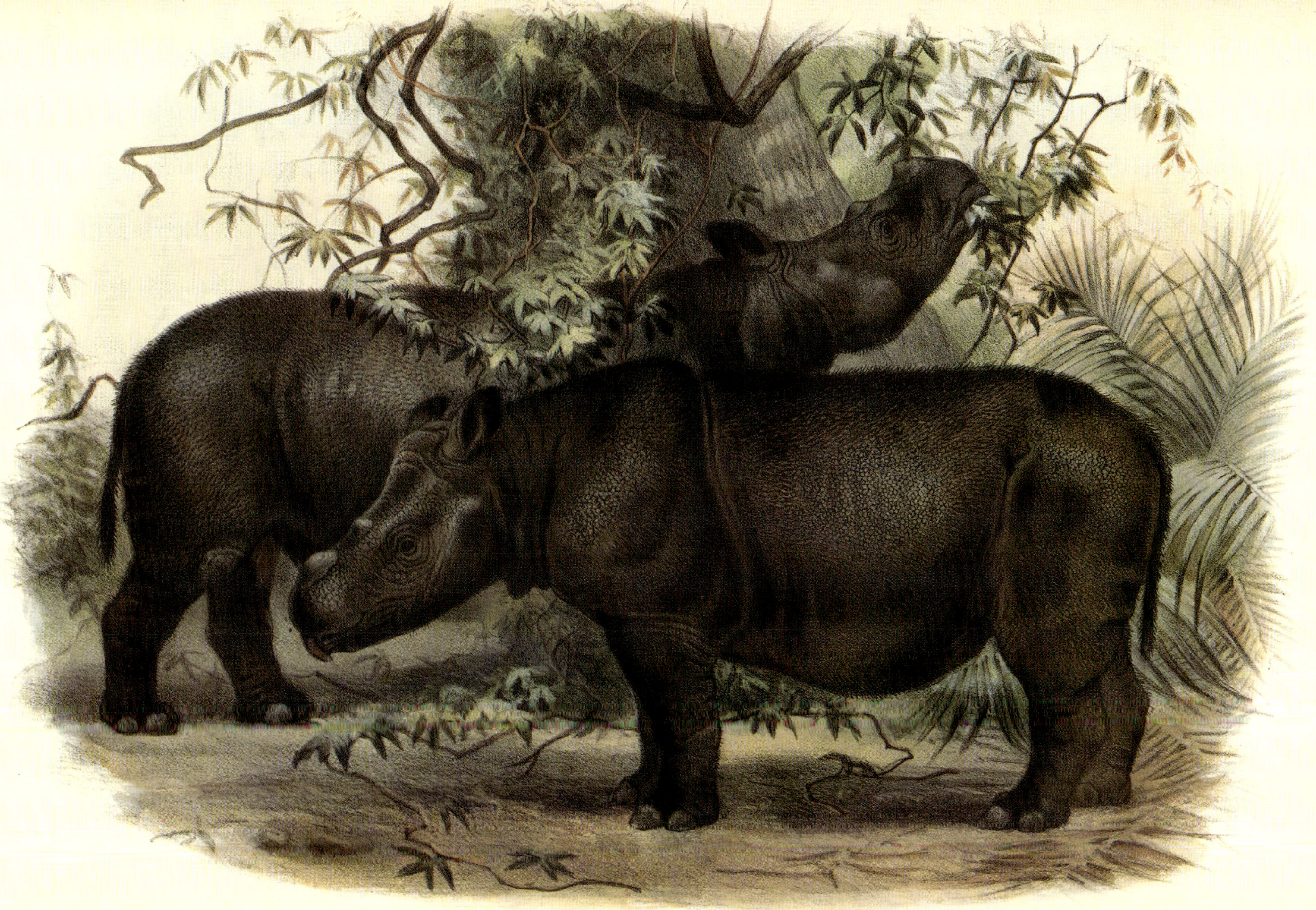

J. Wolf & J. Smit del et lith.

M&N Hanhart imp.

RHINOCEROS SUMATRENSIS

Caribbean Manatee

MANATEE, *Manatus australis* (now Caribbean Manatee, *Trichechus manatus*). Hand coloured lithograph by J. Smit from an original drawing by J. Wolf, pl. 7 from E. R. Alston's *Mammals* (in *Biologia Centrali Americana*, Vol. 2), 1879–82. Size of plate 12½″ × 10″.

This, the commonest of the three existing manatees, attains a length of thirteen feet and may weigh up to 1500 pounds. Already uncommon in Central America when Joseph Wolf's picture of it was published, the Caribbean manatee is now found in coastal and estuarine waters from North Carolina round to the Gulf of Mexico, the Caribbean and the Bahamas. It is herbivorous, slow moving and almost defenceless.

When moving through the water it uses its tail for propulsion and as a rudder to control pitching and rolling movements. As pictured here it rests by apparently hanging suspended near the water surface. In June 1878 a live specimen was exhibited at the Westminster Aquarium in London and it survived there until March 1879. Joseph Wolf was able to sketch it when it was alive and the drawing, as E. R. Alston says, 'well represents the curious position which that animal habitually assumed when at rest'.

A normally silent animal, the Caribbean manatee can emit high pitched screams and squeals. It is hard to understand how a creature so unprepossessing in appearance and with such a limited vocal range could have been mistaken for the mythical mermaid. Perhaps its peculiar way of taking a rest had something to do with it, or the nipples under its flippers may have reminded an onlooker of a human mother nursing her baby.

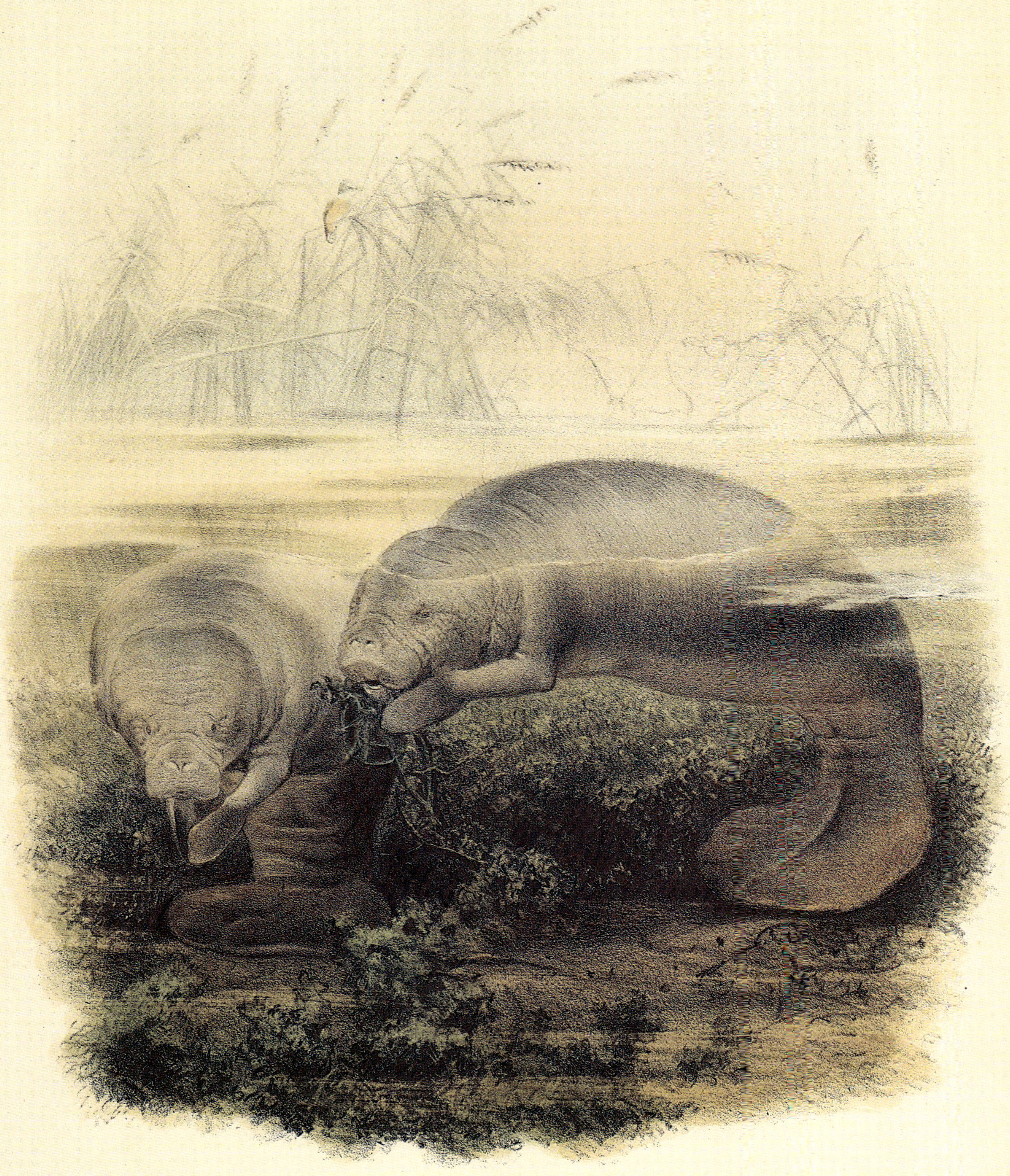

MANATUS AUSTRALIS.

Common Dolphin and Bottle-nosed Dolphin

COMMON DOLPHIN, *Delphinus delphis* (upper) and *Delphinus tursio* (lower) (now Bottle-nosed Dolphin, *Tursiops truncatus*). Hand coloured lithograph from W. H. Flower's *On the external characters of two species of British Dolphins (Delphinus delphis, Linn., and Delphinus tursio, Fabr.)* (in: *Transactions of the Zoological Society of London*, Vol. 2 Part 1), 1880. Size of plate 12½″ × 9½″.

The common dolphin and the bottle-nosed dolphin are now familiar from their appearances on television; and many of us have visited marine aquaria and witnessed their acrobatic performances. The common dolphin was well known to the ancient Greeks and seems to have always been with us, so it is surprising to learn that no adequate figure of it had existed in any zoological work before the upper one in this lithograph was published in 1880. The specimen which had the dubious honour of being the subject of the first adequate portrait was caught in a mackerel net off the Cornish coast in March 1879. The figure shows that it is distinguishable from the very similar but much larger bottle-nosed dolphin by its darker back and the distinct black line along its flank.

The specimen of the bottle-nosed dolphin shown here, a male not quite fully grown, was one of several captured near Holyhead, North Wales, on 5 October 1868. It is not usually as dark in colour as shown here and may have been dead for some time before the artist painted its portrait. This species may reach a length of about fourteen feet, whereas the common dolphin seldom exceeds eight feet. Both, but particularly the bottle-nosed dolphin, are highly intelligent, sociable and playful. They learn tricks rapidly, often play together, invent games of their own and give every appearance of thoroughly enjoying themselves when performing before a human audience. They may also be trained to help divers working in deep water. In the wild, however, they can be fearless in the face of danger. They have been seen to butt at the gills of a large shark which has approached a dolphin family group too closely, wounding the shark so seriously that it has died. We may be able to teach these trusting creatures a trick or two, but perhaps we should try learning a few things from them as well.

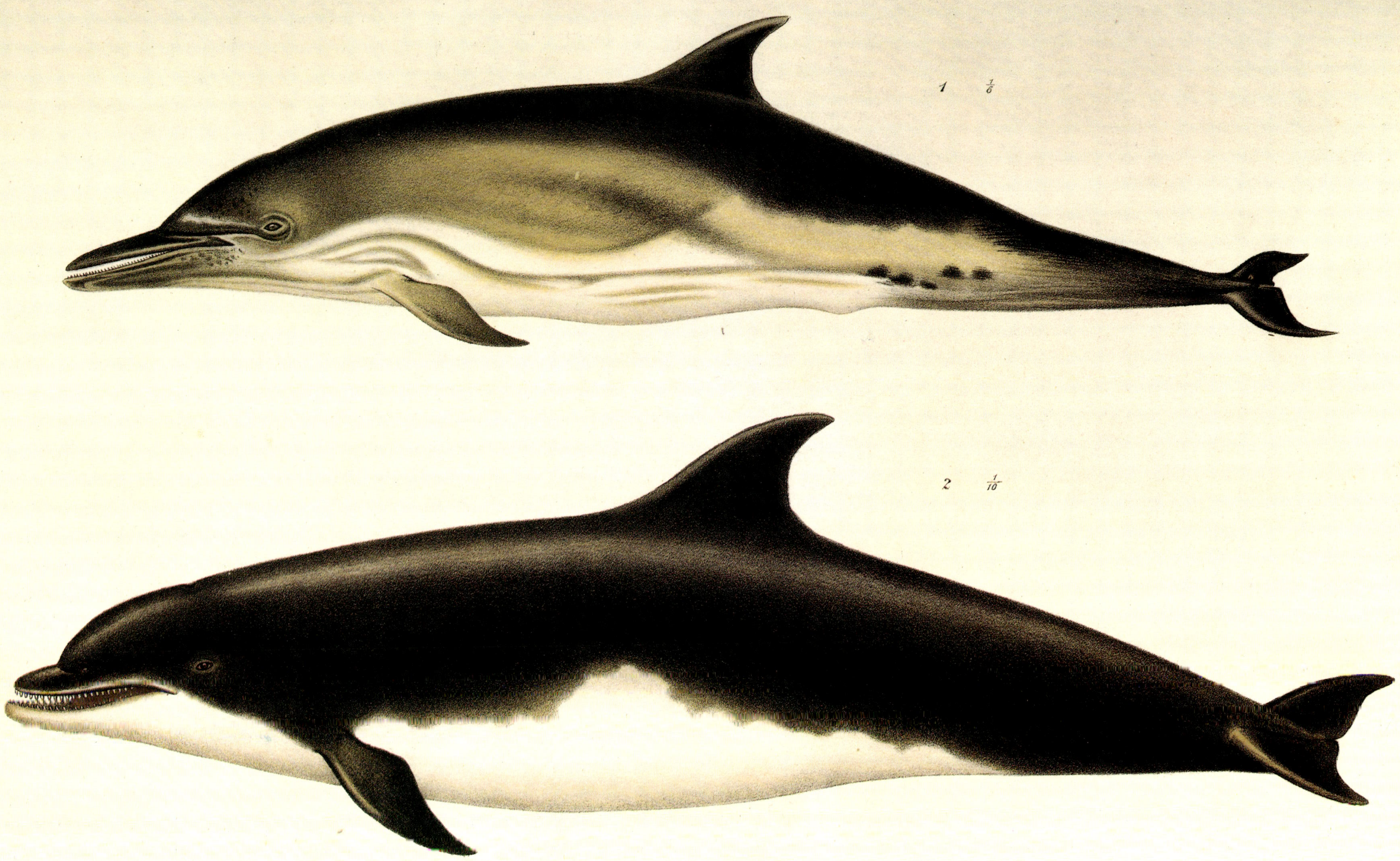

J. Smit lith.

Hanhart imp.

1. DELPHINUS DELPHIS. 2. DELPHINUS TURSIO.

Lion

LION, *Felis leo* (now *Panthera leo*). Hand coloured lithograph by J. Smit from an original drawing by J. Wolf, pl. 1 from D. G. Elliot's *A Monograph of the Felidae, or Family of the Cats*, 1883. Size of plate 23¼″ × 18½″.

Although this picture captures the essential physical features of the King of Beasts it conveys little of the animal's latent ferocity and power. Perhaps it tells us more about the mental attitude of the artist and the conditions under which he worked on his drawing than it tells us about lions. Joseph Wolf may have visited the Lion House at the London Zoo to make preliminary sketches for the picture. He may have seen a frog leap into their water supply, but he was in any case quite prepared to introduce this kind of whimsical touch into his studies of wild life. He knew that curiosity is a feature of cats, big and small, and that for most of the time the lion is not fierce. It is possible that Wolf had never seen one really hungry, certain that he had never seen one in the wild. Being a truthful artist he painted what he had seen, a group of well-fed, contented lions.

Lions are sociable creatures and are rarely seen on their own. A large male, easily distinguished from the female by its mane, may measure up to nine feet from nose to tail-tip and may weigh more than 400 pounds. Wolf's lions may not look fierce but they do look heavy! The lioness in the right foreground also looks powerfully muscled about the shoulders and gives the impression, rightly, that she is as accomplished a killer as the male. Indeed, lionesses kill more often than lions. In the background of Wolf's picture a lion is seen roaring, which it does mainly at sunset or just before dawn; the roar may be heard as much as five miles away.

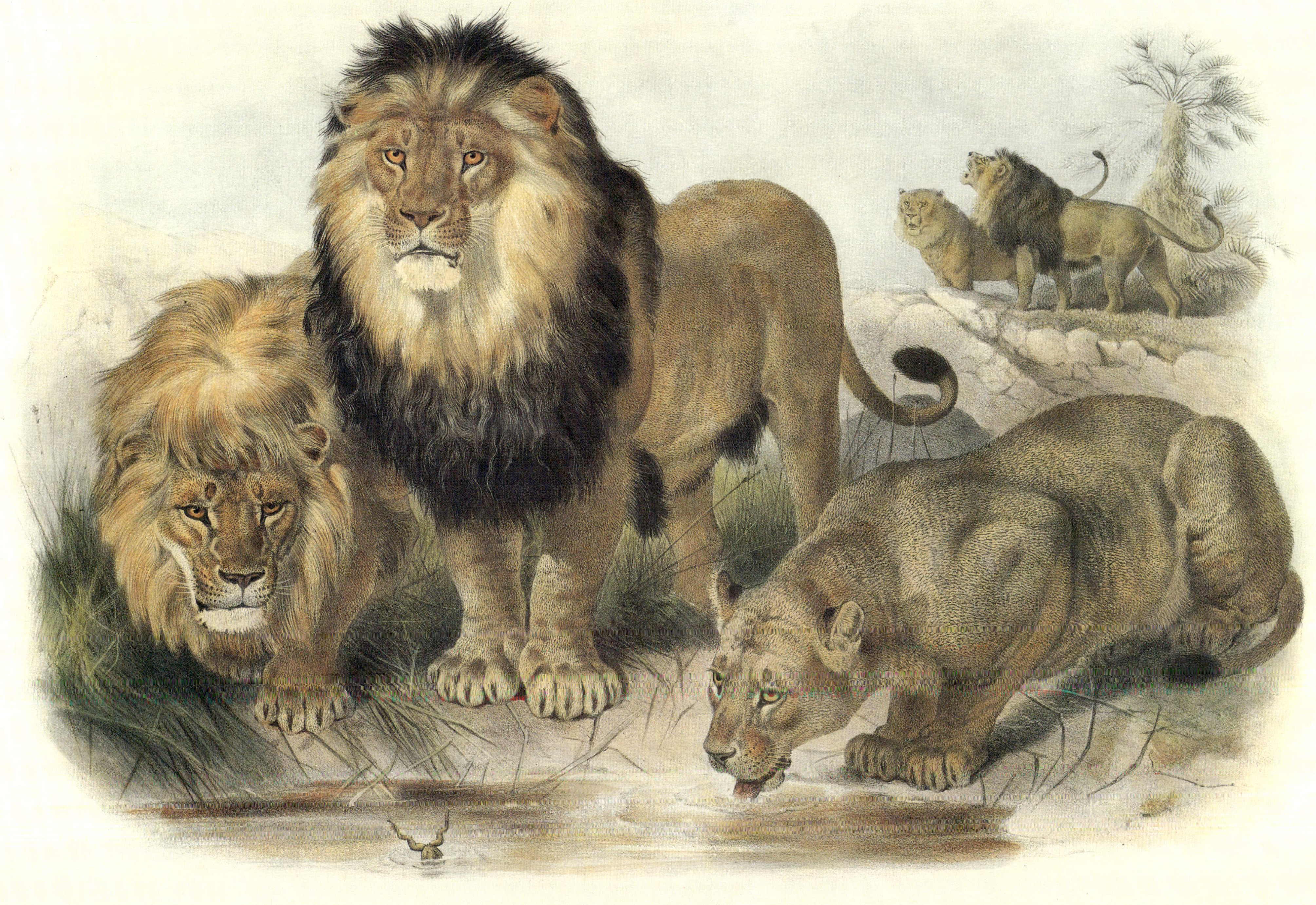

J. Wolf & J. Smit, del. et lith.

M & N Hanhart imp.

FELIS LEO.

Snow Leopard

SNOW LEOPARD, *Felis uncia* (now *Panthera uncia*). Hand coloured lithograph by J. Smit from an original drawing by J. Wolf, pl. 4 from D. G. Elliot's *A Monograph of the Felidae, or Family of the Cats*, 1883. Size of plate 23¼″ × 18½″.

This is a magnificent study of one of the handsomest of the wild cats. Joseph Wolf, famous for his studies of birds of prey, was outstanding for his life-like portrayals of wild life and he was unequalled in the nineteenth century for his ability to place his subjects in naturalistic settings. Here he evokes the spirit of place superbly even though he had never been anywhere near the mountainous regions of Central Asia, the remote haunts of the snow leopard.

With a body length of three and a half feet the three-foot-long tail looks more substantial than it is. This is because the snow leopard has exceptionally thick fur, as much as two inches thick on its back. Living mostly at altitudes between 7000 and 18,000 feet it needs thick fur if it is to stay warm. Of course it does not spend all its time at such extreme altitudes. It preys upon large and small mammals anywhere between the tree line and the snow line, as opportunity allows. In the summer it follows them as they migrate upwards to feed on the higher montane pastures. It will stalk them while they are grazing or resting and sometimes ambushes them, usually choosing the hours of twilight or darkness.

The snow leopard's beautiful fur, so attractively marked with dark grey rosettes, has always been highly prized in the fur trade and has contributed to a marked decline in its numbers in recent years. Although a protected species over much of its range, it is still hunted illegally and its pelt offered for sale.

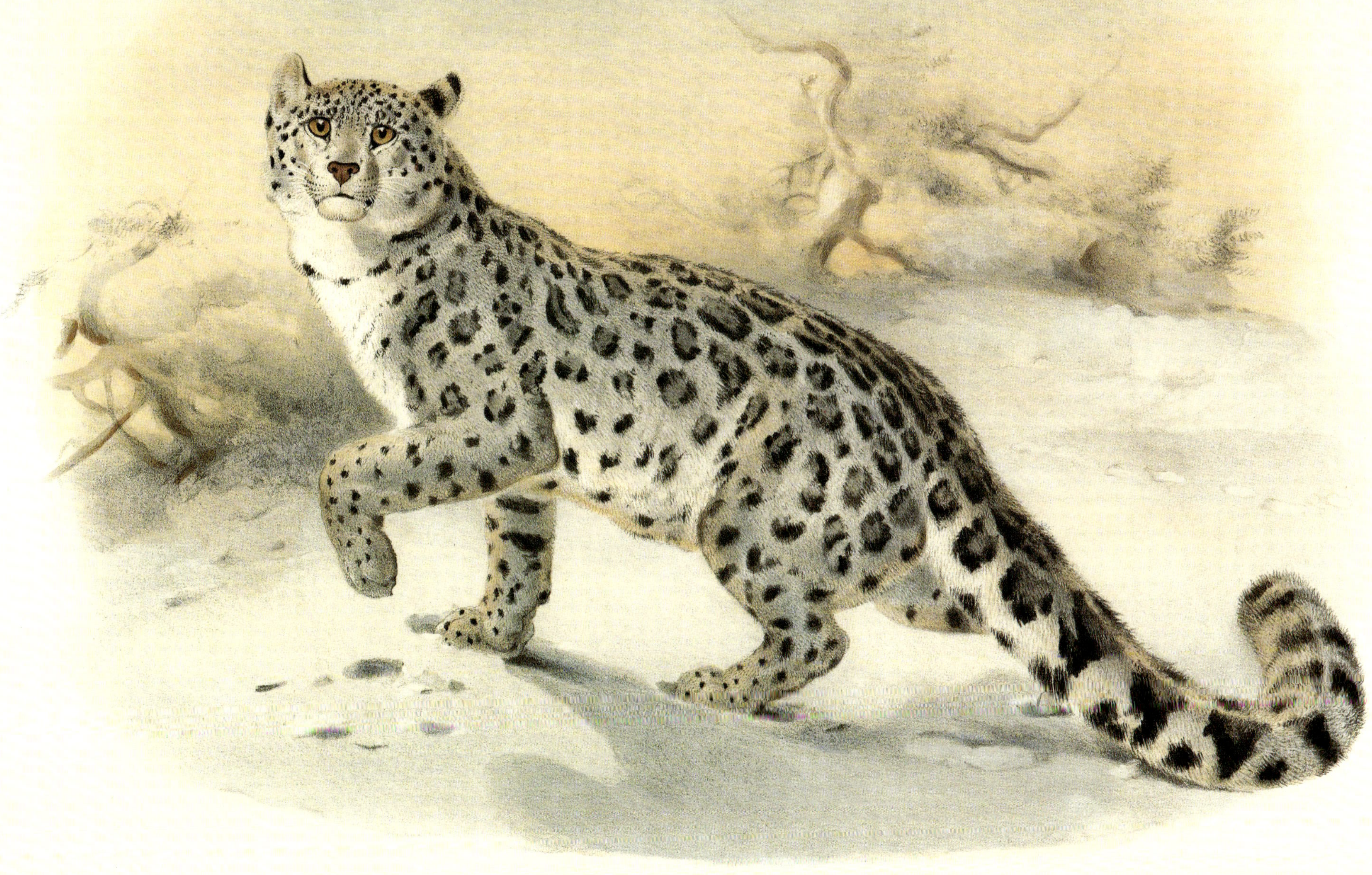

J. Wolf & J. Smit, del. et lith.

M & N Hanhart imp.

FELIS UNCIA

Clouded Leopard

CLOUDED TIGER, *Felis diardi* (now Clouded Leopard, *Neofelis nebulosa*). Hand coloured lithograph by J. Smit, from an original drawing by J. Wolf, pl. 8 from D. G. Elliot's *A Monograph of the Felidae, or Family of the Cats*, 1883. Size of plate 23¼″ × 18½″.

Possibly the most strikingly marked of all the larger cats, the clouded leopard is a forest dweller, sleeping in a tree during the day and hunting at night. Because of its nocturnal habits we know little about its habits in the wild, though we do know that it feeds on monkeys, birds, deer and other small mammals. Using its long and heavy tail as a balancer, it climbs trees easily and seems to be most at home where the jungle is thickest.

As with other cats the spots and blotches decorating its fur seem to be an adaptation to a forest existence and presumably help to make it inconspicuous. Not surprisingly this handsome animal has been hunted for its fur and its numbers are declining. It used to be widespread in south-eastern Asia, but the destruction of suitable habitats in some parts of its range, especially in Malaysia and Thailand, has also contributed to its decline. Fortunately it breeds readily in captivity and may be seen in the larger zoos of the world. The clouded leopard is distinct enough from the larger cats, such as the lion and the tiger, and the smaller cats, such as the ocelot and the bobcat, to have been placed in a genus of its own, *Neofelis*.

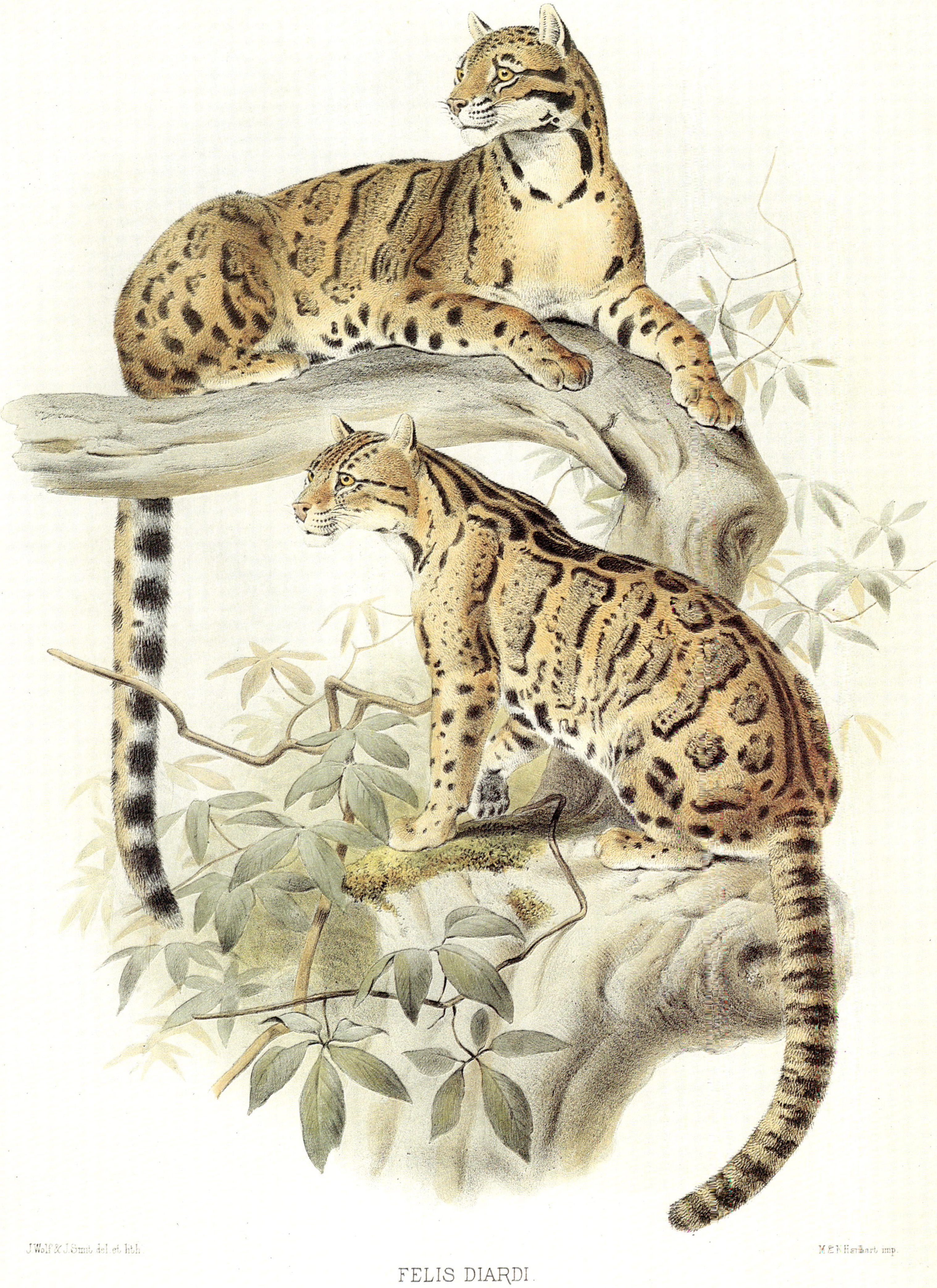

J. Wolf & J. Smit del. et lith.

M & N Hanhart imp.

FELIS DIARDI.

Serval

SERVAL, *Felis serval*. Hand coloured lithograph by J. Smit, from an original drawing by J. Wolf, pl. 26 from D. G. Elliot's *A Monograph of the Felidae, or Family of the Cats*, 1883. Size of plate 23¼″ × 18½″.

Daniel Giraud Elliot, a wealthy American businessman with an enthusiasm for wildlife, commissioned Joseph Wolf to provide original coloured drawings for *A Monograph of the Felidae* and for several lavishly illustrated books about birds. Happily Elliot gave Wolf a free hand and the resulting illustrations include some of the finest wildlife compositions published in the nineteenth century, those in the Felidae monograph being among the most outstanding portrayals of mammals by any artist.

The serval is a slender, long-legged creature, three feet in length plus a foot-long tail. The small head has large ears which are usually seen set wider apart than those of the animal facing us in Wolf's picture. Its fawn coat, ornamented with longitudinal rows of black spots, helps make it inconspicuous in the grassy scrub country which it frequents. A darker form with small, more densely crowded spots was once considered to be a separate species, known as the servaline cat, *Felis servalina*. The serval occurs widely in Africa, the variety being limited to western Africa. One of the faster wild cats, the serval feeds mostly on rodents.

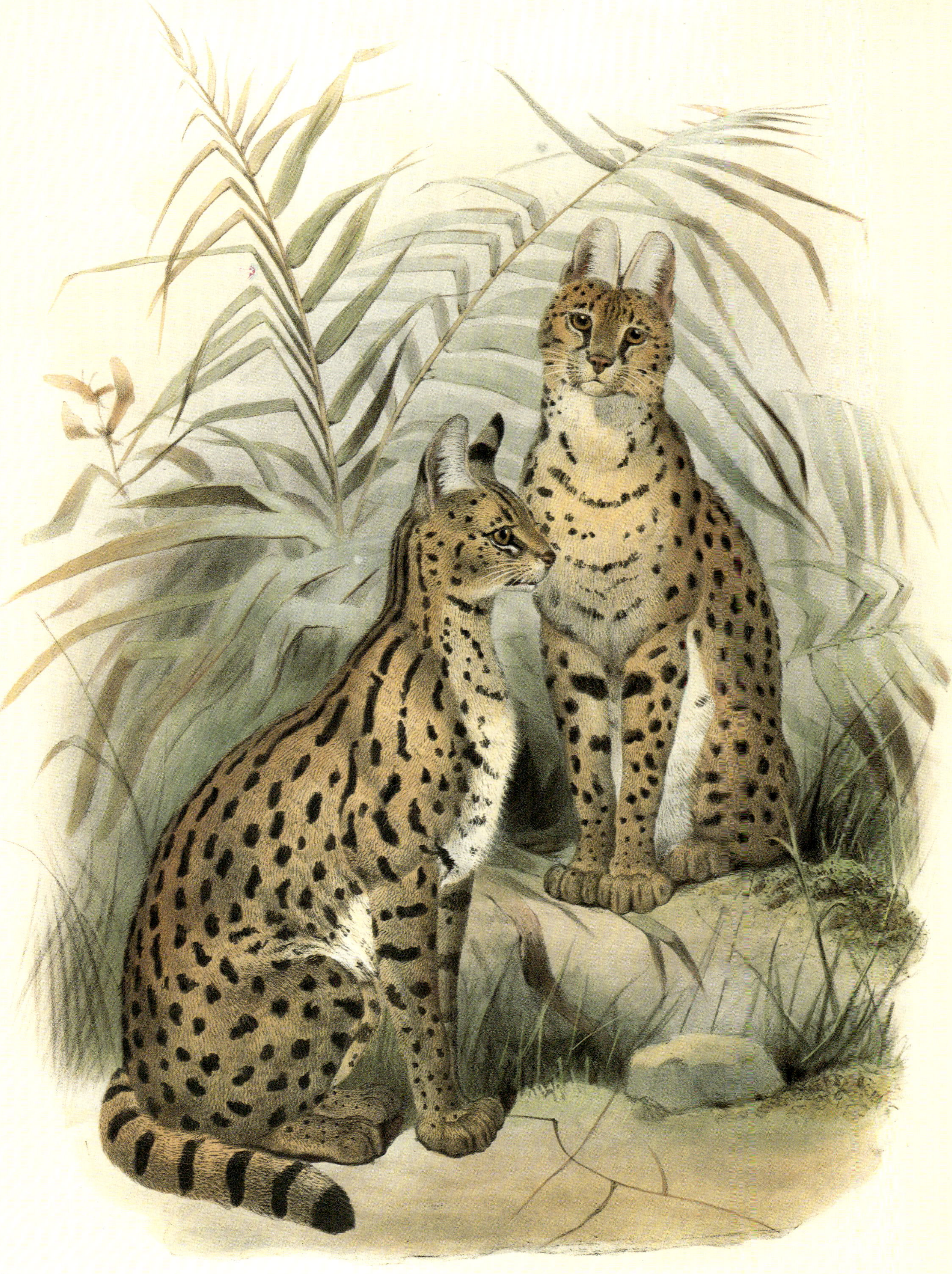

J. Wolf & J. Smit, del. et lith. M & N Hanhart imp.

FELIS SERVAL

Husky Dog

ESQUIMAUX DOG, *Canis familiaris* var. (now Husky Dog, *Canis familiaris*). Hand coloured lithograph by J. G. Keulemans, pl. 38 from St George Mivart's *Dogs, Jackals, Wolves and Foxes: a Monograph of the Canidae*, 1890. Size of plate 10″ × 7½″.

The husky dog is classed among the domestic dogs although, like the alsatian, it is derived mostly from the wolf, *Canis lupus*. It is still largely a wild dog, retaining much of the appearance and character of its ancestors, and is valued for its ability to work rather than for its submissive qualities. St George Mivart says that 'a pack of them was once mistaken for wolves even by so experienced an Arctic traveller as Sir John Richardson'. Eskimos and the earlier polar explorers tried to impose their will on huskies by subjecting them to needlessly harsh and cruel treatment, so the dogs did not give of their best. There has been little selective breeding of huskies with special aptitude for work, but they do reward kind treatment with better service.

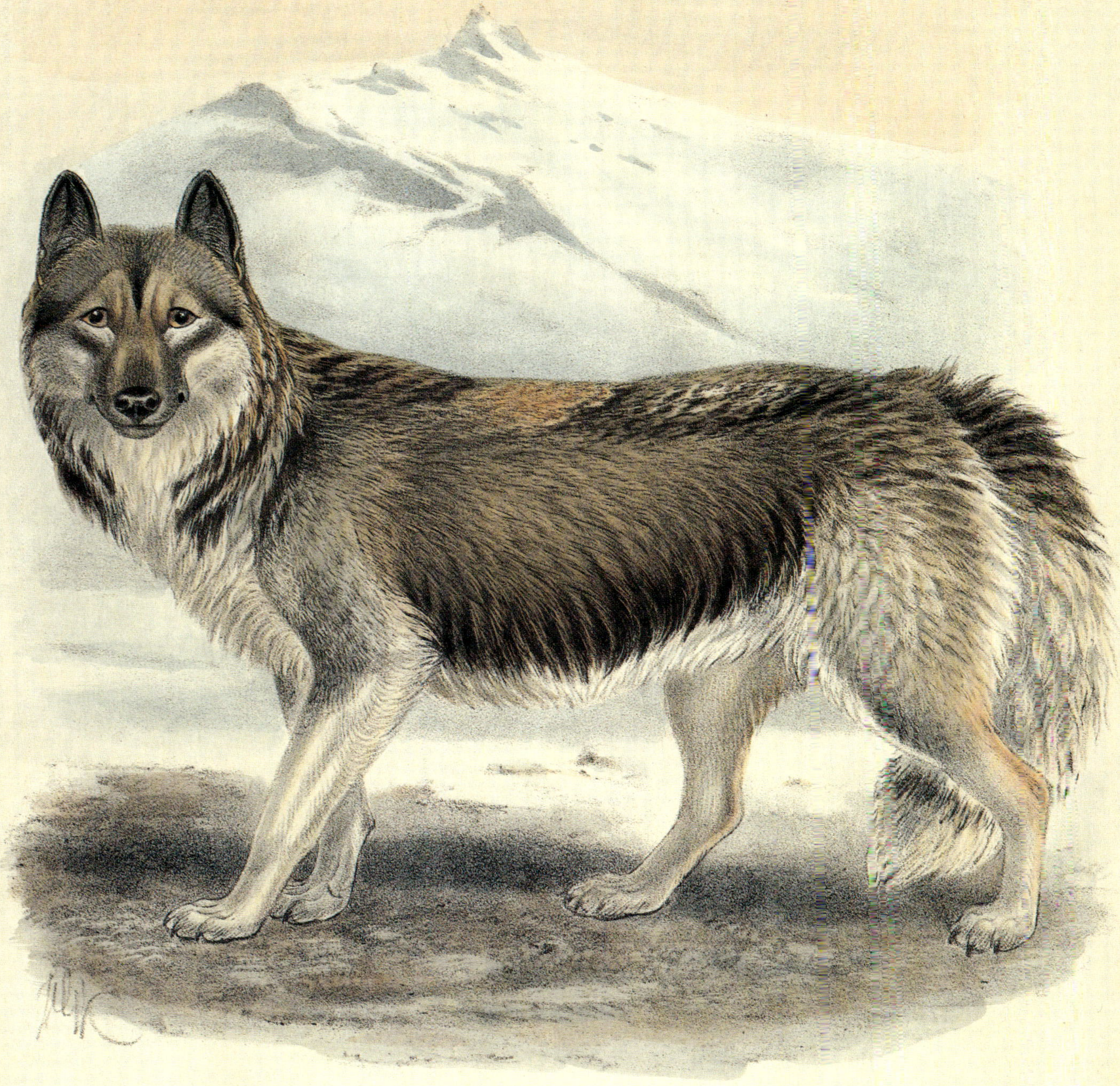

1/6

J. G. Keulemans del. et lith.

THE ESQUIMAUX DOG.

Canis familiaris, *var.*

Mintern Bros. imp.

Mexican Lap-dog

MEXICAN LAP-DOG, *Canis familiaris* var. (now *Canis familiaris*). Hand coloured lithograph by J. G. Keulemans, pl. 39 from St George Mivart's *Dogs, Jackals, Wolves and Foxes: a Monograph of the Canidae*, 1890. Size of plate 10″ × 7½″.

The artist John Gerrard Keulemans, perhaps better known for his studies of exotic birds, prepared this illustration from a stuffed dog housed in the Natural History Museum in London. The dog measured only seven inches from the end of its snout to the root of its tail, making it one of the smallest known. Little dogs, such as the Chihuahua, have been bred in Mexico for centuries, but only recently as pets. To the Aztecs, for instance, the little creatures were appreciated as delicacies for the dinner table and valued in magic, burial rites and medicine.

St George Mivart contrasted the Mexican lap-dog with the Esquimaux dog and said that it had most probably been formed from dogs of European origin. So impressed was he with the variety of breeds of domestic dog that he was moved to say, 'it is absolutely the most wonderful species of animal known to us as regards the number and diversity of the races which compose it.' Many dog lovers will agree with him.

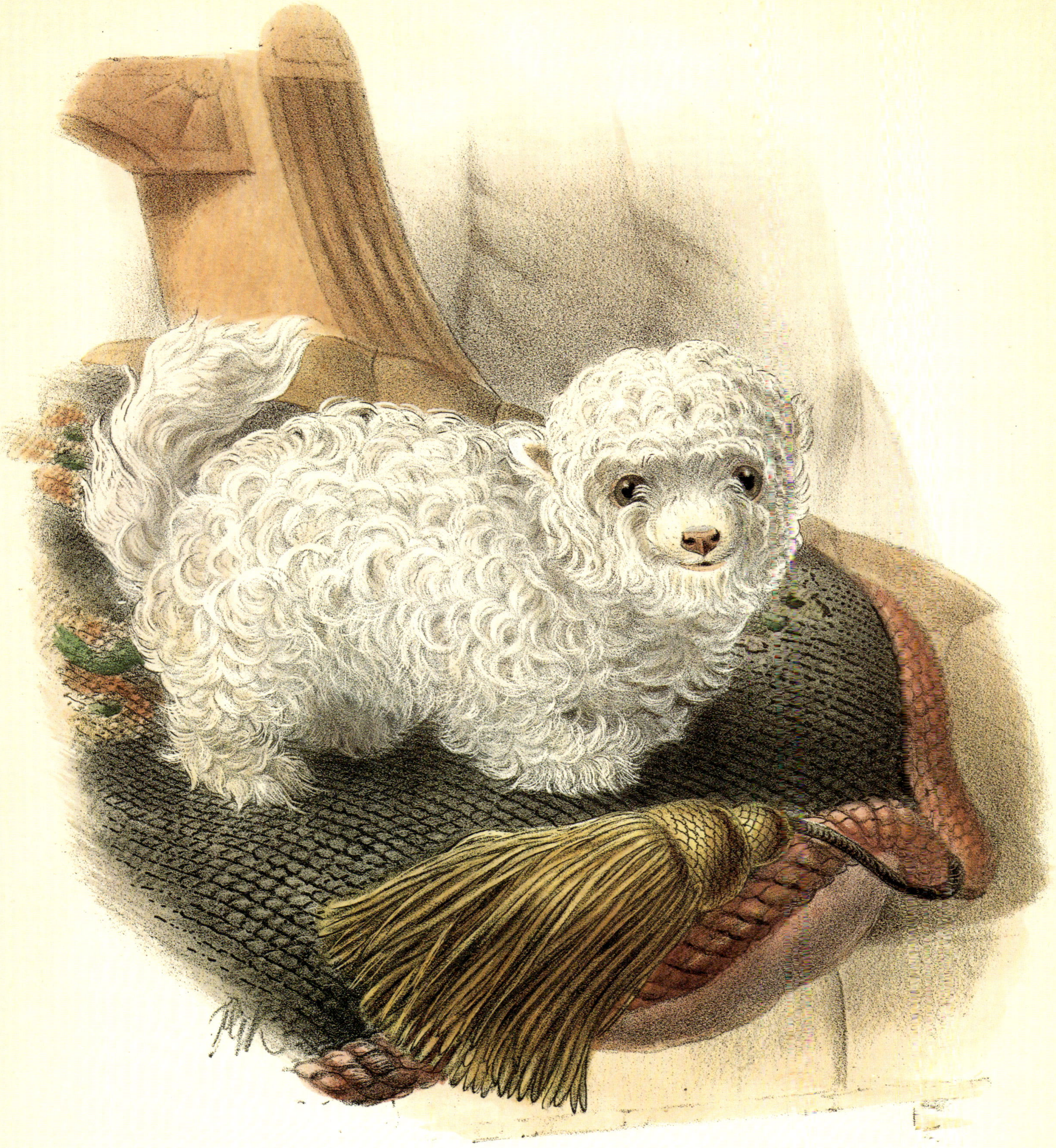

3/4

J. G. Keulemans del. et lith.

THE MEXICAN LAP-DOG.
Canis familiaris, *var.*

Mintern Bros. imp.

Black Wildebeest

WHITE-TAILED GNU, *Connochaetes gnu* (now Black Wildebeest, *Connochaetes gnou*). Hand coloured lithograph by J. Smit, pl. 12 from Vol. 1 of P. L. Sclater and O. Thomas's *The Book of Antelopes*, 1894–1900. Size of plate 11″ × 8½″.

The black wildebeest used to be abundant over much of South Africa but the hunting and agricultural activities of European colonists almost exterminated it. Conservation measures have halted the carnage and increased its chances of survival. This is not the animal featured in television programmes undertaking its dramatic seasonal migrations, thundering along in countless thousands; that animal is the larger blue wildebeest, *Connochaetes taurinus*. The black wildebeest, which numbered less than 4000 examples in 1970, was first seen in Europe in 1776 but was rare in European zoos until the late nineteenth century.

Grant's Gazelle

GRANT'S GAZELLE, *Gazella granti*. Hand coloured lithograph by J. Smit from an original drawing by J. Wolf, pl. 69 from Vol. 2 of P. L. Sclater and O. Thomas's *The Book of Antelopes*, 1894–1900. Size of plate 11″ × 8½″.

This lithograph of a Joseph Wolf watercolour drawing enables us to see at once why Grant's gazelle, a model of symmetry distinguished above all by the beautiful lines of its massive horns, is generally considered to be one of the most beautiful of the antelopes. In 1860, during their exploration of Central Africa, John Speke and James Grant were detained for a long time at Ugogo (in what is now Tanzania) by the drunken native chief Magombo. It was then the explorers first met with the animal that would one day be named after one of them. A creature of the open plains, Grant's gazelle is found in East Africa on each side of the Equator.

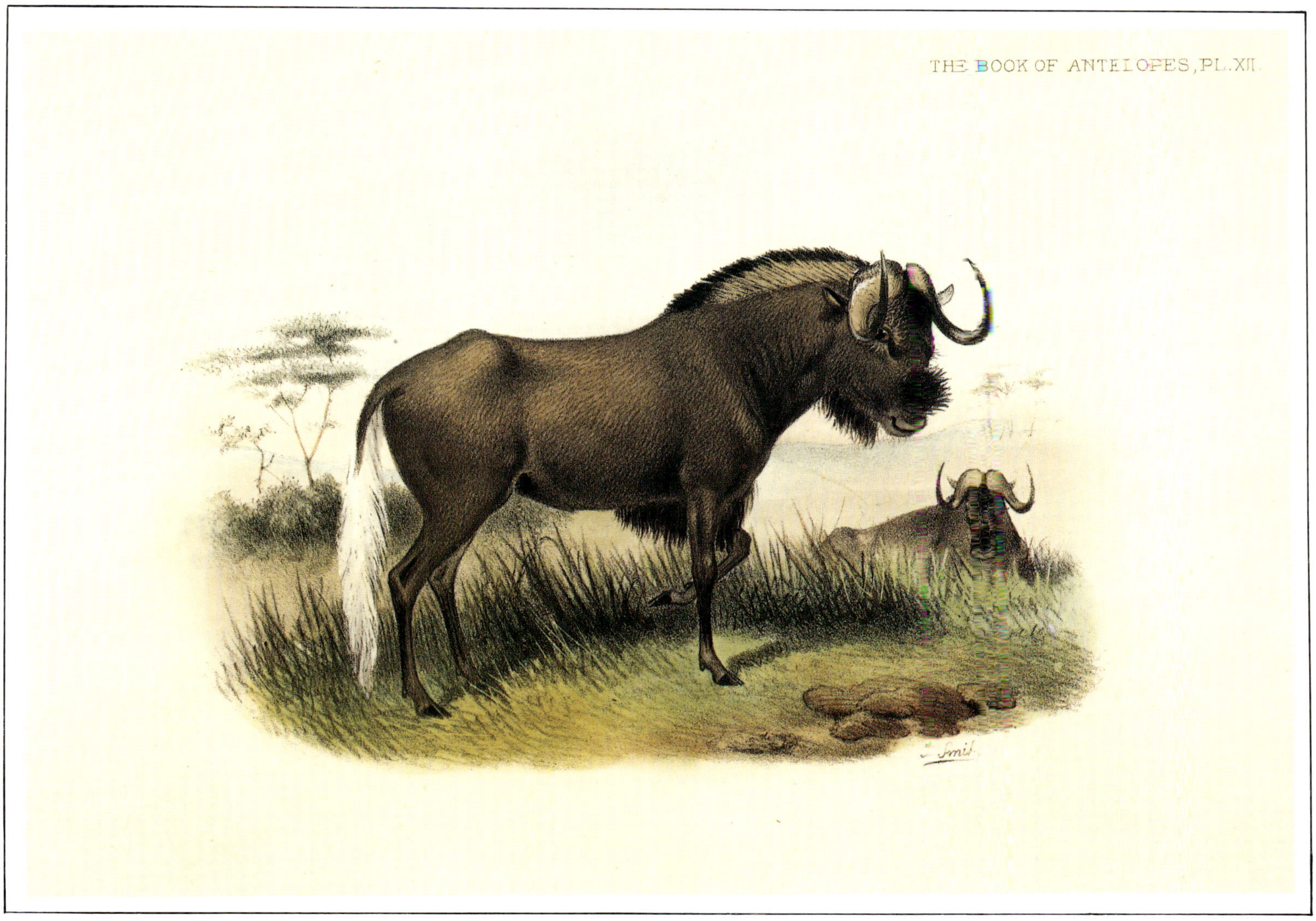
THE BOOK OF ANTELOPES, PL. XII

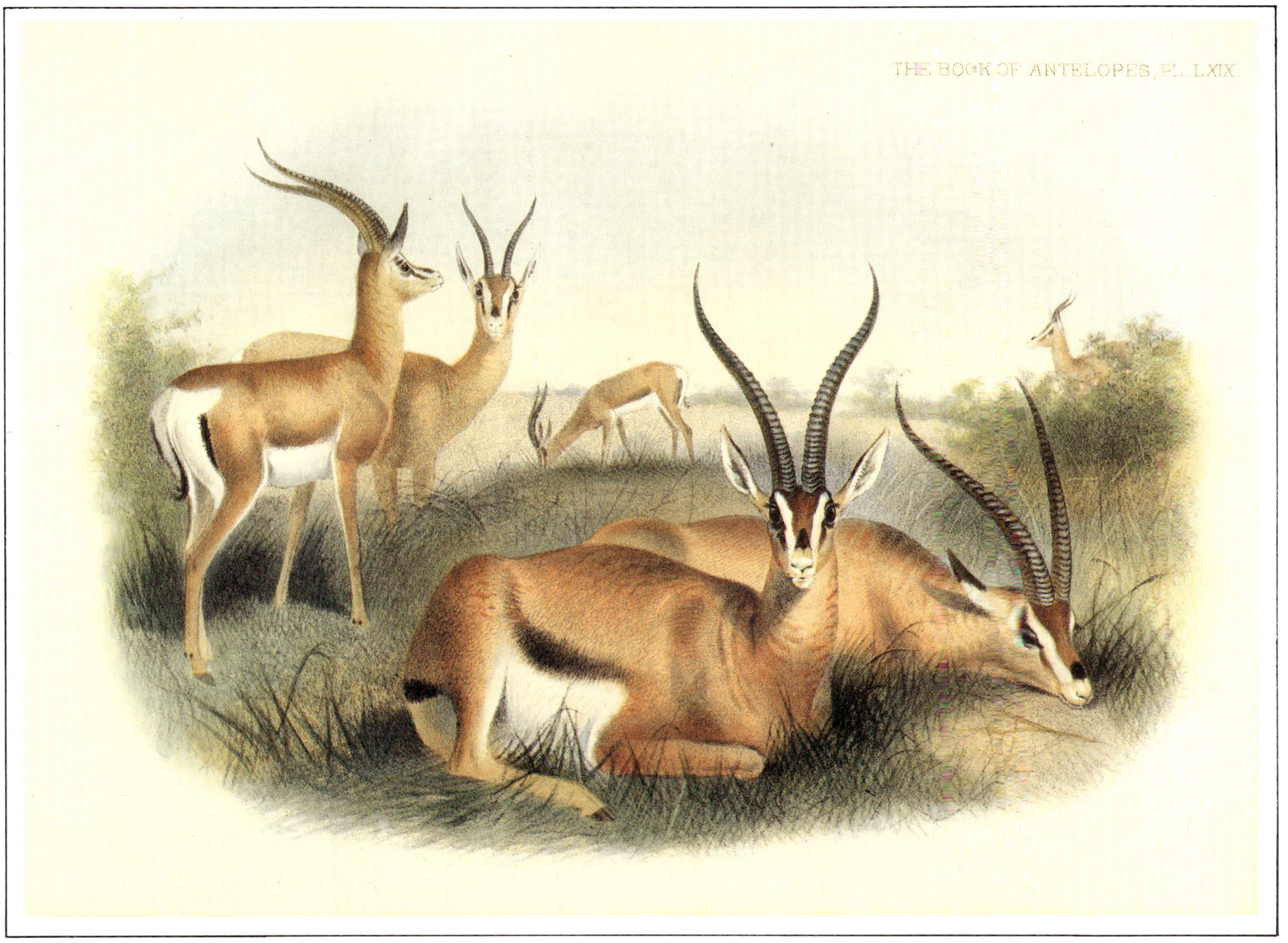
THE BOOK OF ANTELOPES, PL. LXIX

European Bison

EUROPEAN BISON, *Bos bonasus* (now *Bison bonasus*). Hand coloured lithograph by J. Smit, pl. 5 from R. Lydekker's *Wild Oxen, Sheep, & Goats of all Lands, Living and Extinct*, 1898. Size of plate 11½″ × 8½″.

When this lithograph was published the European bison still occurred in the wild in Russia; a large group existed in the Bialowiecza Forest and another in the Caucasus. Formerly protected by Tsar Alexander I, the first group was annihilated during the First World War and the second did not survive beyond 1927. Fortunately a number had been placed in zoos and with three survivors of a wild population a successful breeding programme was instituted. This ensured that the European bison would survive, and it is now resident in many zoos. It has been re-introduced into the Bialowiecza Forest and elsewhere in Russia and Romania.

Originally this large and heavy mammal lived in woodland areas where it ate leaves, ferns, heather, shrubs and bark. Otherwise, little is known about its behaviour in the wild. In Richard Lydekker's book, from which our picture is taken, we learn that these animals 'dearly love a mud-bath, and at times when the flies are troublesome they may frequently be seen plastered over with a coat of dry mud, which forms an efficient protection against their tormentors'. The European bison has longer legs, a smaller head, a longer body and a shorter mane than the American bison. It is also more wary but shares with its American cousin a good sense of smell and poor eyesight.

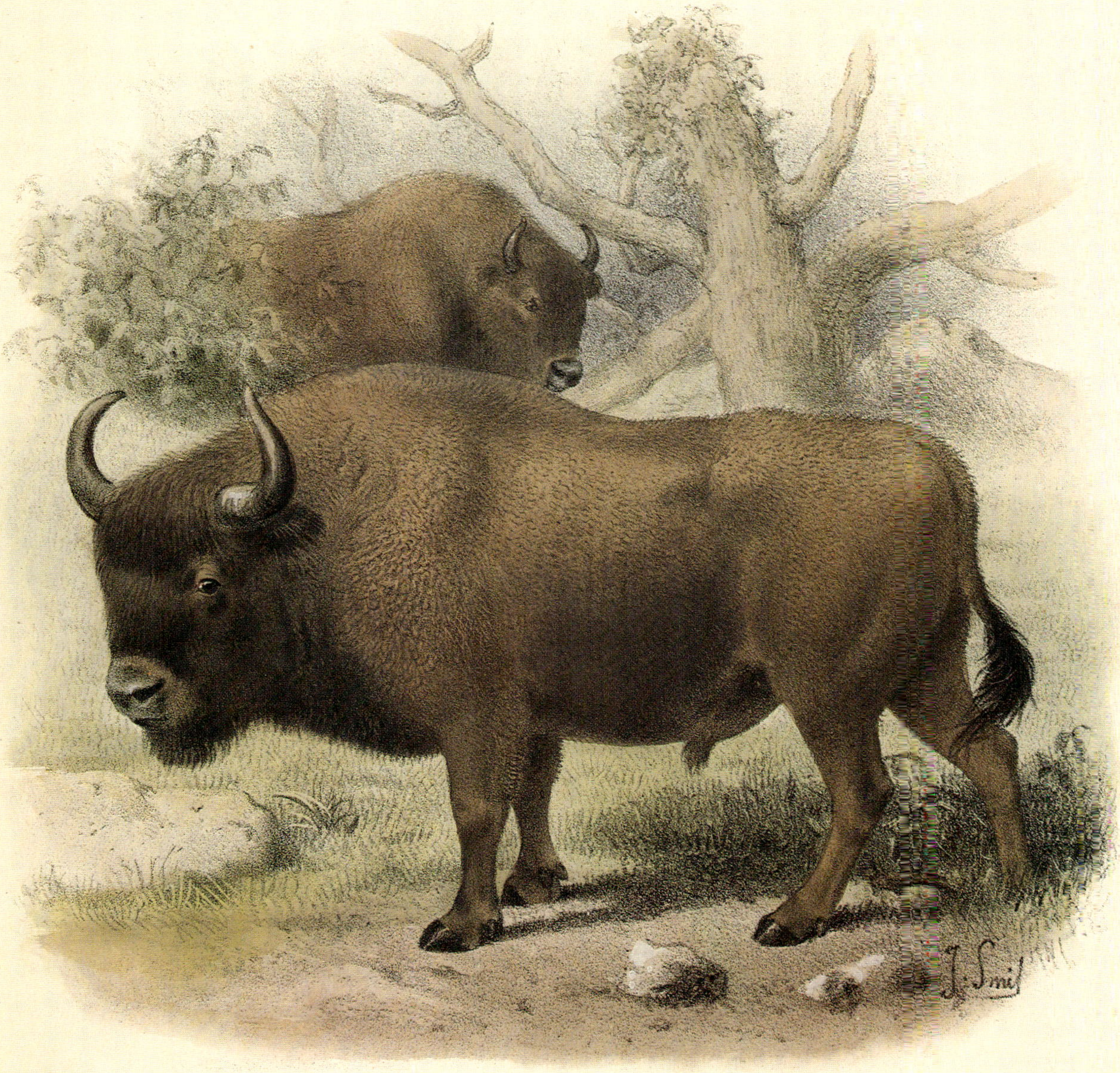

EUROPEAN BISON.

Published by Rowland Ward Ltd.

Markhor

MARKHOR, *Capra falconeri*. Hand coloured lithograph after an original drawing by J. Wolf, pl. 25 from R. Lydekker's *Wild Oxen, Sheep, & Goats of all Lands*, 1898. Size of plate 11½″ × 8½″.

The largest and, to the sportsman at least, the handsomest of the wild goats, the markhor is notable for the variations in the form of its horns, which have been used by some authorities to help define several subspecies of this animal. The variations in the spiral conformation are particularly striking and some pairs of horns show a much more closely wound spiral than those in this picture by Joseph Wolf. As its horns are among the most coveted of all hunting trophies the markhor has been exterminated in many parts of its range.

Standing about 40 inches high at the shoulder and weighing 200 pounds or more, these noble creatures inhabit precipitous and broken ground in arid parts of the Himalayas from Kashmir to Afghanistan, just above the tree line. They are very agile, may congregate in herds and in some places have been seen feeding together with the ibex, *Capra ibex*.

The name markhor means 'snake-eater' in Persian but there is no evidence to suggest that it feeds on snakes. Curiously enough a propensity for eating snakes was once said to be an attribute of the common goat in Scotland, Both animals, of course, are grazers.

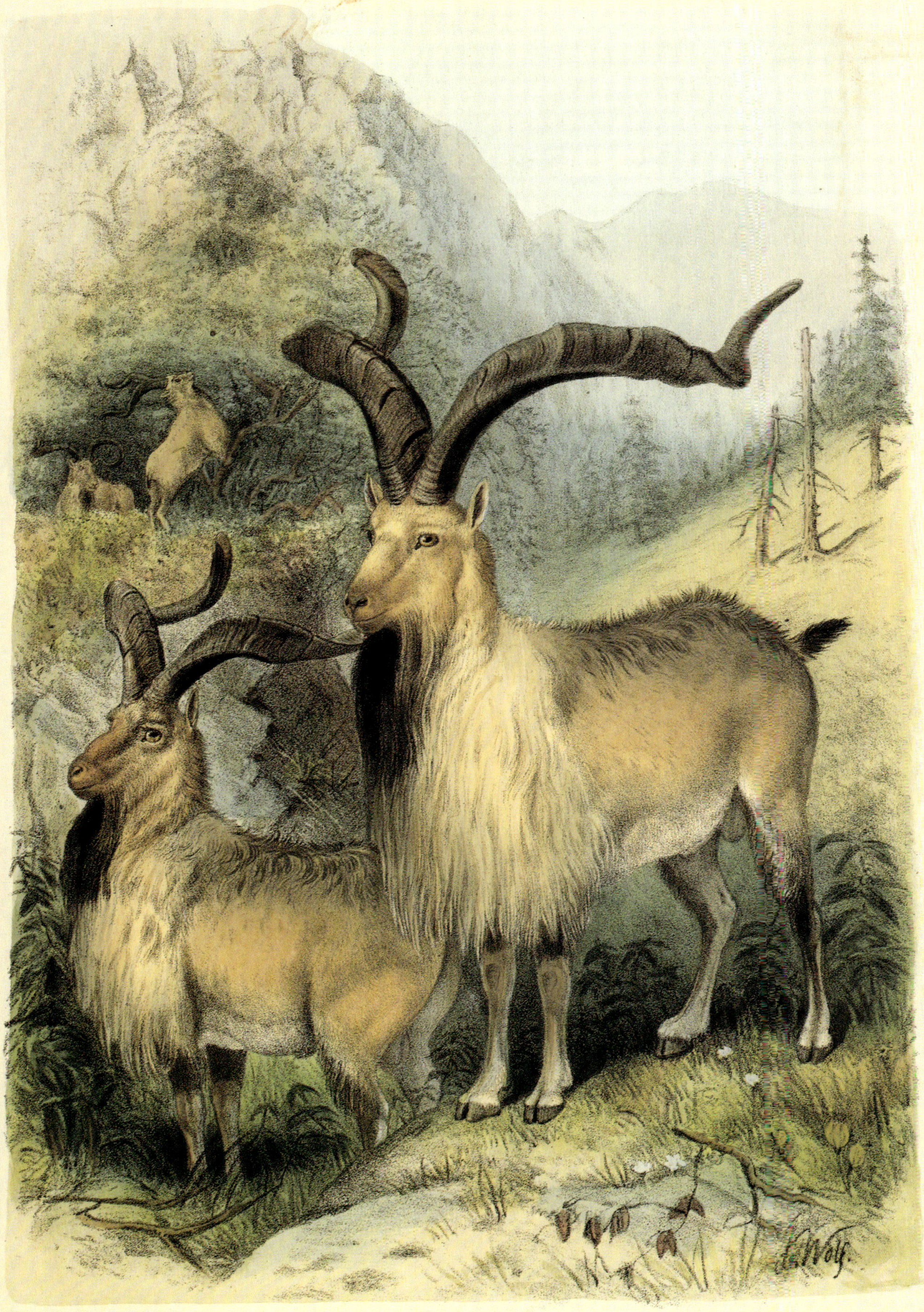

ASTOR MARKHOR.

Published by Rowland Ward Ltd.

Okapi

OKAPI, *Okapia johnstoni*. Hand coloured lithograph by P. J. Smit, pl. 30 from E. Ray Lankester's *On Okapia, a new genus of Giraffidae, from Central Africa* (in *Transactions of the Zoological Society of London* Vol. 16), 1902. Size of plate 12″ × 9½″.

This is a remarkable and historic picture of a large African mammal; remarkable because it is an artist's reconstruction, historic because it is the first published picture of the okapi. Two strips of skin had been obtained by Sir Harry Johnston during a visit to the Congo Free State in 1900 and these were enough for Philip Lutley Sclater to rush into print with the description of a new species of horse, *Equus johnstoni*. Subsequently Johnston received a complete skin and two skulls. These remains enabled Professor E. Ray Lankester, then Director of the Natural History Museum in London, to write an informed article about the exciting new discovery, which turned out to be like a short-necked giraffe with striped hindquarters, a wonderful addition to the pantheon of African wildlife. Smit's fine lithograph illustrating the article proved to be an accurate representation of the okapi when live specimens finally reached the West.

Slender evidence of the okapi's existence had been given in H. M. Stanley's book *In Darkest Africa*, published in 1890. Speaking of the pygmies in the Ituri forests of the Congo he had written: 'The Wambutti knew a donkey and called it "atti". They say that they sometimes catch them in pits.' This, and a discussion with Stanley himself, had been enough to set Johnston on the trail that eventually led him to the okapi.

Trans. Zool. Soc. Vol. XVI. Pl. XXX.

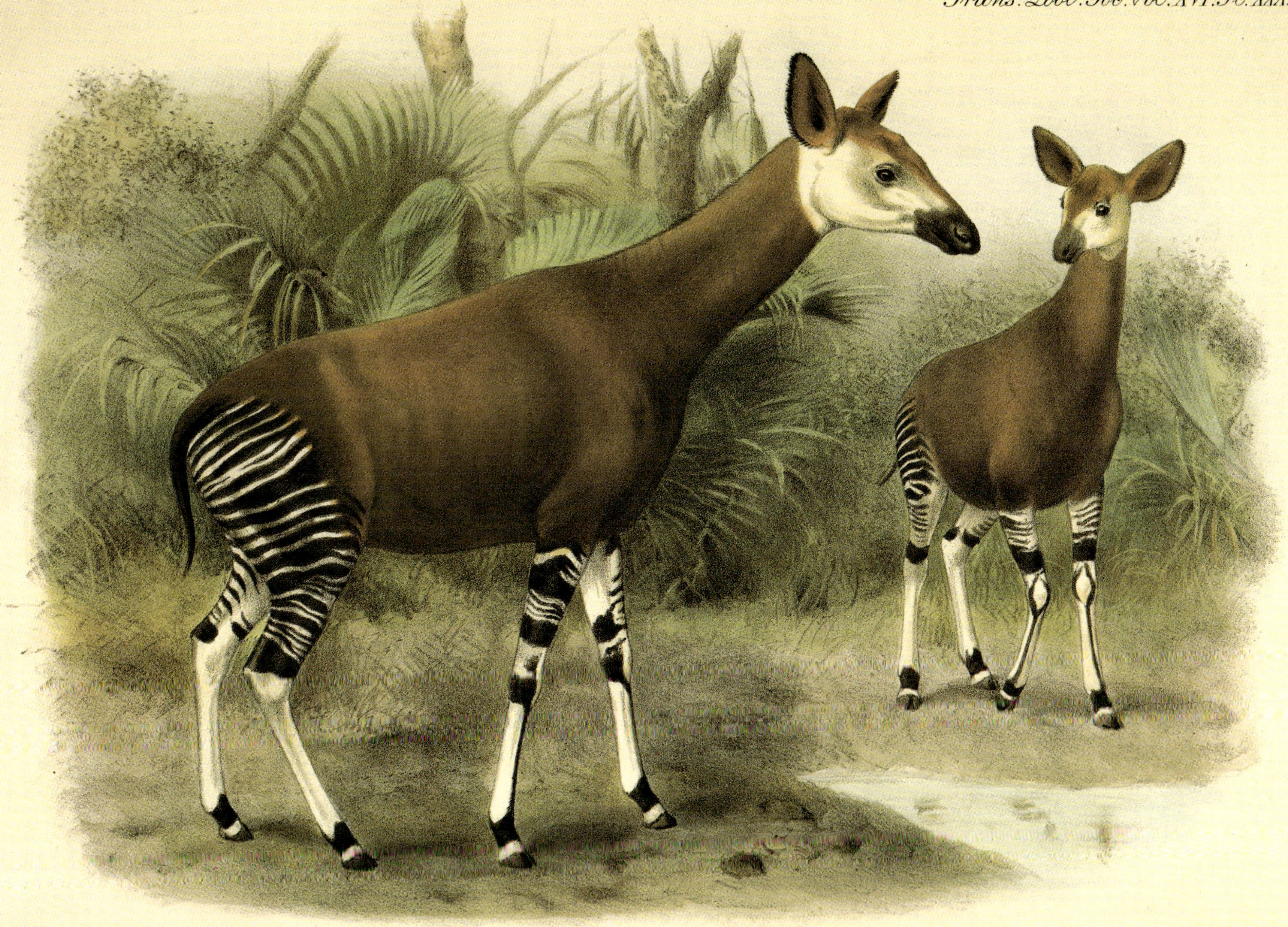

P.J. Smit del. et lith.

THE OKAPI (OKAPIA JOHNSTONI)

Mintern Bros imp.

Crested Porcupine

CRESTED PORCUPINE, *Hystrix cristata*. Chromolithograph by P. J. Smit, pl. 55 from J. Anderson's *Zoology of Egypt. Mammalia*, 1902. Size of plate 12¼″ × 9½″.

The crested porcupine, a large rodent about two feet long and weighing about 60 pounds, is remarkable for its crest of white-tipped grey quills. These quills, supplemented by others which are hollow and open at their ends, are loosely attached to the animal and are easily detached, from which circumstance arose the early and erroneous belief that they could be ejected like darts and used as offensive weapons. When attacked the animal may do no more than charge backwards with its spines erect. The effect, however, can be intimidating and painful. Even the lion learns to treat it respectfully.

Although this picture is an illustration from a book about Egyptian mammals it is unlikely that the crested porcupine still exists in Egypt. It does occur elsewhere in Africa, however, and is common across the central part of the continent. In some places it is all too common and has become a pest to crops. As it is hunted for food and for its quills it may not be a pest for much longer. It may owe its limited occurrence in Europe to introductions by man, probably the Romans. When first seen in Italy it would have seemed a delightfully exotic creature. Unfortunately it has become scarce there now.

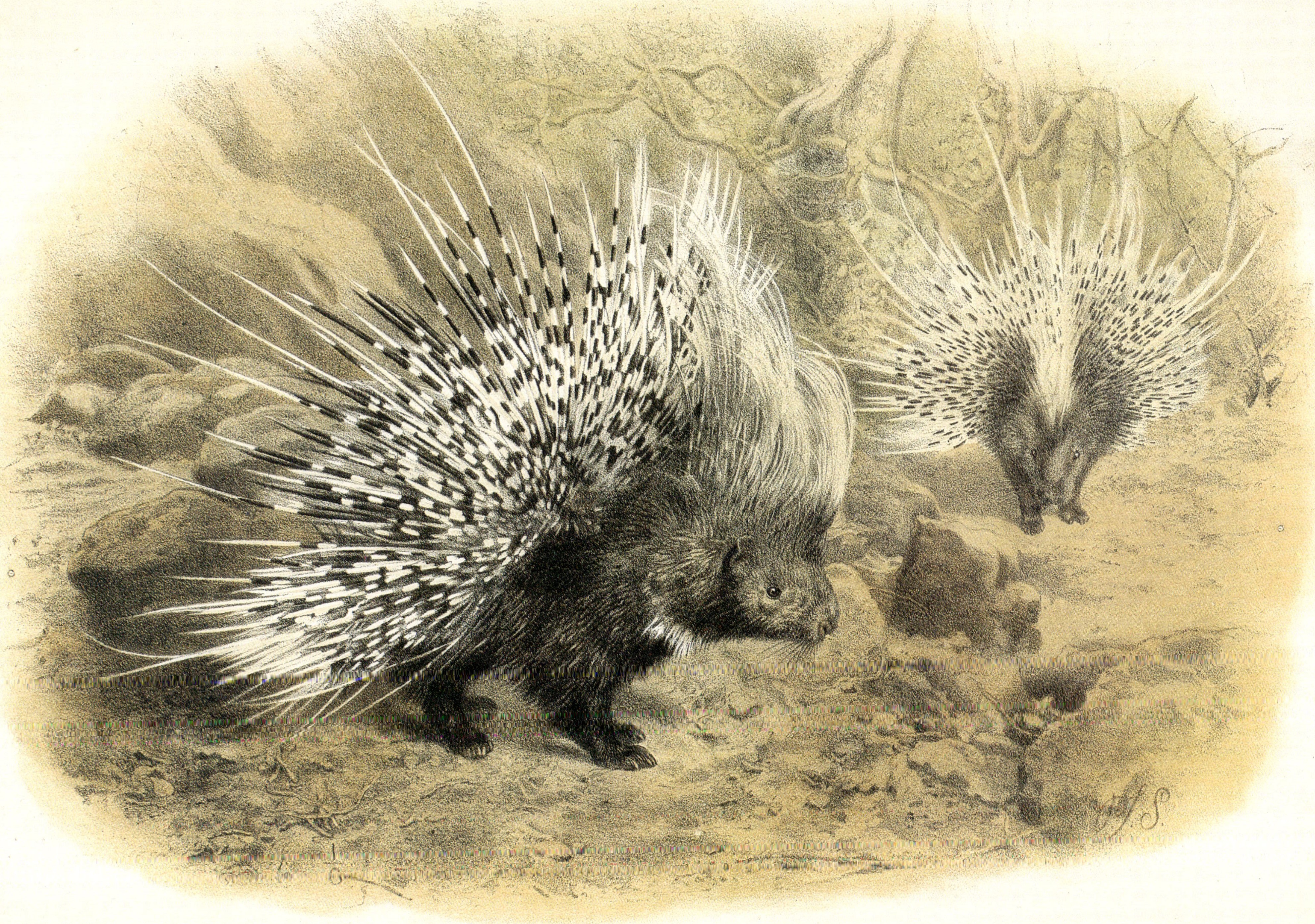

HYSTRIX CRISTATA.

Harp Seal

HARP OR GREENLAND SEAL, *Phoca groenlandica* (now Harp Seal, *Phoca groenlandica*). Colour print after an original painting by J. G. Millais, pl. 35 from Vol. 1 of his *Mammals of Great Britain and Ireland*, 1904–1906. Size of plate 10¼″ × 8″.

The harp seal is one of the smaller seals, measuring five or six feet long when adult. John Guille Millais says it may weigh 'as much as 800 pounds', but it does not normally exceed 300 pounds. Its striking colour pattern of yellowish-white with a contrasting broad black band makes it easy to identify. The black marking on its back recalls the shape of a harp and explains the derivation of its name.

The alternative name, Greenland seal, indicates this animal's preference for living under arctic conditions. Millais gives a graphic picture of its chosen domain. 'The home of the Harp Seal', he writes, 'is near the bleak shores of Greenland and the polar islands, forlorn regions of dreary waste where the accumulations of centuries of winters have formed fields of ice, topped by glittering heights. Near such lands the Greenland seal loves to lie close to the open cracks in the floes, or to fish in the surrounding depths. Its enemies are the Eskimo hunter, the white man from St John's, Trondhjem, Copenhagen, and Dundee, the polar bear, the shark, the swordfish and perhaps the orca [killer whale]; and yet despite the toll these take, it is only the fringe of the great multitudes that are molested. Imagine the abundance of a species of which 200,000 are annually killed in one small area, to the north of St John's, and there is no diminution. Yet it is so.' Millais wrote about the persecution of the harp seal at the beginning of the twentieth century: had he been writing towards its close how different may have been his conclusion!

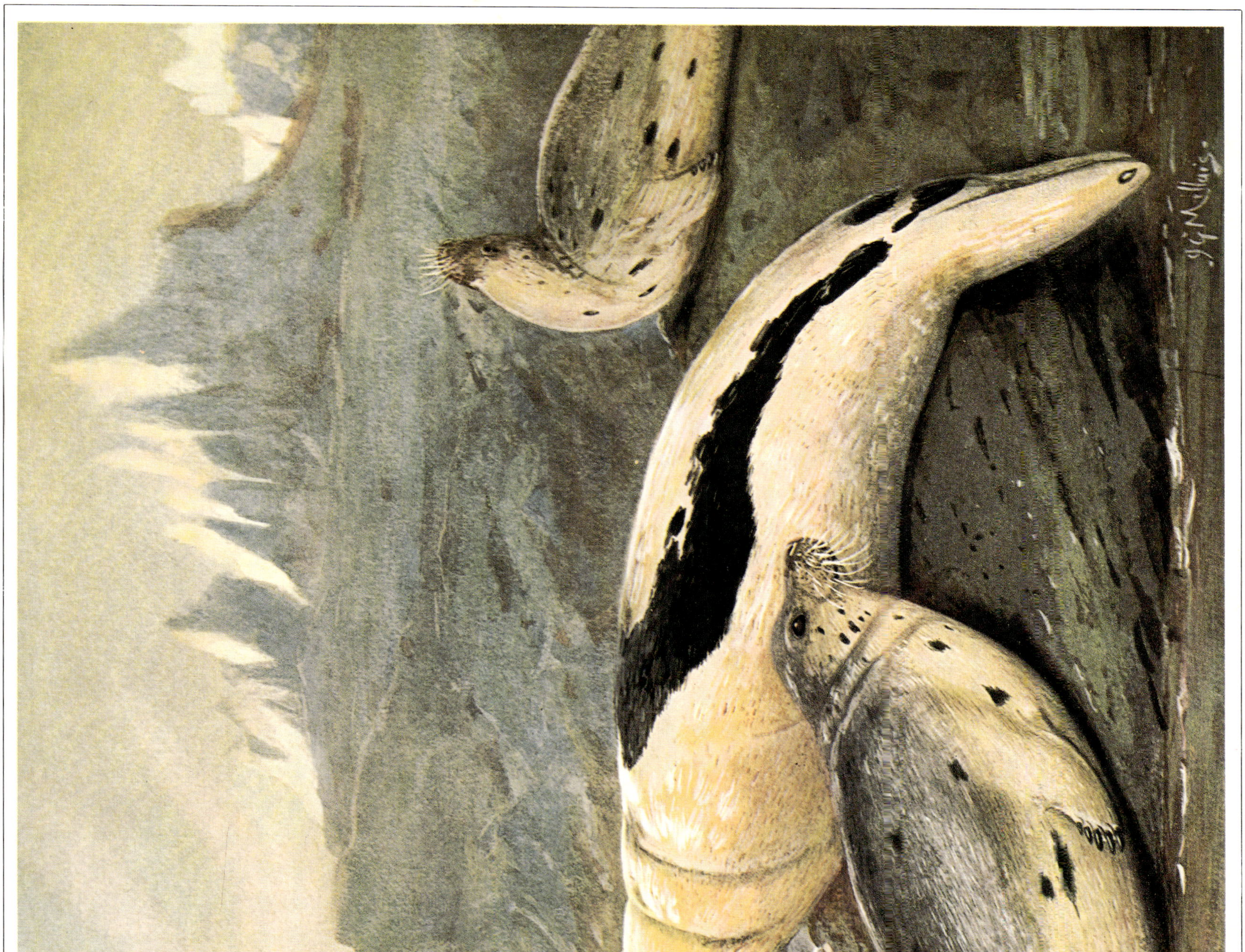
J. G. Millais

Polecat

POLECAT, *Putorius putorius* (now *Mustela putorius*). Chromolithograph after a painting by A. Thorburn, pl. 22 from Vol. 2 of J. G. Millais' *Mammals of Great Britain and Ireland*, 1904–06. Size of plate 10¼" × 8".

The polecat is one of many small, short-legged, elongated animals comprising the Mustelidae, the family which also includes the badger, otter, weasel, pine marten, stoat and mink. It attains a length of about two feet, has small eyes set in a flattened triangular head and is noteworthy for its cream-coloured fur partially obscured by long, black-tipped hairs, these being densest on the belly. This coloration is acquired when the animal is about eight months old, the fur of the youngsters being much paler.

It is bold but careless, which makes it easy to trap. As it is very destructive to small domestic and farmyard animals, such as pigeons, rabbits, hens and chickens, it has been killed in large numbers and is now very scarce or absent from some areas where it was once common, such as Britain. According to John Guille Millais, the author of the impressive three-volume work in which this study of the polecat appears, 'It will attack even so large a bird as a turkey and has been known to kill 16 in one night. One has been seen to attack and hold a fully grown Hare.' It may sometimes be a benefactor to man as it is also known to destroy venomous snakes and vermin such as rats and mice. More than most creatures of its size the polecat loves to kill. Archibald Thorburn's picture shows how handsome is the coat of this efficient little predator, handsome enough to have been used formerly to adorn civic robes in England.

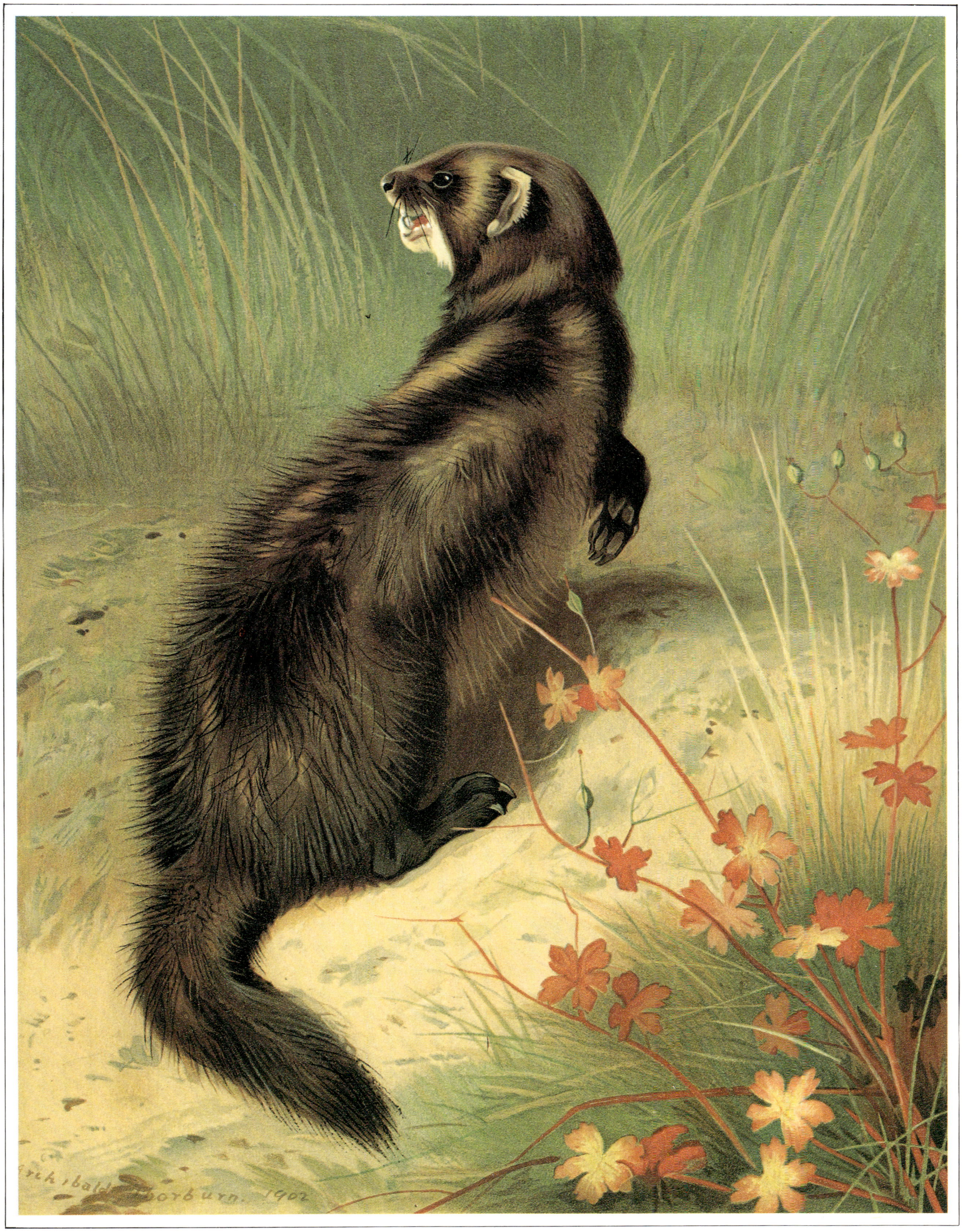

Blue Whale and Fin Whale

Blue Whale, *Balaenoptera musculus* (top), Common Rorqual, *Balaenoptera physalus* (centre and bottom) (now Fin Whale). Coloured print by J. G. Millais, pl. 59 from Vol. 3 of J. G. Millais' *The Mammals of Great Britain and Ireland*, 1904–06. Size of plate 10¼″ × 8″.

Like most early illustrations of whales this one shows them with distended bellies: but, except when feeding, their bellies are flat. Only dead whales would have distended bellies, as shown here, and usually they would have been the victims of whalers. The fin whale was not hunted – and so was not accessible to artists – until the problem of making it float when dead had been solved (by pumping compressed air into its carcase). The top figure in this illustration by John Guille Millais (the fourth son of Sir John Everett Millais) shows an example of the largest animal the world has ever seen. All the statistics of the blue whale are impressive, sometimes staggering. It reaches 110 feet in length and may weigh 140 tonnes. As it surfaces it blasts out a steaming mixture of moisture-laden mucus and trapped water from the blowhole situated on the top of its head, the 'spout' sometimes rising as high as 33 feet and often being characteristic enough to allow positive identification. The stomach may contain a ton or more of krill (a mixture of mature and larval forms of shrimps, crabs and other invertebrates) and several tons may be taken in daily. There are from 60 to 100 grooves on the throat and chest, each groove being about two inches deep. Despite its great size the blue whale is an efficient swimmer and may briefly reach a speed of 15 knots. Regrettably this friendly monster is in danger of being exterminated. In every sense its demise would be a great loss.

The other two figures represent the fin whale, a species which occasionally attains a length of 80 feet and a weight of 60 tonnes. As its blubber is thinner than that of the blue whale it was hunted less vigorously – until the larger species became scarce. It was known to the early whalemen as Razorback because of the pronounced ridge along its back.

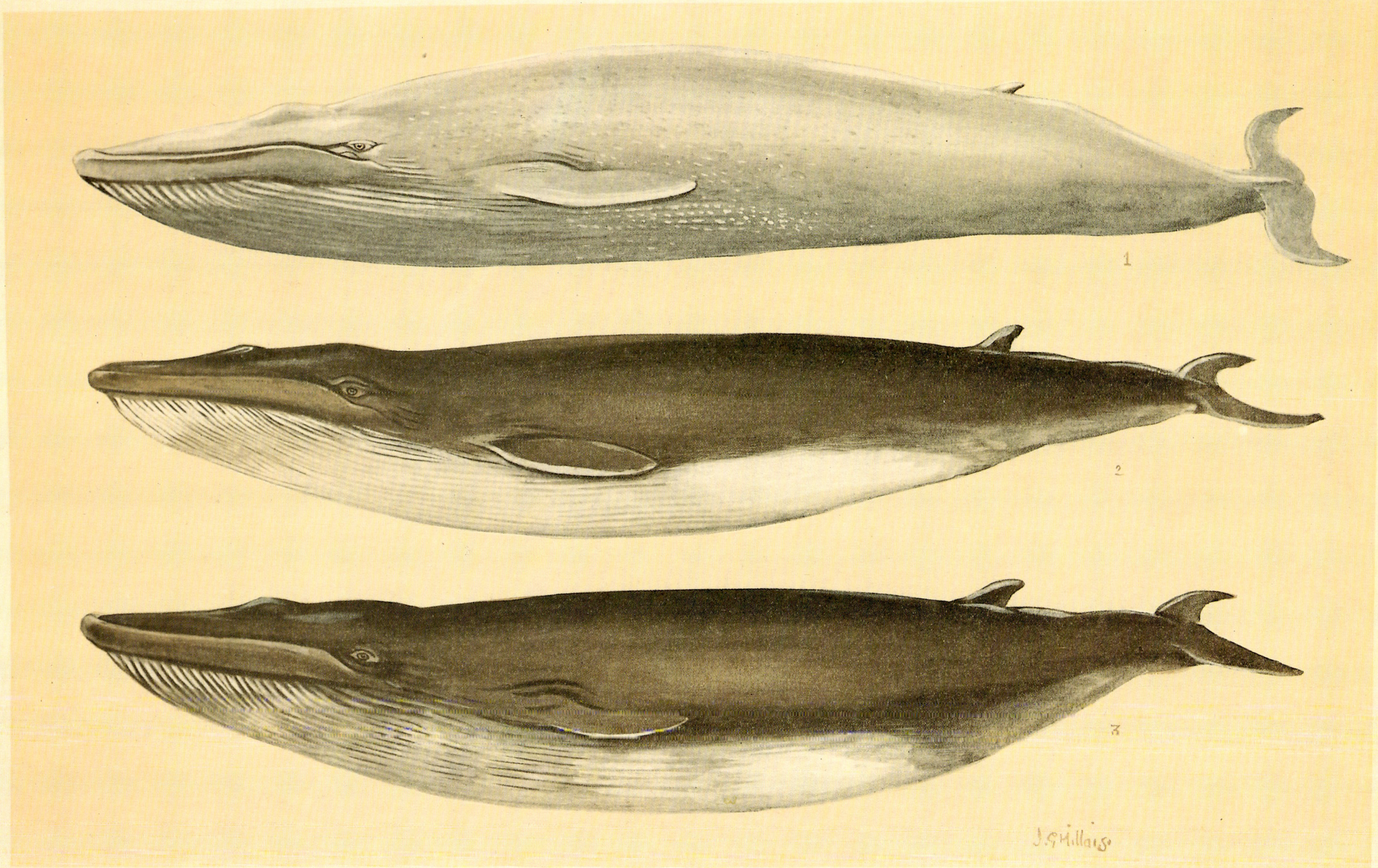

1\. THE BLUE WHALE.

Balænoptera musculus.

2, 3. THE COMMON RORQUAL.

Balænoptera physalus.

INDEX